AF095913

Bigg
Thar
Fash

Bigger Than Fashion

How "Streetwear" Conquered Culture

Tyler Watamanuk

Simon & Schuster
New York   Amsterdam/Antwerp
London   Toronto
Sydney/Melbourne   New Delhi

Simon & Schuster
1230 Avenue of the Americas
New York, NY 10020

For more than 100 years, Simon & Schuster has championed authors and the stories they create. By respecting the copyright of an author's intellectual property, you enable Simon & Schuster and the author to continue publishing exceptional books for years to come. We thank you for supporting the author's copyright by purchasing an authorized edition of this book.

No amount of this book may be reproduced or stored in any format, nor may it be uploaded to any website, database, language-learning model, or other repository, retrieval, or artificial intelligence system without express permission. All rights reserved. Inquiries may be directed to Simon & Schuster, 1230 Avenue of the Americas, New York, NY 10020 or permissions@simonandschuster.com.

Copyright © 2025 by Tyler Watamanuk

All rights reserved, including the right to reproduce this book or portions thereof in any form whatsoever. For information, address Simon & Schuster Subsidiary Rights Department, 1230 Avenue of the Americas, New York, NY 10020.

First Simon & Schuster hardcover edition November 2025

SIMON & SCHUSTER and colophon are registered trademarks of Simon & Schuster, LLC

Simon & Schuster strongly believes in freedom of expression and stands against censorship in all its forms. For more information, visit BooksBelong.com.

For information about special discounts for bulk purchases, please contact Simon & Schuster Special Sales at 1-866-506-1949 or business@simonandschuster.com.

The Simon & Schuster Speakers Bureau can bring authors to your live event. For more information or to book an event, contact the Simon & Schuster Speakers Bureau at 1-866-248-3049 or visit our website at www.simonspeakers.com.

Interior design by Carly Loman

Manufactured in the United States of America

1 3 5 7 9 10 8 6 4 2

Library of Congress Control Number: 2025940860

ISBN 978-1-9821-8286-1
ISBN 978-1-9821-8288-5 (ebook)

"The members of a subculture must share a common language. And if a style is really to catch on, if it is to become genuinely popular, it must say the right things in the right way at the right time."

—Dick Hebdige

Contents

    Introduction | 1

Act One

1. Six Scribbled Letters | 5
2. The Subway School | 13
3. Boosting Silk Crizzys | 21
4. An Accidental Clothing Designer | 29
5. Underground Fashion | 37
6. Tokyo Calling | 47
7. Profanity over Profit | 55
8. It Has to Be *Phat* | 65
9. Blunt Designs | 73
10. Not Really Underground Anymore | 81
11. Played Out | 91
12. Thrasher Fashion | 101
13. An International Machine | 109

Act Two

14. New Kicks on the Block | 121
15. Triple Five Sold | 131
16. Slouching Toward Bowery | 139
17. Internet Magazines | 149
18. Sneaker Frenzy | 157

19. Frontin' | 165

20. Cross-Promotion | 175

21. The Next Level | 185

22. RSWD | 195

23. Most Official Bitch | 203

24. The Hundreds Is Huge | 213

25. Diamond Life | 219

Act Three

26. Fifty Racks | 231

27. The Plastisol Is Fading | 241

28. A 700 Percent Markup | 251

29. Luxury Becomes Essential | 261

30. Supreme's Invisible Man | 269

31. Changing the Game | 279

32. The Hype Machine | 291

33. Armed with a Mind | 299

34. Virgil Was Here | 309

35. A Stüssy Succession | 317

36. World Famous | 325

    Notes and Sources | 339
    Acknowledgments | 344

Introduction

This is the story of a cultural universe that operated under a shared system of underground references and DIY ethos, a youthful provocation of art and fashion and commerce that challenged the by-the-book definitions of artist, designer, stylist, and entrepreneur. I set out to write this book because I sensed there was more here than would ever fit into a single magazine article. In my eight years writing for *GQ*, I watched as the rebellious outliers from this culture and community infiltrated mainstream fashion and menswear with greater frequency. The products they created simply became too covetable to ignore. I was surprised by how sprawling and tremendous the origin story was. The more I researched and the more conversations I had, the bigger and bigger this world became.

I spent four years in conversation—with famous names, lesser-known ones, voices spanning across generations. Hundreds of hours of talking, listening, reading, sorting through archival newspaper articles and old fashion and art magazines. At some point, it became a writer's paradox, a dream and a nightmare. Simply too much material. The story was more expansive than I could have imagined. There was the reality of this book's boundaries—

the constraints of pages we could print, the limits of what could be included—coupled with the realization that each decade could warrant its own book. And so, writing *this* book became an act of reduction—taking nearly fifty years of youth culture, fashion, and collective memory and distilling it into a narrative that could be followed without an encyclopedic knowledge of all the obscure references. This book does not offer a definitive portrait of what the world now calls "streetwear." Even to define it is to attempt to hold water in your hand. For every brand, designer, or personality I could include, there were dozens that I couldn't.

Instead, you will find a book that captures key moments and interconnected stories that amounted to a movement mostly interested in establishing a tradition of its own. These designers, these brands, they didn't just make clothes. They tapped into something else, an idea of connection, to capture the fleeting and shared experience of youth. To me, the most compelling part of this story is the idea of being swept into something larger than yourself, whether you were the one making the T-shirt or the one buying it. It was something distinct, something you could point to and recognize. As streetwear became commodified and diluted beyond recognition, the edges frayed, and the clarity was lost. What was once so tangible became something no longer graspable. Yet a core truth remained. With all of what I could not include in this book, this story that stands is still far bigger than fashion itself.

Act One

1.

Six Scribbled Letters

About five minutes east of the Pacific Ocean, next to the expansive Crystal Cove State Park with looming sun-bleached sycamores and golden California poppies, sits Laguna Canyon Road. The two-lane street, a thirteen-mile stretch entirely located in Orange County, is situated between the Pacific Coast Highway and State Route 73. A sprawling single-story building with dozens of tiny studios stood tucked away at the halfway point. The units were used by locals for things like storage, woodworking, welding, and surfboard making.

It was 1980, and a twenty-six-year-old surfboard shaper named Shawn Stüssy set up a simple studio inside one of the rented rooms. Shawn was one of those lucky people who made everything look effortless and instinctive. With thick dark hair and a wispy black goatee, he was handsome enough and spoke with the languid drawl of someone born and raised in the golden land. The hypnotic downbeat of Bob Marley blared from box speakers as a thick haze of skunky weed floated through the air.

Shawn approached shaping like a stoned engineer, focusing on details to create high-performance shapes. Short and powerful quivers, double-winged thrusters, mid-length twin fins. They gave surfers unmatched power and precision, allowing them to cut through the waves on a dime. He sold them for $300 a board. With different curves and cuts and colors, each looked different from the last, yet every single one was marked with the same scrawly, handwritten six letters: STÜSSY.

The terse signature had an abstractionist quality, like a Cy Twombly painting smashed into something Jamie Reid would have scribbled on a Sex Pistols record. Shawn's inspiration was a nod to the signature of his uncle Jan Stussy, an accomplished painter and university art professor. For someone whose devotion was to surfing and smoking marijuana, Shawn strove for perfection when he wanted. He wrote his last name hundreds of times before picking the best one, the broad-tipped marker squeaking across the paper as his hand twisted and swirled. Shawn had been making boards since he was a teenager, mainly for the mom-and-pop surf shops in the Laguna area, but the namesake boards and studio space were new endeavors.

"The sixties surf culture, after punk, seemed very dated," recalled Shawn. "I knew I was breaking out on my own."

He'd drive from Orange County to Hollywood's Sunset Strip, often to hit the nightclub Rodney Bingenheimer's English Disco to see bands like the New York Dolls. It exposed Shawn to a world of people and clothes he didn't see back in Laguna Beach. He was drawn to Cubist painters and how they used collage, playing with fragmented ideas and abstracted shapes to create striking, off-kilter works. He became obsessive about typography, collecting Letraset sheets, manufactured printed typefaces that could be cut and pasted to create designs. This jumble of interests and styles rendered Shawn's creative sensibility vividly different from the surf scene's status quo.

In the surfing industry of the eighties, there was what was known as the big three: Billabong, Quiksilver, and Rip Curl. The trio hailed from Australia; the companies had been around since as early as the late sixties and sold boards and utilitarian wares like wetsuits and board shorts to committed surfers. Brand licensing deals brought the big three to the United States. Quiksilver sold its goods out of a Volkswagen bus and then a Newport Beach garage that eventually became the company's first American headquarters; Billabong was exported to California and Hawaii first, then to Japan and Europe. The distribution moves signaled that the surfer look had global appeal.

The eighties brought a better economy, and specialist surf shops multiplied in popular tourist regions and coastal towns, creating a greater retail network in the United States and enabling the big three and American surf brands to sell products in larger numbers. In 1981, Quiksilver pulled in $250,000 in annual sales, while Billabong neared $900,000. The surf companies designed specifically for surfers seeking performance and comfort. There was little fashion in it, and style was merely an afterthought.

Shawn Owen Stüssy was born in 1954 to Betty and Kenneth Stussy, who owned and operated a small printing business called Pace Printers. He had three siblings—two sisters, Reggie and Holly, and a younger brother, Brock—and the family grew up in Garden Grove, a city in northern Orange County. Ken was trained as an air force pilot in World War II and later worked in the graphics department of aerospace and defense company Northrop before starting his printing business. Betty took care of the kids and worked as a seamstress part-time. There was no shortage of aunts, uncles, and cousins nearby.

Shawn made his first surfboard in the family garage at thirteen, carving it from Reggie's longboard, and started to make boards for friends. When Shawn entered high school, his woodshop teacher, Bob "Ole" Olsen, was an established local shaper who would go on to be inducted into the International Surfboard Builders Hall of Fame. Once Bob heard about Shawn's extracurricular hobby, he gave him an old power-driven planer called the Skil 100. The next year, Bob offered him a part-time job at his surf shop, providing Shawn with both a paycheck and work experience—and, more important, a master class in creating perfect curved squash tails and boxy rails.

When he graduated high school in 1972, Shawn's main gig was with Russell Surfboards, a shop in nearby Newport Beach, where he shaped boards and occasionally did design work. In the winter months, Shawn packed his clementine-colored Beetle and drove six hours north to Mammoth Lakes, a quirky mountain town where he lived in a tiny trailer and made money as an instructor at the local skiing school. When the snow season ended, he returned to Laguna Beach to shape boards and surf. Shawn also worked as a graphic designer for other nearby surf brands, namely Gotcha, founded by a former hard-partying pro named Michael Tomson. The rebellious label introduced a new level of envelope-pushing that the surf world hadn't yet seen, through bold designs and attitude-heavy magazine ads.

By the late seventies, Shawn's boards had earned him a reputation as a forward-thinking shaper, and local pro surfers were loyal to his work. What Shawn really wanted, though, was to work for himself and play by the rules of a painter.

"It was like my art. The way that I made boards, it was like a sculpture. It wasn't like a job," he would later say.

Shawn eventually made the leap and struck out on his own, quitting Russell Surfboards and taking to that small workspace on Laguna Canyon Road. He officially registered his new business venture as "Stüssy New Wave Designs" with the state. Not long after he set up in his new studio space, his phone rang with a call from a Japanese woman. Her boss, a businessman who owned a surfboard company in the Japanese countryside near Shizunami Beach, had recently traveled to California, and he wanted Shawn to come to Japan for a month to work for him. Shawn packed his tools and went for five weeks, coming home with a stack of neatly folded yen that he'd take to the bank to pay off his credit card.

In February 1981, the year after Shawn opened up his solo studio, a new trade show called Action Sports Retailer (ASR) popped up in Long Beach, a forty-five-minute cruise northward from his studio. It was purely focused on the growing surf, snow, and skate industries. The show's founders badly wanted the young and in-demand shaper at their show. They offered Shawn a small booth for free.

On a whim, Shawn screen-printed his scribbled Stüssy signature—the same one that marked his boards—on Hanes T-shirt blanks. The design concept was simple, inspired by the tees made by Tony Alva, the long-haired Venice Beach skateboarder famous for skating in empty swimming pools. These shirts served as self-promotion, a way to help Shawn sell more of his boards and to make his company look more established than it was. He didn't even have a line sheet with prices.

By the end of that trade show, he'd sold about two dozen boards. But his last-minute T-shirt design booked orders for over one thousand Stüssy tees.

Oh fuck, Shawn thought. *Are you kidding me?*

One thousand shirts at eight bucks a pop was $8,000. That was a mountain of money to him, even more than he made from his boards. More significantly, it was easier money. While other shapers churned out five boards a day, Shawn preferred to spend the entire day on a single board, putting on Marley or the Pistols and sparking an oversized joint, stretching the process into something more serene. The unexpected T-shirt orders provided an opportunity to pocket more cash without having to become, as he put it, a "production" shaper.

Shawn showed up at his second ASR trade show with his surfboards and two new T-shirt designs, and found himself with another unexpected fashion hit. This time it was in the form of some homespun shorts: He had taken chino pants from a local army-navy store and hacked them above the knee, giving them a slightly longer silhouette than the thigh-baring Ocean Pacific style popular among surfers at the time. To Shawn's surprise, buyers and shop owners kept asking about his DIY shorts throughout the day. By the end of the trade show, he had hundreds of orders for a Stüssy garment that he hadn't even thought to try and sell. He went out and bought every pair of chinos he could find, close to four hundred of them, clearing out every surplus store in the area.

Toward the end of 1981, Shawn had generated about $25,000 in sales.

"It was never like, *I'm going to start a clothing line,*" he recalled. "It was just kind of a street-smart flea market kid going, *Well, fuck, I could make a hundred of those. That's easier than making ten boards, and I make more money.*"

Shawn kept running into one problem: The T-shirt orders were getting bigger and more expensive to print, and he never had enough cash to cover the up-front costs. (Stores typically pay vendors on "net 30" terms, meaning one is paid a month *after* delivering the product.) One trade show forced him to borrow money from his accountant, a fellow surfer named Frank Sinatra Jr. (no relation to the famous singer). When that money got eaten up, Shawn went back to ask for another loan.

I'm not going to lend you any more money, Frank told him.

Instead, the accountant proposed a partnership. The surfboards were a labor of love. The two Californians knew the money was in the clothes. Together, they set out to get it.

2.

The Subway School

Leonard "Lenny" McGurr threw up his first tag in 1970 at the start of what became known as the Graffiti War, a decades-long battle between outlaw graffiti writers and New York City officials. Most New Yorkers hated these paint vandals for covering the subway system they rode in messy scrawls and depleting their hard-earned taxpayer money in cleanup costs. The city spent millions upon millions in prevention, adding a skyscraper's worth of razor-wire fencing to subway yards and increasing aggressive policing; the kids fought back with a reckless verve and enough spray paint to fill the Hudson River. At the time, Lenny was a dark-haired and lanky teenager, often mistaken for much younger than he actually was. For him and his peers, it was how they pursued self-expression.

Futura 2000 was his tag, a new-wave spin on the classic writer-name format. Most writers used an alias and a number that often matched the street they lived on: TAKI 183, C.A.T. 87, Frank 207, Joe 136, Phase 2. Lenny took his by combining the name of a sleek-looking Ford with a futuristic Stanley Kubrick reference. In high school, he linked up with an uptown crew known as the Soul Artists of Zoo York, started by a childhood friend named Marc

André Edmonds (ALI). Over an autumn weekend in 1973, Lenny and Marc had an experience in the subway tunnels they'd never forget.

In the ultra-flat black of night and armed with fifty spray cans in an overstuffed bag, their plan was to tag six trains—or *wagons*, in the argot—parked in the layup tunnel under Broadway. They were in the midst of spraying when, without warning, the train's lights buzzed on, and Lenny saw an enormous flash. It was the sweepers. When the train's power clicked on, so did the rail's electricity, which ignited the pressurized aerosol cans and sparked the aerosol vapors in the air, creating the blast of fire and shrapnel. Marc survived but was badly burned and wounded. One month later, Marc, identified only as "Ali," gave an interview to the *New York Times*, warning the masses of the dangers of subway graffiti. "People ought to have canvas to work on."

After the incident, Lenny enrolled in a globetrotting four-year stint in the Merchant Marines and eventually returned to New York in 1979 to find the graffiti scene drastically different than when he left. The art world had started to pay attention, and some of his old crew had evolved beyond train yards. He reconnected with Marc, who had set up a studio storefront called the Soul Artists on 107th Street and Columbus Avenue, near the very top of Central Park. Marc pushed graffiti as an established and legitimate art form by bringing it indoors and to the canvas. Lenny became a regular at the space, as did Eric Haze (SE3, HAZE), a prolific tagger from the Upper West Side, and Lee Quiñones (LEE) from the Lower East Side.

Their uptown crew had started to bump shoulders with the lively East Village art scene, thanks to Fred "Fab 5 Freddy" Brathwaite (Bull 99, Showdown 177), a charismatic and nattily dressed Brooklyn-born tagger who befriended the arty eccentrics below Central Park. Freddy moved through both worlds with ease, bringing his downtown cohorts to the uptown Soul Artists studio. Lenny met Jean-Michel Basquiat (SAMO), a poetic graffitist who ran wild around Lower Manhattan, and Keith Haring, a bespectacled art-college student who filled subway stations with his illustrations. Other clued-in New Yorkers filtered through 107th Street, too: artist-impresario Andy Warhol, fashion scribe Glenn O'Brien, photojournalist Martha Cooper.

Lenny experimented with new visuals and techniques, leaving the cartoonish wild-style lettering of the seventies behind in favor of more abstract fare. He learned that angling the paint canister afforded him greater control of the nozzle, allowing him to manipulate the aerosol pressure to deliver lines as fine as spiderwebs. This new mode of working yielded his *Break* mural in 1980. It was an otherworldly painting that spanned an entire subway car—sixty feet of metal teeming with effulgent hues of red, orange, and yellow—and it was immortalized in a photograph by Martha Cooper. Most graffiti artists relied on DIY cardboard cameras or Instamatics to document their work. Martha's photo—of the painted and moving train suspended in crisp stillness on elevated tracks—was shot on luxurious Kodachrome film and delivered the rich colors of a professional photographer. The painting and the photograph put the twenty-five-year-old on the map, elevating him from Lenny to *Futura*, from wagon writer to graffiti artist.

In 1980, the *Village Voice* published a cover story on graffiti's slow drip into the art world, written by journalist Richard Goldstein, who likened what was happening in train yards to the birth of rock 'n' roll. The article, titled "In Praise of Graffiti," featured Futura, HAZE, ALI, and Fab 5 Freddy and noted that Freddy had started reading *Artforum* magazine and that a few of the writers had even begun to *buy* their paint, as opposed to stealing it. "The possibility of a career in fashion, graphic design, or even art is making inroads into traditional assumptions about what graffiti is," wrote Goldstein. The older Lenny and his peers got, the less appealing scaling barbed-wire fences seemed. They spent fewer hours in train yards and more time in studios, working on canvas and navigating an antiquated art establishment that was slowly warming to their talents. When Martha Cooper looked to publish a graffiti photo book, it was rejected by every American publisher it was submitted to. (It was eventually published in 1984 by London-based Thames & Hudson as *Subway Art*; her photograph of Futura's *Break* train was given a two-page spread.)

As the graffitists received more ink in major newspapers, New York City was in the midst of an art boom. In 1970, there were 73 galleries listed in *Art Now: New York Gallery Guide*; by the mid-eighties, that number had shot up to nearly 450. The surge, and an increased commodification of art, was fueled by new money on Wall Street and the strength of the Japanese yen. The white-collar art dealer Jeffrey Deitch gave Jean-Michel Basquiat his first major press hit, comparing him to famed abstract expressionist Willem de Kooning.

At first, Futura started on the outskirts of the gallery system; his earliest shows were at downtown queen Patti Astor's Fun Gallery in the East Village. In early 1981, Futura and Fab 5 Freddy co-curated *Beyond Words*, a show at the super-trendy Mudd Club that included works from Jean-Michel Basquiat, Keith Haring, Kenny Scharf, Eric Haze, and others. The same year, a massive and epoch-making exhibition at PS1 Contemporary Art Center (now MoMA PS 1) titled *New York/New Wave* debuted, featuring Futura and his friends alongside buzzy names like Nan Goldin and David Byrne—over one hundred artists in total. In a review for Warhol's *Interview* magazine, Glenn O'Brien proclaimed, "Here's a whole new art world ready to replace the old one."

"That show brought us into a bigger picture now, where we weren't just subway vandals," recalled Futura.

Two years later, Futura's works were again featured alongside Basquiat's and Haring's in *Post-Graffiti*, a big-time exhibition hosted by blue-chip gallerist Sidney Janis, who saw graffiti as continuing "the tradition of Pop Art." Futura quickly became a known entity in downtown circles and a small-time graffiti sensation. He bumped elbows with Madonna and Andy Warhol and swirled around SoHo, Tribeca, and beyond. He remained one of Fun Gallery's top sellers, with prices reaching $6,000 a canvas, and received sanctioned mural projects, like one he painted with Eric Haze on Park Avenue. But Futura didn't find the transition into the art world as easy or as lucrative as some of his contemporaries; he could not crack the art of securing patronage.

"Comparisons were being made to me and other well-known artists, like Kandinsky or whoever. I didn't really get it. I get it now. But at that time . . . I had a rough time of it," he said.

In 1986, Keith Haring opened the Pop Shop, an experimental retail location at 292 Lafayette Street in the city's SoHo neighborhood (its name short for *south of Houston*). People whispered it was an Andy Warhol stunt, but it was all Haring with his own money. The small but slick storefront split the differences between fashion boutique, art gallery, and nightclub. It was coated in floor-to-ceiling graffiti, and the T-shirts hung on the walls like paintings; dance music blared incessantly. A Keith Haring canvas cost six figures, but at the Pop Shop you could buy a Haring poster or T-shirt for twenty dollars and a sweatshirt for thirty. The shop also sold items from Keith's friends: Kenny Scharf, Jean-Michel Basquiat, Eric Haze, and Futura. This was not Basquiat's first foray into clothing: In the late 1970s, when the graffitist was still a teenager, he produced hand-painted clothing under the label Man Made. Basquiat took items like trench coats and sweatshirts, often found on the street, and branded them with his art. At one point, the clothes were sold in Patricia Field's small boutique in the East Village.

"Keith encouraged me to do my first T-shirt," recalled Eric. It led to his T-shirts and stickers getting picked up by Wheels, a skate shop in Santa Monica, and a Rough Trade record store in London. The move from subway cars to T-shirts made Eric realize that graffiti writers were essentially typographers and designers. At around the age of twenty-three, Eric enrolled in the School of Visual Arts in New York City to formally study graphic design. "I was in that last generation before the computer . . . to come through an educational system with a T-square ruler, spray mount, and hot wax." Eric leveraged his street sensibility with his graphic acumen and became a pioneering hand in shaping the visual language of hip-hop during the eighties, working with the Beastie Boys, Run-DMC, LL Cool J, and Public Enemy.

In 1987, Def Jam Recordings flew Eric and Dante Ross, a former graffiti writer turned "street-smart B-boy" A&R representative, to the Action Sports Retailer trade show in San Diego. The duo was sent to land Beastie Boys a skateboard partnership; they came close with Brad Dorfman's Vision Street Wear, a category-bending skateboard and fashion company that had just crossed $30 million in annual sales. The deal ultimately fell apart, but the trip proved worthwhile anyway. "We hooked up and became friends with like, Shawn Stüssy, Gonz [Mark Gonzales] . . . and the whole Dogtown crew," recalled Eric. "I spent a night smoking out in a hotel room with Shawn when we first met. We were both struck immediately that we both had these graphic languages—his was born out of surfing, and mine was born out of graffiti—which were so much sort of these parallel underground worlds." Eric and Dante had a blank-labeled copy of Public Enemy's *Yo! Bum Rush the Show* and the latest Beastie Boys tracks that they played for the surfers and skaters. "We sort of turned everybody on to these beats and albums that week. To me, that was one key flash point for East Coast meeting West Coast, hip-hop meeting surf and skate. . . . After a week at the trade show wilding out, we just felt like, *Yo. We're part of this scene now.*"

In New York, Futura focused on making it within the downtown art scene, even after he learned that crossover artists like Basquiat and Haring were much better at the game of securing patronage. "These people had a bit more art knowledge, whether they went to school or had read books about art history," Futura said. "I was a bit more ignorant then, because it simply wasn't my backstory. I didn't go to art school." Basquiat made paintings that sold for upward of $25,000; Haring's work climbed to $40,000 a canvas and rose to $350,000 by the decade's end. Futura's profile never rose beyond $6,000 paintings, and the red-hot buzz of spray paint on canvas cooled down as the eighties came to a close.

"I just couldn't make it as a gallery artist. It just wasn't working, and people weren't really interested anymore in graffiti per se. So it was my exit," recalled Futura.

By the end of the eighties, the decade's downtown art boom came to an end with the untimely deaths of Basquiat in 1988, then Haring in 1990. It was nearly impossible to write illegal graffiti in the train yards. The Graffiti War was over, and the city had won. Futura took odd jobs to make ends meet. He had married a Frenchwoman named C.C. he'd met while on tour in Europe with British punks the Clash, and the couple now had a young son. A new sense of responsibility kicked in. The art world money was no longer there, and bills needed to be paid. He worked as a bike messenger, drove for an off-book cab service, and sorted mail at a Queens post office. He didn't abandon his art completely thanks to the French fashion designer Agnès Troublé of the label agnès b., who secured him an art studio in Williamsburg, Brooklyn, and paid for two years' rent.

The gesture was enough for Lenny to keep painting and writing the Futura 2000 name, hoping that the next wave would hit.

3.
Boosting Silk Crizzys

On a brisk Friday morning in 1988, Rack-Lo sprinted through Midtown Manhattan as fast as his heavy Timberland boots let him. He darted out of the Lord & Taylor department store, but the sticky-fingered teenager wasn't in the clear yet. He had a thousand dollars' worth of Polo Ralph Lauren clothes stuffed into his jacket and one store detective chasing after him, inching closer and closer with each step.

Your ass is going to jail, motherfucker! shouted the guard.

Hell motherfucking no . . . Rack-Lo thought, picking up his pace.

The guy lunged at him and grabbed on to his backpack, yanking at it like a linebacker going for a nasty tackle. But Rack-Lo, trim and quick-footed, was an expert booster who had done this dozens of times before. The backpack was empty, a cheap nylon decoy. He shimmied out and let his chaser have it, a booster's olive branch. The guard almost lost his footing but stayed upright, gritting his teeth as he steamed onward, making up the distance with each stride.

Rack-Lo was not about to get busted that day. He pulled up the back of his jacket and let two or three shiny silk tops flutter onto the dirty sidewalk. The store cop slowed down slightly to pick up the shirts, which gained Rack-Lo a few extra steps, but the pursuit continued. He realized he'd have to give it all up to get this tenacious guard off his tail. He admitted defeat and lifted his shirt again so the remaining armful of shirts fell out. It was enough to stop the detective in his tracks, picking them up and looking ahead as Rack-Lo disappeared into the Midtown bustle.

Rack-Lo cut around the block's corner and bolted into the nearby subway station. He stomped down the stairs, shoving through the turnstile and onto the train platform. He moved through the station without making eye contact with anyone and hopped down on the tracks to escape through the West Thirty-Ninth Street tunnel. He headed south to Thirty-Fourth Street station, where he hopped up on the platform and joined the crowd waiting for the next subway like he was just another commuter.

"The only thing about that day I regret is that I wish I came home with those silk crizzys."

Rack-Lo and his friends had snappy, slangy vernacular for everything. A *silk crizzy* was the Polo Ralph Lauren silk shirt with a vibrant, ornate crest on the front. It was a women's piece, but that didn't matter to them; his crew turned any Polo piece into a totem of cool. When you wore something so fly that people in the neighborhood practically strained themselves to catch a glimpse, you were *breaking necks*. Polo Ralph Lauren, the American designer's sportier sub-label, was *Lo*, and to *rack* was to steal. The shoplifting gang of Brooklyn teenagers he ran with had a nickname of their own: They were the Lo Life Crew, or the Lo Lifes for short.

Ralph Lauren was founded by a Jewish designer named Ralph Lifshitz, who grew up in the lower-middle-class Mosholu Parkway area of the Bronx. He started off as a salesman at the ultra-preppy Brooks Brothers before designing a collection of wide neckties under the name Polo and eventually expanding to a complete menswear line. By the eighties, Ralph Lauren had become a full-blown lifestyle brand for the country's upper middle class. Its advertisements pictured well-heeled families sailing expensive yachts, playing polo, and relaxing on lavish estates. The Ralph Lauren family was almost always white, and the prices were always high. A basic oxford shirt cost nearly $70, and a suit could run well past $1,000. It symbolized a new kind of American luxury.

The Overspent American, a book later published by economist Juliet B. Schor, explored how an excessive and uniquely American concern with social status fueled the Reagan-era consumerism of the eighties. Schor also examined the psychology that drives those who cannot afford it toward these aspirational symbols. "For many low-income individuals, the lure of consumerism is hard to resist," she wrote. "When the money isn't there, however, feelings of deprivation, personal failure, and deep psychic pain result. In a culture where consuming means so much, not having money is a profound social disability."

An emerging class of upwardly mobile young professionals, more concerned with image and status than previous demographic groups, spent money on the luxury symbols of the decade: private education for their children, color TV sets for their homes, and designer clothes for their closets. The Ralph Lauren label appealed directly to this new group. By the late eighties, Polo/Ralph Lauren reported annual revenues of $700 million. Everyone who could afford to, it seemed, wanted to buy a piece of Ralph Lauren's fever dream of white upper-middle-class America. And those who couldn't afford to buy it decided they'd just steal it.

As the rapper KRS-One rhymed on a 1987 Boogie Down Productions track: *Manhattan keeps on makin' it, Brooklyn keeps on takin' it.*

The Lo Life Crew officially came together in 1988, a united front made from two Brooklyn shoplifting crews: Ralphie's Kids, from St. John's Place in Crown Heights; and POLO U.S.A., for United Shoplifters Association, from Marcus Garvey Village in Brownsville. Neighborhoods like these especially felt the brutal downward force of eighties New York: the crack epidemic, aggressive stop-and-frisk policing, rising crime and homicide rates. The two groups boosted individually, sometimes playing nice with each other and other times fighting. Rack-Lo, né George Billips, wanted to make them whole. Each guy brought his own moral compass to the group. Some sold drugs, some robbed, and some earned straight paychecks. Almost all of them schemed.

They learned how to empty a pay phone's money box with a hammer, chisel, and nail, sometimes making off with a hundred dollars' worth of quarters. They'd snatch gold chains from passersby or ransack apartments for TVs and stereo systems. Or purposely jam up a subway turnstile and then extract the tokens. Sometimes they'd even rob a rival booster.

"I've always been poor, so I always stole. . . . I had a thousand ways to take the things I wanted. I would stick up a booster after they went boosting," recalled Victor "Thirstin Howl the 3rd" DeJesus, then known as Big Vic Lo, who cofounded the crew alongside Rack-Lo. Almost everyone who was serious about boosting had a nickname: Rack-Lo, Big Vic Lo, Boostin' Billy, Bek-Live, Fi-Lo, Prance-Lo, Uncle Disco, B-Bob Lo.

The Lo Lifes found strength and success in greater numbers. Some of the younger crew started out as "bag men." You'd enter the store with an older and more experienced booster, and they'd be the one to throw the clothes into the bag and hand it off to you, and it was on you to run out with it. Within the crew, there was a brotherly competition. If you had some really exclusive Ralph Lauren pieces, you stood out as an original. It wasn't all just for fashion, though. Many Lo Lifes also stole merchandise to flip on the streets.

"It was about survival. Coming to places like Bloomingdale's enabled us to survive. To put food on the table for our families and to pay bills," recalled Rack-Lo.

They tormented retailers of all kinds in every corner of the city. Higher-end Manhattan department stores—Bloomingdale's, Bergdorf Goodman, Lord & Taylor, Saks Fifth Avenue—were frequent targets. But they'd do the same to lower-rent spots, like Bargain Factory Outlet in Yonkers or Joey's Kids in Long Island, sporting goods stores with marked-down Polo at the season's end. Over the years, they'd even venture out to New Jersey and Connecticut for missions, sometimes traveling as far as New Hampshire and Pennsylvania. "These were items of respect and gave you social status in your neighborhood," remembered Victor. "To actually come back with some high-end stuff from Fifth Avenue and wear it in the projects, it made you somebody."

When stores made shoppers check bags at the door or added alarm sensors, the Lo Lifes found clever ways to circumvent. A store had a no-backpack policy? They'd stuff merchandise down the front of their pants, or wear women's girdles to conceal the goods. Those pesky alarms? The crew devised bags from aluminum foil and thick gray tape to fool the sensors so the security system wouldn't be activated as they walked out. But perhaps the most brazen and fearless method was what they called the million-man rush. "We would go into the store with fifty heads," explained Rack-Lo. "You snatched what you wanted and just ran out, like a hit-and-run."

The crew became well-known among the NYPD, and the New York City tabloids loved to cover their boosting sprees. The goal, obviously, was to get away with it, no matter what. But even the best boosters could only avoid handcuffs for so long. "If somebody got arrested, we still went on. Getting arrested was a part of the game," explained one Lo Life member.

Beyond the law-breaking methods of acquiring the gear, the Lo Life crew wore the Ralph Lauren gear in a fresh way. It was showy and bombastic, full of swagger. The crew would color-coordinate and stack logos on logos. You'd match your cap to your jacket to your tee. It was a whole new way of wearing the clothes, as opulent and maximalist as the Apthorp building on the Upper West Side. The showier the style, the better. The stuntworthy attitude of wearing as much of one label as possible, a total devotion to a singular brand, was new to the city's sartorial canon.

When Black teenagers in the Bronx first started to remix and rhyme over rock 'n' roll and disco records, they were taking existing forms and making them their own. The Lo Life Crew did something similar, taking Ralph Lauren's beautiful dream of white upper-class affluence and inventing a new type of streetwise style along the way. It was the same for Daniel Day, better known as Dapper Dan, in Harlem, who designed opulent garments out of leather printed with the logos of Louis Vuitton and Gucci; he called them knock-*ups* because they were too luxurious to be called knockoffs. "When I was growing up, if you had diamonds and furs, that gave you clout," Dapper Dan once recalled. "When the big fashion brands began to come out, I noticed how people gravitated toward them, and that what identified these brands was their logo." Ralph Lauren was perhaps the first American designer whose logo inspired similar envy to a Louis Vuitton one.

The *Lo Life look* went from a Brooklyn thing to a citywide thing. The streets of Harlem were no longer full of fur coats and velour tracksuits. The rising hip-hop scene—from MCs and DJs to entourages and other hangers-on—adopted the look as well.

"When Lo Life started wearing Polo, it was all eyes on us, like *Who are these kids with all these bright colors?*" recalled Rack-Lo. The way he and his friends wore Polo was unique to their worldview, different from what you'd see in the magazine ads or on billboards. They paired Polo parkas and sweaters with denim as stiff as wood planks, with Nike and New Balance sneakers or Timberland boots on their feet and baseball caps rested artfully askew on their heads. The official Polo ads of the era were more likely to feature herringbone trousers and tweed blazers. The look the Lo Lifes invented was big and baggy and bold—or as Rack-Lo put it, "We looked like the millionaires of the hood."

The Lo Life Crew, alongside the likes of Dapper Dan, were early to transfer aspirational power from luxury materials to a logo. They rewrote the codes of inner-city status, expanding the definition from opulent fur and gold chains to include logos and branding. It was only a matter of time before garments with the right logo held as much street-ready prestige and power as monogrammed patterns imported from Europe on garments made in more costly fabrics. To Rack-Lo and his crew, the Ralph Lauren logo was everything in one neat package. It symbolized the lifestyle aspiration, the feeling of belonging. That finally, a singular American fashion brand could be worthy of religious devotion. It marked the dawn of a new kind of designer and hinted at the rise of the megabrand.

4.
An Accidental Clothing Designer

Instead of cash, Shawn Stüssy sometimes paid his tax accountant the currency of a fresh surfboard. Frank Sinatra Jr. was aware of Shawn's reputation and the mythical Stüssy board. "It was like getting in a sports car versus being in a Chevrolet Impala," he recalled. Frank knew he wasn't doing taxes for just any average surfboard shaper.

Frank was a year older than Shawn and grew up in Hacienda Heights, on the outskirts of Los Angeles, and later relocated to Orange County. His father was from New York City and worked as a presser for a suit manufacturer before moving to California and starting a business producing made-to-order uniforms for police departments. Frank used to help with his dad's company on weekends, but had zero interest in taking over one day. It was a dead business, in his mind. When Frank graduated from college, he started working as a certified public accountant at a large firm that dealt with emerging businesses preparing to go public. He often helped local businessmen with their taxes and kept his ears open for any opportunities outside of his day job.

"Shawn and I would have conversations while I'm interviewing him about his taxes. We talked about his dream for the business, what he wanted to do, and I'd offer my advice," recalled Frank. "We became close enough that we would be talking about these ideas that evolved into the business."

Toward the end of 1981, Frank put up $5,000 of his own money to become a part owner, with a 50 percent ownership stake in the company. The division of labor was simple: Shawn handled all the creative duties, while Frank managed the reality of running a profitable business. By the second year, around 1982 to 1983, Stüssy's sales had doubled, from $25,000 to $50,000.

Frank kept the company's overhead low; he worked for zero money, and Shawn worked for very little. Each season, the collection expanded in scope to include more graphics and clothes. The T-shirt remained the main attraction, but they added an easy-wearing "beach pant" and a striped knit top with a mock neck. The surfboards faded into the background as the apparel ramped up. It was clear they were onto something.

"Each season was a little bigger than the last season," said Frank. "But Shawn was pretty frustrated that we weren't bigger, which would give him the resources to do more things from a fashion point of view. Fashion in surf shops was just starting to take off, but we weren't Gotcha. We weren't Quiksilver. We weren't Ocean Pacific. We weren't doing big numbers."

The next year, the brand caught a break in the form of Ken Engstrom, an old-school salesman of a different era. He was nearly twenty years older than Shawn and Frank and had worked for Warnaco, selling brassieres and underwear before moving over to the surfwear industry. Frank knew a connected sales rep was key to getting to the next level. "When you're that small, it's hard to hire a rep, because your rep can't afford to feed himself from an order of three dozen T-shirts," he said. But Ken had approached Frank; he was unhappy at his current gig working for the surf label Gotcha.

Ken, your commission at Gotcha is twice our revenue, Frank joked.

Gotcha was booming, shipping to department stores across the country. But the company had cut Ken's commissions, so he was willing to take a chance with the smaller brand. When he signed on with Shawn and Frank, his impact was instant. Ken brought in $1 million in that first year because of his established relationships with all the buyers. He brought Stüssy to Nordstrom and Vans, expanding the brand outside of California. The shops trusted him.

A Stüssy collection was still streamlined, maybe fifteen products within a line sheet: T-shirts, one pair of shorts, one pair of pants. To help with the growing business, Frank brought on his younger sister, Emmy Coats (then Sinatra). Fifty percent of the sales volume was T-shirts, which made things even easier to produce.

"Once you get to a million dollars in a couple of visible volume stores, everybody else notices," said Frank. "And they start talking about it."

Surfwear became a booming industry and grossed more than $1 billion in 1987. Shawn's former employer Gotcha approached $100 million in annual sales; Quiksilver hit nearly $34 million; and the industry juggernaut Ocean Pacific (OP) was tracking toward $380 million, boosted from global distribution and licensing.

That year, an article in the *Los Angeles Times* called Orange County's beach towns the "Silicon Valley of rad threads." It was estimated that there were now about four hundred surf companies, with over one-third of them based in Shawn's neck of the woods.

Stüssy was a minnow among sharks. The de facto way of doing business was to plaster advertisements in surfing magazines and to sponsor surfing contests and pro surfers. Gotcha planned to invest half a million dollars in surfing contests, and OP spent $300,000. Shawn and Frank knew they couldn't make that type of investment in advertising and marketing. They needed to find an alternative way to get the word out about Stüssy, and it had to be cheaper.

In 1987, as the worlds of East Coast hip-hop and West Coast surf and skate continued to merge, Shawn flew out to a trade show in Manhattan, where he met a guy a decade younger than him named Paul Mittleman. Paul was fresh out of high school, a grown-up New York City kid whose parents owned one of the most popular new and vintage stores in the city, Pandemonium, on Broadway near Seventy-Fifth Street. He was plugged into the city's nightlife scene and he worked at Pandemonium from time to time, helping out the family business when needed. Paul's father occasionally sent him to trade shows to scout new labels.

Paul noticed the Stüssy booth right away. He recognized the handwritten logo from surf magazines but didn't otherwise know much about the brand. He walked up to the booth, and the two started talking. Shawn mentioned that he didn't know anyone in the city, so Paul invited him out to dinner. "A night or two later, I took him out to some nightclubs. He started meeting my friends, and I guess in a very random way that's how the whole 'Stüssy Tribe' thing really started," recalled Paul. The two became fast friends.

The International Stüssy Tribe (IST) was born out of that group, Shawn's growing international friendships, and others like it. Shawn's friendship with Paul wasn't a one-off. He started to form bonds with many across the globe throughout his travels, "an oddball eclectic group of people," as he later put it. In New York, there was Paul, Dante Ross, Albee Ragusa, Jules Gayton, and Lono Brazil. London had a strong showing: filmmakers, DJs, and musicians, including Michael Kopelman, Mick Jones, Alex Turnbull, Goldie, brothers James and Mark Lebon, and eventually Malcolm McLaren, the famed impresario and image architect behind the Sex Pistols. In Italy, there was Slam Jam founder and clothing distributor Luca Benini, and in Tokyo, Shawn befriended Hiroshi Fujiwara, a young magazine writer and perhaps the first DJ to start playing American hip-hop in Japan. This group started out small but grew alongside Shawn and the brand, expanding to include painters, taggers, record producers, musicians, DJs, club promoters, impresarios, and every type of hip scenester in between. These were the arbiters of emerging culture, the cutting-edge tastemakers from all over the world.

"We couldn't afford high-fashion brands, so the way you put together an outfit was the best way to express your style," recalled New York IST member Jules Gayton.

"We liked music. We knew about art. We liked to go out at night. We had nothing else to do. We liked to smoke pot and drink beer. We liked to skateboard," said Paul. And most notably, "We all had a certain fashion style." This group mind fed into Shawn's thought process about the fashion direction for Stüssy. The ragtag crew quickly became the cultural driving force that powered the brand and Shawn's target audience.

"I don't think of myself as a designer by any means. I'm a clothing man who makes what he and his friends like to wear," Shawn said at the time.

The downtown New York way of dressing was an amalgam of several styles, one that fused skate culture and hip-hop with a dose of American workwear and a wink and nod to sharp runway fashion. This assembled street aesthetic became the calling card for how the otherwise effortlessly cool were dressing—and it was exactly how Shawn was designing.

"Shawn started looking at things a little bit differently when he started going to New York," recalled Paul. "He was always into reggae, but he knew nothing about hip-hop. Then he saw it was the soundtrack of what was going on."

Shawn gave the New York City look a wholehearted embrace. Stüssy played into those cultural references like no other, and Shawn blended high design, downtown coolness, and a tough attitude into his collections. "Shawn's outlook for culture and fashion completely opened up," said Frank. "The rest of the surf industry wasn't doing this. They were surfers. Shawn was much more than that."

"I got no inspiration from the surf world," Shawn later said. "I just fell into hip-hop and the club culture in New York."

As the Tribe grew, so did Stüssy, from a humble California surf label to a global in-the-know fashion brand. It didn't take long for the clothes to land on the radar of stylists, editors, and the otherwise influential. The clothing began to regularly appear in editorial layouts in fashion magazines in the United States, England, Germany, and Japan. London Tribe member Michael Kopelman launched the label in the United Kingdom with his new distribution company, Gimme 5. Shawn's reputation as a shaper and graphic designer had turned him into a cultlike figure in Japan, and the label found itself stocked in a growing network of shops in Tokyo and beyond. The sales orders from the American trade show circuit were bigger than ever before.

"London and New York and Tokyo are seen as major fashion centers, and I think they put Shawn on the map as far as vibe, as far as legitimizing his place in fashion," one international Stüssy distributor said at the time.

Shawn sent notes and sketches from all over the world via fax to Emmy and Frank in California. He was spending three months of every year traveling: New York, London, Paris, and Tokyo, visiting fashion boutiques by day and hip clubs by night, soaking up a city's style and collecting inspiration for his own designs. Shawn would return to Laguna Beach with an armful of garments he'd found while exploring a flea market or vintage store. It could be a flannel shirt or a pair of workwear trousers, and he'd give it to Emmy, who had to reverse-engineer the style and then put it into production with the help of a local patternmaker named Cynthia. It was an unconventional way for a designer to work, but Shawn had no formal fashion training and didn't know how to cut a pattern himself. There was a magic to it that worked. Neither Frank nor Emmy wanted to risk messing with it—so they rode it out. Plus they didn't have anywhere else to turn.

"Shawn was the creative director, Shawn was the designer, Shawn was the advertising director. He was the entire design team," recalled Frank.

Each season, the orders placed by stores at the trade shows grew, and the label added more and more styles. The sudden growth was tricky to navigate, but luckily the bulk of their collections still centered on the graphic tee.

"The beauty of a T-shirt is you could schedule out some blanks with your vendor and deliver it to a screen printer, get it delivered and ship it, and get paid by the store pretty much in time to pay the bill for all that," Frank said. "In the parlance of the industry, we call that inventory turns. At a standard clothing company, your inventory turns four times a year. Our inventory turned like ten times."

With a smooth-running production system in place and the IST spreading the Stüssy gospel in major cities across the globe, the company had reached that next level. It was no longer just one surfer making clothes for other surfers in his workshop. Thanks to the IST and their clued-in friends, you could wear a Stüssy shirt to a nightclub, or to a hip-hop show or to skate in. The *Los Angeles Times* proclaimed, "If anyone can bridge the gap between beach and street fashion, it is probably Shawn Stüssy."

"A lot of people tell us we're blowing it by not growing faster, but we see it more as a matter of not being greedy," Shawn said at the time. "Because we have controlled our growth, we have evolved naturally and called the shots our way."

In 1988, Shawn and Frank hit around $10 million in sales.

Word bounced around the industry that Stüssy could have easily pulled in twice that.

5.
Underground Fashion

Deep in New York's SoHo, the pulsing sound of rap filled up the room and then spilled out onto the sidewalk. It came from the fishbowl clothing boutique on Spring Street. At just three hundred square feet, it was about the size of a tiny studio apartment. It was called Union NYC, perhaps the first shop of its kind in America to cater to this new underground look: baggy and big and full of attitude. The name was meant to convey the inclusion of diverse trends under one roof and the crowd that shopped there: a mix of graffiti writers, skaters, club kids, aspiring graphic designers, and hip-hop heads. Once inside, you couldn't hear yourself think, let alone ask the clerk if you needed help with something.

Union opened its doors in 1989 and immediately felt more like a clubhouse than a clothing store. The employees wore some combination of voluminous pants and oversized hoodies and high-top sneakers. The store carried an experimental mix of classic English brands that were hard to get in the States, American workwear, some imported sneakers and footwear, and clothes from new up-and-coming T-shirt labels. Four-hundred-dollar Maharishi military pants were displayed next to $20 T-shirts from brands like

CONART, Pervert, and Freshjive. Plus the shop's in-house backpacks, constructed of vintage vinyl. It was one of the few places in the city to get the London label Duffer of St George, a personal favorite of the owner, an American British man named James Jebbia who ran the shop with his girlfriend, Mary Ann Fusco.

"Mary Ann was probably one of the first people in New York to resell sneakers," recalled Agustin "Augie" Galan, who worked the floor at Union. "She would go to London and bring back all the hot New Balances and Clarks and resell [them] for like three hundred dollars."

James was born in West Virginia in 1963, to an American father in the United States Air Force and a British mother, who raised the kids and later worked as a teacher. The family moved to England when James was a toddler, and his parents divorced when he was ten. James and his brother lived with their mother in Crawley, West Sussex, about twenty-eight miles south of London. As a teenager, he took the train into the city and spent his spare cash on clothes at its hidden gems. James loved the needle-haystack hunt of it all. When he turned nineteen, he moved to New York and lived in an apartment on Staten Island, paying $500 in monthly rent.

His first job in fashion was at Parachute, an avant-garde boutique that opened on SoHo's Wooster Street in 1980 and sold futuristic, high-end fashions and an innovative pick of Japanese brands to clientele that included David Bowie, Mick Jagger, and Andy Warhol. The shop was housed in a booming loft with grandiose pillars, industrial shelving, and buffed concrete floors. It felt like a modern art museum.

James applied the same week as Eddie Cruz, a gravel-voiced Bronx native who also held a deep passion for clothes and style. Both guys were hired, and the two became fast friends. "We hit it off. I could tell this guy was super ambitious," recalled Eddie. "He was the best salesman in the store. He made the most commissions." James was promoted to manager, and with the blessing of Morgan Allard, one of the store's partners, he opened his own booth at a nearby flea market. He purchased wares from the city's Garment District and imported British clothing to sell. For a short period, he even produced small batches of clothing under the label Blast with the help of Eddie, as Eddie's mother had a factory in the city. After five years of working at Parachute and running the stand with Mary Ann, James upgraded the booth to a proper brick-and-mortar shop, and Union was born.

Union wasn't the only store in downtown Manhattan trying to hit the bull's-eye of how the young, hip, and wild were dressing. There was Liquid Sky on Broome Street, more geared toward the New York rave scene, which sold everything from drum machines to giant wide-leg trousers and oversized graphic T-shirts. One block north of Washington Square Park was Patricia Field, the come-as-you-are boutique owned by the flame-haired woman of the same name. She sold arty fashions, including T-shirts by Keith Haring and Kenny Scharf. The SoHo neighborhood had been changing, too. Within the past decade, it went from eccentric vintage stores, art galleries, and live-work lofts to a more expansive shopping experience. There were now world-class boutiques like Comme des Garçons, Yohji Yamamoto, and agnès b.

Another newly opened downtown shop was called 555 Soul, on the Lower East Side, about a twelve-minute walk from SoHo. It was the project of Camella Ehlke, a petite and pixieish blond woman with the upbeat attitude of someone who always sought out the sun. Originally from Cleveland, she was studying fashion and art at the Pratt Institute in Brooklyn. And while 555 Soul was a storefront, it was also her clothing brand and her apartment.

The earliest 555 Soul designs were colorful, striped, and bold. Camella's influences borrowed from African tribal patterns, California surfwear, graffiti writers' lettering styles, and the nascent New York rap scene. Stocking caps and oversized hooded shirts. At first, things started out really slow. It was more of a hobby than a profitable business. "People just wanted things that looked new and interesting," she recalled. Everything was custom-made for her circle of friends, many of whom were up-and-coming DJs and MCs. Camella's store was proudly less official than a place like Union. She thought of herself not as a retailer like James but as more of an artist and designer. She had friends like Josh "Stash" Franklin come by to paint on fabric that she'd then turn into clothes. "I'd just buy all the spray cans and forties of malt liquor, and we would just make a party of it," Camella recalled. "It was easy in New York to be broke and creative." She sold T-shirts from her friends' labels like PNB Nation and SSUR, a T-shirt label started by Ruslan Karablin, a graphic designer and artist who moved from the Soviet Union to Brooklyn when he was five. "I started courting the 555 Soul store on the Lower East Side," recalled Russ. "Through Camella and [her] store, I got to meet people like Stash and Futura."

In 1991, the *New York Times* wrote about the shop, and its popularity grew. "Ludlow was trife back then," recalled Union's Augie. "I remember going to her shop and she was in the back sewing and I was like, 'Wow, this short white lady is hanging out on this really dangerous block.' Lower East Side was no joke. It was drugs, violence, anger . . . That's what attracted us to 555 Soul, too. Just the brazenness of it. That Camella just set up a shop on Ludlow to sell her stuff." Camella's clothes frequently turned up on hip-hop concert stages and in fashion magazines. A young Uptown Records A&R guy named Sean "Puffy" Combs once came in, wanting to hire her to make custom velour tracksuits for an R&B group he worked with called Jodeci. But Camella never rushed and kept her overhead low. The store didn't have a register, and she kept the cash from sales in a Phillies Blunt box. The sign on the door read: OPEN AT 12 P.M. OR WHENEVER I FEEL LIKE IT.

Union had been trying to get Stüssy on its shelves for a while. Everyone wanted Stüssy—the kids that shopped there asked for it directly—but landing an account with the label wasn't that easy. When James first reached out to one of the brand's sales managers, he was told that they weren't accepting any new accounts at the time. Both Shawn and Frank still worried about the label getting too big and losing its demand. Through a mutual friend, David "Shadi" Perez, James caught word that Shadi's friend Paul Mittleman had befriended Shawn while the designer had been in town. The next time Paul stopped by Union, James asked if he might pull some strings.

Funnily enough, I think Shawn is going to be here this month, Paul told him. Why don't you guys just meet?

The next week, Paul and Shawn were having lunch at a red-booth diner in SoHo on Prince Street. Paul walked the Californian over to Union, where Shawn checked out the shop and gave the store the thumbs-up on the spot. Stüssy quickly became the store's bestselling and most popular brand. James had never seen this type of sell-through before, not at Parachute or the flea market. Every time new Stüssy gear hit Union's shelves, it would immediately sell out. It bolstered James's business in a real and tangible way.

James knew the demand for the brand was so high it could easily support a standalone storefront. He approached Shawn with the idea. He'd be able to put whatever photos on the wall he wanted, play whatever music he wanted. It took little convincing for Shawn to get on board with the idea. The designer returned to Laguna Beach and pitched the idea to Frank.

Not in a million years, Frank replied. We're wholesalers, not retailers. That's a kiss of death.

Shawn was undeterred. He'd formed a friendship with James; the two just clicked. Plus he sensed how important New York was. He wasn't going to take no for an answer. Frank knew there was no talking him out of it. Shawn partnered directly with James, licensing his name for retail back to himself for one dollar a year.

In 1990, the first-ever Stüssy store opened on 104 Prince Street, just a short distance from Union. The store only made up about 5 percent of the label's total sales, but as Shawn put it, "New York ended up being one hundred percent of our image. That ended up being the best decision I ever made."

The more time Shawn spent in New York, the more fashionable his designs seemed to get. He was heavily inspired by the city's street fashion, which became known as the *Stüssy look* among certain retail circles. No one was really sure what to call it. It was borrowed from rappers and taggers, from skaters and art-school kids. It was an improvised fashion, a studied collision of seemingly disparate elements cobbled together from army-navy stores, sneaker outlets, classic workwear shops. These were not clothes, but signals. It was how the Black and brown youth in the city dressed, eventually making its way to the white kids, too.

"It was sneakers. It was Timberlands. It was Carhartt. It was more stuff you'd wear in the Northeast, because it was cold. It was

Adidas Gazelles and Kangol hats," recalled Paul. "Shawn started noticing these things and bringing them into Stüssy."

These Northeasterner clothes had an unusual journey from wares of longshoremen and tradesmen to New York City staples. In the late eighties, drug pushers discovered the utilitarian qualities of the Carhartt jacket. "They needed to keep warm, and they needed to carry a lot of stuff," a regional salesman for the company once explained. "Then the kids saw these guys on the street, and it became the hip thing to wear." The journalist Rob Walker later echoed something similar about Timberland in his book *Buying In*, writing that "the first urban buyers of Timberland boots were New York drug dealers—guys who had to stand on the street all night and needed the best possible footwear to keep them warm and dry." By the early nineties, both were staples of the city's street-level fashion.

The new Stüssy store greeted shoppers with a massive floral arrangement of orchids while Ice Cube and other hip-hop blasted from a booming sound system. A larger-than-life primitivist sculpture stood outside the changing rooms, made by Shawn's aunt. On the railings around the walls hung graphic T-shirts for $20, button-up shirts for $60, and higher-end pieces like leather jackets for $590. It didn't look like a surf shop; it was something new entirely. A write-up in *New York* magazine at the time of the opening described the new store as "hip sophistico" meets "downtown money."

The move also represented a step up, legitimizing what Stüssy was doing to new groups of industry insiders. One night, Shawn and James were sitting across the street in a diner when they saw the designer Giorgio Armani, flanked by two assistants, peering through the Stüssy store's windows.

One of the first breakout hits was the brand's "S" cap. The shop was selling hundreds of them every single week. Shoppers collected them, buying them in every single color and often returning to the shop to grab new colorways as they were released. Throughout his retail career, James had never seen anything like that before. Employees at Union recalled seeing John F. Kennedy Jr. wearing a Stüssy hat with his suit while biking around SoHo; the moody heartthrob actor Matt Dillon was spotted wearing one, too. "I think it made people feel like they were kind of in the know about what was going on in the world," recalled Eddie Cruz, who eventually became Union's manager.

Each season, Union and Stüssy sold more than the one before it. James let Eddie and Mary Ann focus on running Union as he put more energy into the Stüssy shop, working there most days. Frank admitted he'd been wrong about the New York store.

The International Stüssy Tribe (IST) became a beacon of next-level style so compelling that it was impossible to miss. The guys showed up in magazines like *Thrasher* and *Details* in the United States, *The Face* and *i-D* in the United Kingdom, and *CUTiE Magazine* in Japan. A Stüssy ad from the late eighties showed five IST members—painter caps, B-boy jackets, cuffed denim—posing in front of a tagged SoHo stoop. This was no longer a surf brand. Showing up in glossy fashion magazines only made the brand more alluring, giving it an edge that was unheard of for one that mostly sold graphic tees, hats, and sweatshirts.

By the end of 1991, Stüssy hit $40 million in annual sales, but the demand was much, much higher—orders totaling nearly $100 million had been requested. Frank and Shawn turned down over $60 million that year, not wanting to risk overexposing the brand and losing cachet.

"We frankly didn't have the money to grow any faster," Frank added.

Back in Laguna Beach, the Stüssy team did its best to keep pace with the explosion of growth. "We were always trying to catch up," recalled Shawn's design assistant, Emmy. "There was so much demand for the label." The brand had staked its claim on both American coasts—and at department stores in most of the states in between. And thousands of miles away in Tokyo, a crew of young Japanese men admired the *Stüssy look* from afar, studying the T-shirts and baseball caps and baggy pants like textbooks.

6.
Tokyo Calling

If you want to know what's happening in New York, ask Hiroshi. The name had echoed around Tokyo's hip and evolving Harajuku neighborhood since the eighties. No one in Japan was as clued in with America's baggy fashions or boisterous hip-hop as Hiroshi Fujiwara. He transported emerging music from New York and London to Tokyo with vivid, passionate detail. He also brought the clothes that went along with it, an entire city's worth of underground style stuffed into his suitcase.

Hiroshi grew up in Japan's coastal countryside and traveled into the bustling city as a teenager to shop for records and clothing. He especially loved Seditionaries, a British punk-infused label started by Londoners Vivienne Westwood and Malcolm McLaren. Hiroshi moved to Tokyo around 1981, when he was eighteen, and started DJing parties and writing for men's magazines. The following year, Hiroshi won a fashion contest, and the prize was a free trip to London. There he met McLaren, the English impresario behind the fashion label he loved dearly. The man quickly rerouted Hiroshi on his quest for cool, telling him London was boring and that the real action was in New York.

Once Hiroshi landed in Manhattan, he stayed for three weeks, catching sets by DJs like Afrika Bambaataa and Grandmaster Flash at the Roxy. "It was an amazing mixture of people," he recalled. "You would find Black kids, nerdy-looking people, and the yuppies in suits." At one point, Hiroshi even bumped elbows with Andy Warhol.

Hiroshi was already spinning in Tokyo, but the way of the American DJ blew his mind. In Japan, a DJ played vinyl that belonged to the club or was rented from a larger disco company. "No one was carrying their own bags of records," he later said. The New York DJs used *two* turntables, scratching and cutting between the records. On another trip, Hiroshi noticed kids in Stüssy shirts at the clubs. Before he left, he made sure to purchase at least one from Patricia Field.

The trip plugged him into a world that hadn't yet reached Tokyo. Hiroshi brought his own records to gigs, introducing many to the sound of hip-hop, and he wore his new Stüssy threads. Word about the thumping foreign music he played and his *New York clothes* started to spread within the city's creative circles. He became an in-demand DJ, spinning at a popular Harajuku club called Rise Bar and founding a trailblazing hip-hop group called Tiny Panx with his friend Kan Takagi, all while still writing for the Japanese monthly magazines.

In the mid-eighties, Hiroshi interviewed Shawn Stüssy for *Takarajima* magazine. Shawn, a decade older than Hiroshi, was on one of his surfboard shaping trips. A few Japanese stores sold Stüssy's clothes, but Shawn's cutting-edge boards had earned him a reputation in the country. The two became friends, and the American designer sent Hiroshi boxes of Stüssy clothing in the mail. Hiroshi became the first Japanese member of the International Stüssy Tribe.

His magazine editor asked him to write about this New York music and its clothes, and Hiroshi, along with Kan, launched a column called Last Orgy for *Takarajima*, sharing with readers the latest and greatest in the world of hip-hop, skateboarding, sneakers, and American fashions. By 1990, *Last Orgy* had launched as a late-night series on Japan's FM-TV. The format and tone were informative and rebellious at once, blending the styles of Glenn O'Brien's arty public-access show *TV Party* and *Yo! MTV Raps* hosted by Fab 5 Freddy.

That same year, Hiroshi launched GOODENOUGH, a clothing brand and storefront, in the quiet residential backstreets of Harajuku. The shop was an outlier in the neighborhood of mostly nameless vintage clothing shops and obscure record stores. He partnered with Toru Iwai, an industry veteran who previously ran VAN, an Ivy League–inspired Japanese brand founded in the fifties. The GOODENOUGH T-shirts were designed by a young illustrator and graphic designer named Shinichirō Nakamura, who approached Hiroshi with the idea. Shin had been spending endless hours on a Macintosh computer, teaching himself all the design programs. Hiroshi promoted GOODENOUGH in the magazines he wrote for, but did not reveal his involvement until years later. He wanted the label to stand on its merit, not trade on his expanding celebrity.

As Harajuku's fledgling scene grew, Stüssy became increasingly popular in Japan. To open the first Japanese Stüssy store in Shizuoka, Shawn partnered with the same businessman who hired him to shape surfboards; a handful more shops opened quickly. To celebrate Stüssy's warm Japanese embrace, in 1990, Shawn decided to throw a big club party: the first gathering of the International Stüssy Tribe. The group flew into Tokyo for the occasion: Paul, Jules Gayton, and some New York crew; Michael Kopelman and Marc "Fraser" Cooke from London. Hiroshi was booked as one of the DJs that night, and he brought along his own crew: Nigo, Jun, and Shin, to name a few.

Throughout the eighties, Japanese teenagers started to break further from the more traditional fashions of their parents' generation. Many dressed in a style called *amekaji*, or "American casual," which had evolved since it first emerged in the sixties and seventies. Japanese youth had loved American fashion for decades, an obsession that dated back to postwar Japan, as meticulously documented in W. David Marx's *Ametora: How Japan Saved American Style*. However, this new amekaji way of dressing was more easygoing than the semiformal "Ivy style" that had been popular for decades prior. The teenagers and young men of the eighties preferred more casual fare like printed T-shirts, athletic sneakers, sweatpants, and baggy jeans. A circuit of Japanese magazines like *Men's Club* and *Popeye* often showcased uniquely American ways of dressing, which style-inclined Japanese men followed like manuals. Still, the nebulous "street fashion" born from the graffiti, hip-hop, and skateboarding subcultures swirling around New York was more challenging to grab, making Hiroshi a singular source of truth for the authentic *Stüssy* look.

As a teenager, Nigo read Hiroshi's Last Orgy column like it was his favorite novel. The boy idolized the young man.

Tomoaki "Nigo" Nagao was born in 1970, only six years later than his hero. His interest in clothes started at twelve, when his parents bought him Levi's 501 jeans and white Adidas Superstar sneakers. Tomoaki became further enamored with clothes from reading magazines like *Popeye* and *Takarajima*. At eighteen, he moved to Tokyo to attend Bunka Fashion College—not to become a fashion designer but for the editorial classes it offered aspiring writers. He wanted to work in magazines like Hiroshi.

In his first year, he befriended a classmate and aspiring fashion designer named Jun Takahashi. Jun cut a slim figure, had spiky dyed hair, and performed in a cover band, singing Sex Pistols songs in Japanese. He wore ripped jeans and ratty flannels and wanted to design avant-garde fashion like Rei Kawakubo and Martin Margiela.

"Something interesting about Tokyo is that people aren't defined or limited by the genre that they're into. You can be into hip-hop or punk and still mix. It doesn't matter," Tomoaki said later.

Jun took Tomoaki to punk clubs and introduced him to all the names he had grown up reading in his favorite magazines, including his idol Hiroshi. Someone remarked that the two guys even looked alike, so he was given a nickname among the small social circle: Fujiwara Hiroshi Nigo ("Fujiwara Hiroshi Number Two"). Everyone in their crew had a nickname. Jun was Jonio, after Sex Pistols frontman Johnny Rotten; Shin Nakamura, shy and obsessed with skateboarding, became Sk8thing. What started as a juvenile nickname, teasing the younger student for looking like and idolizing Hiroshi, was embraced. From then on, he was simply Nigo.

Nigo quickly immersed himself in this new world. He started working as Hiroshi's assistant while still in college and became a protégé-in-waiting. "I learned so much from him, just his way of working," Nigo recalled. "The relationship is like a master-student situation, but Hiroshi would treat me like I was one of his friends, and that was very different from how things normally work in Japan." His association with Hiroshi opened doors.

In the early nineties, Nigo landed a part-time job working for

Popeye, following in Hiroshi's footsteps and building an image as a man of many talents: a magazine editor and writer, but also a DJ and fashion stylist. Inspired by GOODENOUGH, Nigo and Jun opened Nowhere, a small storefront split into two micro-boutiques. On one side, Jun sold his new label Undercover, which he launched while still in college; on the other, Nigo curated imported American workwear and casual fashions. He traveled to the United States on buying trips, where he purchased sneakers, varsity jackets, and other secondhand clothes that weren't available in Japan. That same year, Hiroshi opened a second storefront, Ready Made, that focused on limited collaborations with his friends' labels.

"We opened [Nowhere] and published a column in *Takarajima* announcing it," Nigo recalled. "We had a lot of fans who knew us from doing the column, and they would come to the shop."

The free promotion from the magazine meant Nowhere had curious shoppers from the start. Within the first few months of opening, it became clear that Jun's Undercover was a hit, but shoppers seemed less interested in Nigo's imported wares, and the international travel of the buying trips wore on him. Jun saw his friend becoming stressed and nudged him: *Why don't you start making your own clothes?*

Throughout the seventies and eighties, the three temples of Japanese style sculpted how the world viewed the country's fashion: Rei Kawakubo's Comme des Garçons, Yohji Yamamoto, and Issey Miyake. Their collections wooed the Parisian set, planting the flag that Japanese fashion was layered and dramatic. The overarching aesthetic was austere, long and layered, with avant-garde tailoring and reconstructionist silhouettes. It was not *casual*. But Hiroshi and Nigo were rewriting the definition of Japanese fashion.

A critical cultural difference between America and Japan gave them an advantage. At the time, personal style was not considered a masculine hobby or worthwhile pursuit in the United States. In a *New Yorker* article on the youthful Japanese shopper, American journalist Rebecca Mead wrote that "in Japan, the right T-shirt or cap is sought with a kind of dogged intensity, and not just by a fringe group of fanatics," and later noted how "utterly nerdy they can be in their pursuit of cool." On weekends, high school and college students in slouchy clothes flocked to Harajuku's streets, searching for rare T-shirts, sneakers, and caps like it was a sport.

This harked back to the long-standing collector culture in Japan, back to the seventies and eighties, when generations lusted over preppy Ivy League blazers and hard-wearing American blue jeans. The concept was refashioned for the contemporary (and rebellious) look of oversized T-shirts and baggy pants. Popular men's magazines like *Popeye* and *Hot-Dog Press* grouped the work of Hiroshi and his disciples under their own genre called Ura-Harajuku-kei. Author W. David Marx deconstructed the term as "classic American casual items with neat presentation: camouflage jackets, crisp brand-logo T-shirts or striped skater shirts, rigid dark denim, Clarks Wallabees, Adidas Superstars, Nike Air Max 95s."

Nigo went to Shin, who had established himself as the group's default graphic designer, for help with the label he wanted to launch. After watching the *Planet of the Apes* movies, the two created a cartoonish ape head graphic and named Nigo's new brand A Bathing Ape. Nigo borrowed about 4 million Japanese yen (approximately $34,000) from a friend and started small, printing T-shirts in batches up to fifty, giving half away to his friends and selling the remainder. Less than a year after he opened Nowhere's doors, the first A Bathing Ape (BAPE) clothes hit the shelves.

"We carried on like that for two years, producing very few of them, giving away half and selling half," recalled Nigo. The fact that his trendy friends had the shirts—and that such a small number were available to the shopper—drove the exclusivity. The pressure of scarcity was at work, even if he'd stumbled into it by accident. "I didn't intend to create demand by limiting supply. I just didn't like the idea of a lot of people wearing the same clothes."

Another demand-driver arrived when *Takarajima* magazine approached Nigo and Jun to write and curate their own column. The two friends named it Last Orgy 2, an homage to Hiroshi's column that they loved so much. (It later moved to another magazine, *Asayan*, as Last Orgy 3, with Hiroshi, Jun, and Nigo all contributing to the column.) They used the pages to promote their projects, driving readers to the trio's mini-network of retail shops. Nigo was early to align the label with the nascent Tokyo hip-hop scene, further boosting its appeal.

Hiroshi and Nigo had more passion for American vintage and the *underground fashion* of New York than for walking in the footsteps of Rei Kawakubo or Yohji Yamamoto. Their template was Shawn Stüssy. While they stuck with graphic T-shirts and hoodies, Jun veered into a more fashion-driven lane, designing high-concept clothes and putting on Undercover fashion shows in warehouses. All three men took what was happening in New York and California and gave it the Japanese homage, elevating the quality and aesthetics while playing into the limitedness of it all.

The Ura-Hara crew went from spectators to players. By joining the fray, they raised the bar for every upstart T-shirt brand in New York, Los Angeles, and beyond.

7.
Profanity over Profit

Making a single FUCT T-shirt design required an academic level of effort. There was none of the looseness and speed as when Erik Brunetti wrote graffiti as a hardcore punk teenager out east in the eighties. Born in 1967, Erik dropped out of high school his senior year and left New Jersey for New York City. By his early twenties, he had found himself on a cross-country trip with a bunch of skateboarders. They drank heavily, smoked pot, and dropped acid on their way through Texas and then California, where Erik settled into his new life and an apartment in ragtag Venice.

In 1990, he started FUCT, or "Friends U Can't Trust," from that one-bedroom apartment.

FUCT's graphics took a swing at the world. They repurposed familiar imagery to lure you in, extending an open hand until it bashed you over the head with whatever message Erik had hidden behind his back. He questioned the importance of authorship in contemporary culture, building on what Andy Warhol, Richard Prince, and David Salle did. Except Erik did it with the more ferocious bite of an appropriationist reared on Void records and Krylon spray paint. An early FUCT design featured a photo of a man on the subway jamming a pocket-sized revolver into the head of another. The image was lifted from photographer Bruce Davidson's acclaimed 1986 book *Subway*. (Erik ripped the page out of a library copy.) One T-shirt graphic included the Rolling Stones "Hot Lips" logo redrawn with an acid tab resting on the tongue; in another, he gave Pepé Le Pew a fat joint and hazy, stoned eyes. Erik leveraged the red boxes and white typography of artist Barbara Kruger with text displaying a tart Brunetti zinger: "Fight crime; buy a gun."

These designs were not made with computer magic; Erik did almost everything with ink and paper, using vellum overlays and graphite pencils to ensure the crispest graphics.

"You can totally rip off any image you want," he later said. "All that happens is you get a court order. But by the time that happens, you've already made a lot of money."

Erik ran FUCT with his friend Natas Kaupas, a trailblazing West Coast street skater who ran his own company called 101 Skateboards. As a teenager, Natas landed on the cover of *Thrasher*, and the sponsors came calling. He first signed with Santa Monica Airlines before moving to World Industries, perhaps the most foul-mouthed and influential skate label of the nineties. The company's designs featured everything from crack pipes to cartoon executioners, and it parodied everyone from major corporations to fellow skate brands. Nothing was off-limits, a mentality Erik brought to FUCT. "My background is affirmably rooted in punk rock, so naturally I gravitated toward rule-breaking and antiestablishment."

Steve Rocco, one of the founders of World Industries, recruited skaters to launch their own labels under his umbrella of connection and infrastructure, taking some of the profit for his troubles. Natas started 101 Skateboards with Rocco's backing; Erik designed skate decks for 101 and World Industries. One day at work, Rocco saw one of Erik's FUCT graphics and offered to plug the label into the World Industries machine. Together they'd turn it into a real company. Erik and Natas would do the fun, creative stuff while Rocco handled the manufacturing, distribution, and sales. With World Industries' connection to nationwide retailers, the brand printed and sold more shirts than ever. But Erik's payout wasn't adding up.

"FUCT was being sold everywhere, and I was getting nothing," he recalled.

He felt shortchanged. That was enough for him. Erik went to Rocco and Natas and told them he was leaving and taking the brand with him. Natas had 101. FUCT was *his* project.

Erik knew he had to start over from scratch. His first step was finding some startup cash.

———

By the end of the eighties, the surf industry was a $1.5 billion business, and the nascent skateboard industry was its rebellious younger brother, sitting at $490 million, including clothes, shoes, and gear. Skateboarding had a tougher and more rebellious look than surf. Many surf clothes were still neon-hued and beachy, while skate brands were drafted from a darker palette. In the early nineties, the influence of street skating gained popularity, reshaping the skate industry and making it more accessible. Skaters no longer needed access to halfpipes and ramps, just the naturally occurring concrete slabs, stairways, handrails, and pavement sidewalks of urban and suburban life. The barrier to entry was suddenly lower.

A major cultural shift in America was brewing. Thanks to a cranked-up music genre billed as grunge, the likes of rebellion, flannels, and DS-1 distortion became fashionable overnight. Nirvana's second album, *Nevermind*, hit no. 1 on *Billboard*'s pop chart and further ushered wayward angst into the mainstream. MTV hired its first grunge VJ, and the men's fashion magazine *Details* published an ode to the flannel shirt. In 1993, two years after the release of *Nevermind*, the small yet influential literary magazine *The Baffler* proclaimed that the "teen rebel" was the "model consumer."

Capitalism and the influence of the nineties counterculture further entangled into what was later called "rebel advertising" by *Alt. Culture: An A-to-Z Guide to the '90s—Underground, Online and Over-the-Counter*, a profoundly detailed guidebook to all things alternative, coauthored by journalist Steven Daly. The book named MTV the home of this phenomenon and highlighted its significant role in blurring the lines between faux counterculture and consumerism, asserting that successful Generation X advertising required "some sense of consumer rebellion." The book pointed to a slew of TV commercials and magazine advertisements: The elder Beat poet William Burroughs appeared in an ad for Nike Air Max sneakers; former Black Flag front man Henry Rollins modeled for a Gap campaign; Subaru ran a commercial in which a grungy, long-haired kid waxed about the Impreza being a "punk rock" car. In the nineties, selling rebellion became a corporate trend.

Erik restarted FUCT by printing two hundred "Oval Parody" T-shirts—his riff on the automotive Ford logo—with $2,000, money he earned painting a commissioned graffiti mural. In 1991, on a trip to New York to visit family, Erik stopped by James Jebbia's Union boutique on Spring Street. He spoke with the British man working the floor, unaware it was the shop's owner. At some point in the conversation, Erik mentioned the small label he ran from Los Angeles.

Oh yeah, I know about FUCT, James told him. I've been trying to get it in the store, but Rocco won't sell it to me because we don't carry hard goods. (The World Industries owner had a rigid policy for all his brands: They only sold to "core" skate shops, and because Union didn't sell hard goods—decks, trucks, wheels—that meant James couldn't get a wholesale account with FUCT.)

I'm not working with Rocco anymore—I'd love to sell to you, Erik told him. But we're a tiny operation now.

James told Erik to fax him a line sheet.

When Erik landed in California, he drew up a FUCT catalog specifically for Union and faxed it over. "I would make it according to what he ordered, and he would put it out, and it would sell out immediately," he recalled. "Getting into Union was a pivotal point for FUCT, followed by a lot of rebuilding the brand after leaving a major existing infrastructure. James was a huge help."

It was a turning point for the brand, allowing Erik to bank some money and rebuild inventory after breaking away from World Industries. James introduced Erik to Slam City Skates, a London shop that had just started selling Stüssy and was doing quite well with it. The English market took to FUCT immediately. Soon Erik's designs showed up in British magazines like *i-D*, *Dazed & Confused*, and *The Face* so frequently that people thought the brand was based in the United Kingdom. Then he received a bump in visibility stateside, thanks to a duo of high-profile musicians.

The singer of Rage Against the Machine, Zack de la Rocha, wore an Oval Parody shirt in the music video for the band's 1993 "Bullet in the Head" music video. He kept wearing it at concerts and for TV performances. "Zack wore the tee so often during his performances that he created a big demand for it," Erik recalled. Dave Grohl, Nirvana's long-haired drummer, wore a baseball cap with the logo in a promotional photo shoot, sitting on the floor next to front man Kurt Cobain. It was the band's last photography session, in July 1993, before Kurt died by suicide.

Erik had gotten FUCT back on its feet and bigger than it had ever been, now selling out of shirts in quantities of ten thousand. He teamed up with another Los Angeles label, X-Large, and opened the joint X-FUCT storefront on Beverly Boulevard. There was one problem. Erik partnered with a young art student and graffiti tagger because he needed some up-front cash to help guide the growth. Within a few weeks, he realized he had made a terrible mistake. The guy turned out to be an "artistically talented wannabe seeking street credibility but with no talent for business," in Erik's words. The two kept clashing over money until the tagger showed up furious at the FUCT office and only left when Erik unloaded his pistol into the ceiling. Erik later told this story to a journalist named Jeff Spurrier, who was writing a profile of the brand for *Details*. (Jeff described FUCT as "fashion vandalism" and Erik as "a tattooed entrepreneur with a bad attitude.")

The aftermath was messy, but Erik carried on, living the life of a hard-partying artist. He did his best work late at night, usually waking up around noon. He started an upmarket brand called Dorothy's Fortress, played in a band called Lucifer Wong, and started his own record label. He spent much of his time working on art projects—moody drawings with India ink in the vein of the unsparing punk illustrator Raymond Pettibon.

FUCT was just one of the many things Erik did. It was not his endgame.

A few New York designers and retailers moved to Los Angeles in the early nineties. The graffiti artist Eric Haze lived in Los Feliz, where he ran his eponymous T-shirt label and steadily worked as an in-demand graphic designer. James Jebbia sent Eddie Cruz to open the Stüssy Union, a hybrid boutique with Stüssy gear on one side of the shop and a selection of Union's downtown Manhattan stock on the other. Camella Ehlke started to visit, looking to open a 555 Soul store in the city.

The city birthed its own crop of new West Coast T-shirt brands, too. A twenty-two-year-old design student named Rick Klotz, a self-described "white B-boy who's into fashion," started printing Freshjive T-shirts in 1989. After selling $300,000 worth at one ASR trade show, Rick dropped out of art school the next day. Eli Bonerz and Adam Silverman opened the X-Large storefront in 1991 in Los Feliz, selling workwear, local graphic T-shirt labels, and the store's namesake signature designs. Los Angeles graffiti writers started to get into the T-shirt game: One named Luis Pulido founded a label called GAT (Gypsys and Thieves), and The Seventh Letter, a sprawling crew boasting nearly one hundred members, started printing and selling their own shirts. Farther south, in San Diego, brothers Bobby and Joey Ruiz founded Tribal, a brand that incorporated influences from lowrider and Chicano-style graffiti culture.

The man who launched the careers of Andy Warhol and Roy Lichtenstein read the article about Erik and FUCT in *Details*. His name was Ivan Karp, and he liked daredevil, catch-me-if-you-can artists. He was one of the first gallery owners to plant a flag in SoHo in the late sixties and was always looking for the next big thing. The famed pop art dealer called Erik from New York to tell him that he was a fan. The work reminded Ivan of what Warhol was doing in the eighties, and he invited Erik to do a show at his gallery.

The resulting exhibition was *Lost*, a collection of seventy lost-pet posters tacked to the gallery's white walls. Erik had picked his favorites from the five hundred posters he gathered from nearby Los Angeles neighborhoods. Most posters referenced lost dogs and cats, but others mentioned lost rabbits, turtles, and parakeets. Erik ensured a duplicate poster was hung nearby before removing one for his collection.

"I don't think that this collection is something that somebody is going to want to own," Erik told the *Los Angeles Times* in a write-up of the exhibition. "It's more or less an installation, a conceptual art piece."

The article compared his work to that of the late Marcel Duchamp, the French artist famous for playfully ridiculing existing norms with metaphysical wit. Erik was evolving beyond the medium of T-shirts. He scanned all the *Lost* posters and published a limited-edition zine, creating only fifty copies. He later sold hand-pulled silk screen posters of FUCT's Oval Parody logo with the master printmaker Richard Duardo, who also worked with David Hockney and Keith Haring. Erik went on to show work in a few more exhibitions, but unfortunately, the chaos of juggling a clothing company and an art practice became too tough, and he scaled back his efforts.

"I could not maintain a balance between my fine art career and the brand," Erik recalled. "I felt like if I could not give my entire life to my art, then I was cheating myself and the viewer."

With FUCT, he was not interested in selling to department stores or playing nice in the apparel industry. The brand passed on exhibiting on the trade show circuit, and he also defiantly bucked any comparison to his perceived contemporaries. "We don't even categorize ourselves as in the same league as Freshjive or GAT or Stüssy. All those companies are garbage as far as we are concerned," Erik told *i-D* magazine at the time.

FUCT was singular. While some designers opted to legitimize and scale up their clothing brands, Erik thrashed in the steel cage of commerce. He was more at peace in his art studio. FUCT turned him into a pathbreaking original, even if he showed sour reluctance about it and yearned for an ascent in the art world. His fucked-up graphics and pop culture references influenced the attitude silk-screened on T-shirts for years to come.

8.
It Has to Be Phat

Back in New York, a millionaire hip-hop mogul from Queens named Russell Simmons wanted to start a clothing line. He was on his way to celebrity, with a bombastic rags-to-riches story that swirled around him: a low-level drug dealer turned local party promoter and an eventual major-label playmaker. His brother Joseph was one-third of Run-DMC, one of hip-hop's first breakout groups. Russell cofounded Def Jam Recordings with a virtuoso, grungy white-boy producer named Rick Rubin, and the duo released hit albums from the Beastie Boys, LL Cool J, and Public Enemy.

Music had made Russell rich beyond his wildest dreams. Now he wanted to get into fashion.

It was 1991; not a full year had passed since Shawn Stüssy and James Jebbia opened the doors to Stüssy's Prince Street storefront. Russell had become a regular in SoHo, enamored with the glossy platter of fashion and infatuated with the side dish of runway models that went along with it. One of his frequent stops was the high-end boutique Bagutta, originally on West Broadway. He and the owner, Marc Bagutta, struck up a friendship.

"I was in there all the time buying dresses for girls," Russell recalled. "We started talking about the fashion business—how it worked at retail, wholesale, marketing."

One thing about Russell was he moved fast. He tasked a producer and rising A&R man named Dominique Trenier with assembling a team that could build him a clothing brand and do it quickly. There was only one catch: The name had to have the word *Phat* in it. Dom called his good friend Alyasha Owerka-Moore, a fashionable twenty-one-year-old skateboarder from Clinton Hill, Brooklyn. Alyasha designed flyers for his friends in hardcore punk bands, made beats, and worked at Skate NYC in the East Village. He also designed the first logo for Camella Ehlke's 555 Soul. The two friends put together some flat sketches. "Russell hires us . . . we're just like, *holy shit*. We don't know anything about the garment industry," recalled Alyasha.

Alyasha only knew one person with ties to the fashion industry: his friend Paul Mittleman, whose reputation as Stüssy's New York consigliere was only growing stronger. Paul was hired. The group needed a graphic designer and got Russell to bring on Eli Morgan Gesner, an energetic skater from the Upper West Side who had once designed for SHUT Skates, essentially New York City's first skateboard company. "He was the only dude we knew that knew how to use Photoshop and Illustrator," said Alyasha. Eli was a bit of a tech and creative wonder; he had designed a logo for SoHo Skates when he was fourteen. "One morning, I'm just getting phone calls from Dom, Alyasha, and Paul, and I don't even understand what they're talking about," recalled Eli. "They were, like, 'Yeah, we're going to start a clothing line . . . like Stüssy, but for Russell Simmons. *Imagine the Def Jam version of Stüssy.*'"

With a small team in place, trying to turn Alyasha's sketches into a full-fledged clothing brand proved to be frustrating. Sometimes they met at Time Cafe, a hip spot in SoHo that Russell frequented, where models and fashion insiders hung out. Other times, the group convened in Rush Communications' offices or Russell's three-story penthouse in NoHo's famous Silk Building. He'd often be yammering away on his cell phone, encircled by his entourage, or distracted by some other matters of the day. It was an uphill battle from the start. "Russell was always surrounded by yes-men that didn't have any fashion sense, and didn't really know what was going on in the street," recalled Alyasha. "Every meeting you had to battle back a bunch of fucking dipshits that hung out with him."

Russell's young and streetwise design team had a crystal clear idea of what they wanted to do. They wanted to play into the rugged and outdoorsy look—Ralph Lauren Polo, Timberland, the North Face, Carhartt—that had been on the rise. That fashion wasn't even on his radar yet. Russell had something else in mind: He wanted a look similar to the industry darling, a vibrant brand from Los Angeles called Cross Colours. Jumpsuits in primary shades, color-blocked T-shirts, and backward jeans. "He was looking at Cross Colours because he had already lost his eye on the street. Russell was just looking at the millions," Alyasha said. "It was the highest-volume brand that he could compare for Black inner-city youth. We were like, 'You're missing the mark.' All the kids were wearing Timberland and Polo at this point." The three friends pushed against the idea of doing anything remotely close to Cross Colours.

At another meeting, Eli showed up before Alyasha (who was late), walking into Russell's lavish penthouse armed with a notebook full of sketches. The hip-hop impresario was annoyed that Alyasha wasn't with him; Russell waited for no one and pushed Eli to get started anyway. "Alyasha and I were really trying to emulate the Polo look. We're making rugbys and sweaters," said Eli. "With just me presenting, it's like the *whitest* thing ever. I'm trying to plead my case to do Polo-looking shit, and Russell's not having it."

Alyasha finally walked in, immediately jumping in to back Eli up. He explained how they wanted to reference how the hip-hop heads from Brooklyn to the Bronx dressed. These city kids wore Polo Ralph Lauren and Tommy Hilfiger. This was the next wave, they told Russell, but the mogul wasn't buying it. He was stuck in the past. "Run-DMC was at a point in their career where nobody gave a fuck about them . . . and their look was corny and dated," Alyasha recalled. "Hip-hop was evolving at the time." Then Alyasha referenced Grand Puba, a rapper and MC from the hip-hop group Brand Nubian who had just emerged as a solo artist. In Brand Nubian, Grand Puba carried an Afrocentric style, wearing beads and pendants with brightly colored patterns. He now gravitated toward a preppier, all-American look: baggy sportswear, oversized rugby tops, and bold graphic T-shirts. And *lots* of Ralph Lauren and Tommy Hilfiger. This proved the magic trick; the reference clicked in immediately for Russell. The visual of the always stylish Grand Puba was all it took.

Alyasha persuaded him on the name, too: Phat Farm, a gesture toward Ralph Lauren's Polo Country, perhaps Ralph's most rugged sublabel yet. Phat Farm would do something more cunning—they'd take the outdoorsy workwear and preppy attire already being repurposed through the lens of Black street culture and build an entire new brand around it.

In 1990, the Action Sports Retailer trade expo moved south, from Long Beach to San Diego, to accommodate an expanding industry. More than nine hundred companies exhibited their wares at nearly two thousand booths. (The previous venue couldn't have handled half of that.) Within the $1.5 billion action sports industry, a business report in the *Los Angeles Times* noted, the "most striking growth . . . was in 'street' fashions, a melding of 'rap-gangster' styles with skateboarders' durable wear."

Cross Colours, a label that helped establish a specific fashion market based around hip-hop fans and Black youth, was launched in 1989 from a warehouse in downtown Los Angeles. The two founders, Carl Jones and Thomas "TJ" Walker, were inspired by a swatch of green-and-yellow kente cloth. Both men had already found success in the Californian apparel industry; Carl had founded and sold a profitable screen-printing company that produced shirts for major labels like Guess. Together, Carl and TJ had partnered on Surf Fetish, a beachwear brand notable for bringing a more fashion-conscious look to the category. As surfwear cooled, the label added skateboarding and then biker wear.

The bright clothes of Cross Colours were a hit. Big Daddy Kane, Queen Latifah, Tupac Shakur, and Kris Kross donned the flashy, baggy clothes. The label appeared throughout MTV and even on NBC's *Fresh Prince of Bel-Air*. The brand held a constant presence in the trade magazines, featured in stories about this emerging "urbanwear" category, with Cross Colours touting projections of $40 million in annual sales. Russell wanted those millions to be his.

———

Russell and Marc had already found an empty storefront for Phat Farm on the same block as Stüssy on Prince Street. They started a $175,000 renovation with plans to open in early 1993. Russell revved into promoter mode and started the press blitz. The hype-building began before the brand had a single item in stock. "We're in all these magazines and doing promotional photo shoots, but we don't have any clothes made," recalled Eli.

It quickly became apparent that while Alyasha and Eli had the talent to deliver flat sketches and designs and the prowess to print graphic T-shirts, they had no clue how to make proper clothes. (Paul was on and off with the brand as he finished up college.) They figured they should start simple and found a manufacturer in Midtown's Garment District. They produced a luxed-up version of the M-65, a military bomber jacket. Their Phat Farm twist was to create it in grandiose cream-colored leather with fur accents. To the design duo's surprise and delight, the finished sample looked incredible, and they immediately approved a production run of one hundred units. Things were finally starting to look up. Until a few weeks later, when they were told that their entire order had been stolen from an idling delivery truck. The pressure was back. They knew it was on them to fill the empty store with Phat Farm clothes.

The following week, the two designers had their prayers answered. A chance meeting at Time Cafe led to two Canadian businessmen who ran a clothing company called Roots, their country's answer to the Gap. With Russell seated at the table, they offered up their expertise and facilities. Eli and Alyasha flew back and forth to Toronto over many weeks, and they soon had samples of thick hooded sweatshirts, canvas pullover jackets, and leather jackets. Combine that with the graphic T-shirts they had printed in New York, and the first Phat Farm collection was ready just in time for the grand opening.

Phat Farm debuted on Prince Street in April 1993, nearly three weeks behind schedule. The shop was designed to resemble an upstate barn, complete with dim lighting, weathered finishes, and wood paneling. Almost half the clothes were made by their new friends in Canada. (The stolen M-65 jackets never showed up.) The debut collection was about fifty pieces, including a $650 leather jacket, $70 hooded sweatshirts, and $25 graphic tees. The rapper Queen Latifah swung by and left with a canvas jacket.

"It's fun, and I can afford to do it," Russell told the *New York Times* about his frenetic expansion from hip-hop into fashion. "So if I lose a lot of money on it, I had fun. If I make money, I'll have even more fun."

The year prior, Russell's companies had pulled in $40 million. Phat Farm clothes populated the pages of magazines with a few phone calls. Where Shawn and Stüssy spent years organically building a following, all Phat Farm needed was Russell's status and deep pockets. He had the world watching on day one. In the first year, the SoHo store alone grossed $2 million.

Behind the scenes, the small design team was cracking. Eli and Alyasha felt overworked and grew tired and unhappy. "I would just bark at 'em. I was young and didn't know any better," recalled Alyasha. "I was just so frustrated that I had to take these meetings."

Alyasha was often late or didn't show at the Phat Farm offices, and Eli had to cover for him in front of Russell. None of the guys liked dealing with Russell, his ego, or his entourage. It caused tension among the group. Paul was studying at Hunter College and working as the unofficial New York promoter and liaison for Stüssy. "It was such a blur. We all left and came back at some point. It was revolving doors," recalled Paul.

The three friends were designing for a multimillion-dollar brand with little oversight and little experience, and it was a tremendous pressure on the young designers. They felt like they were as much the brand as Russell was but didn't get the respect they craved. "We came up with the name and the logo and the marketing," Eli said. "At the end of the day, we didn't have any ownership; it was entirely owned by Russell Simmons, and we were just his employees." Eli went to Russell and Marc to talk this out, hoping to get a minor ownership stake in the label.

This is what you signed up for, they told him. *Why are you complaining?*

Not long after the Phat Farm boutique opened its doors, Eli and Alyasha left and both started skateboard companies. Alyasha headed for California and cofounded American Dream Inc. with pro skater Ron Allen. Eli held on at Phat Farm until he had saved enough money to buy a new Macintosh computer and then cofounded Zoo York with Rodney Smith, a cofounder of SHUT Skates. The name was inspired by a group of skateboarders and graffiti artists, the now-defunct loose-knit collective known as "the Soul Artists of Zoo York," going so far as to get founder Marc "Ali" André Edmonds's blessing to use the name.

The departures didn't slow Russell and Marc. They hired new designers, and later that year, they signed a licensing deal with USA Classics to take the operational reins of Phat Farm. It was a manufacturing and production deal that put the brand in mall retailers nationwide.

What started out as "the Def Jam version of Stüssy" had become a widely popular beast of its own. Both Stüssy and Phat Farm hinted at a shift in how the American youth at large wanted to dress—how New York's graffiti, hip-hop, and skateboard circles bumped together with newfound intensity, ready to morph into a superscene of sorts. Still, no one had any idea just how widespread the outsized style of rappers was about to get.

9.
Blunt Designs

By the early nineties, Leonard "Futura 2000" McGurr was working the graveyard shift at a Kinko's copy shop on Twelfth Street, running copy machines while the city that never sleeps slept. He became so proficient at the work that he often found himself with a few free hours toward the end of his shift, which ran from midnight to eight a.m. He was in his late thirties now, and most of his coworkers were college students, stoned and tech-savvy kids who taught him how to use the Macintosh computers and emerging software like Photoshop and Illustrator Ink. The new technology felt like a rocket ship, and he was ready for the ride. Art was driven by innovation; the spray can combined the brush and paint into one instrument and birthed a new art form.

"This was the second coming of this graffiti culture," Futura recalled. "The seventies were on trains, and the eighties were transitioning from trains to the gallery. In the nineties, the next sort of segment was going to be this graphic design stage."

He teamed up with two friends, Jeremy "Gerb" Hurley and Josh "Stash" Franklin, to form a new design collective and T-shirt label; they called themselves GFS (Gerb, Futura, Stash). Gerb was a well-connected club guy and downtown DJ, and Stash was a fellow tagger, a wunderkind of the city's graffiti-art scene. Twelve years younger than Futura, Stash caught the graffiti bug as a teenager. He missed the era of peak trains and tunnels but tagged every surface in Lower Manhattan within reach: mailboxes, brick walls, subway station steps. The older graffiti writers embraced Stash. He was damn good. At seventeen, he showed his work at the renowned Fun Gallery alongside originals from Futura, Jean-Michel Basquiat, and Keith Haring.

The young tagger—short, with sandy brown hair, and broad enough for manual labor—was early to the self-made graphic T-shirt. He printed bootleg tees from his apartment's bathtub with a silk-screen kit he bought from Pearl Paint. "I wanted to make some Krylon T-shirts because nobody had them. I wanted to make them for me and other graffiti writers because that was the premier brand of choice," Stash recalled. He printed Rust-Oleum ones, too, referencing another revered paint company of the scene. He started this in the mid-eighties, and they were an immediate hit within his social circle, so he kept it up.

"You're just reppin' brands from the culture," said Futura. "These are spray-can companies that we were respectful of. Any writer in his right mind would rock them."

The T-shirts jumped to the next level when Gerb gave one to Mick Jones, a cofounder of the Clash and later of the band Big Audio Dynamite, who wore it on TV during the American Music Awards. The exposure put the T-shirts on the radar of graffiti writers across the globe. On a zigzagging trip through Europe with Futura, Stash brought a backpack stuffed with Krylon and Rust-Oleum tees to sell outside of museums and concerts along the way. He brought them to a graffiti art show on the Rue Chapon in Paris but spoke zero French; Futura taught him how to say *fifty francs* and how to make change with the foreign currency.

After this trip, Futura and Stash came to Gerb, and the three formed GFS. They decided to start a clothing company together, too, and named it Not From Concentrate. At the time, *fresh* was the word du jour. Not From Concentrate poked at that.

"The eighties spit out all these ex-graffiti, creative people. But that art-world thing wasn't really viable [for them]—people were getting into other ways of creative expression through graphics. We started clothing companies," recalled Futura. "My attention went very much away from the art world."

Their company logo paid tribute to the NYC MTA subway signs, with the letters GFS each set inside a different color circle in the style of train lines. One of their first designs was an homage to their beloved Phillies Blunts. All three of them were potheads. Weed was a 24/7 thing for them. Someone was always burning. And in New York City in the nineties, you smoked a hollowed-out cigarillo filled with pot. You smoked a Phillies Blunt.

As the name suggested, the company from Philadelphia produced flavored cigars and cigarillos with a unique earthy flavor and sweet scent. They were readily available at every corner bodega. An editor from marijuana's magazine of record, *High Times*, explained that the practice of "blunting" was started by Jamaicans in New York, who preferred rolling marijuana in tobacco leaf instead of paper. You cracked the Phillies Blunt open down the middle, hollowed out the tobacco, licked the wrap so it didn't crack, packed it with ground-up weed, licked it again, and rolled it back up. It also offered some camouflage to the scent of burning marijuana. As with any novel idea, word spread throughout the boroughs until it blossomed into a citywide practice, beloved by rappers like Nas and the Notorious B.I.G. *Vibe* later called the Phillies Blunt "the first cigar to truly reign supreme in hip-hop."

The GFS design first started as a parody. The guys took the Phillies logo and reworked the graphic to read ILLEGAL BLUNT. Then they had the idea to go more direct with it: The company didn't sell official Phillies Blunt T-shirts, so they made their own, inspired by Stash and his Krylon and Rust-Oleum shirts.

"All of this kind of appropriation stuff was going on, where you took logos that you knew in culture and you flipped them a little bit and tried to be clever," Futura recalled. "Well, we weren't even trying to be clever. In the end, we just straight ripped it off."

They printed all the Phillies Blunt T-shirts in their small downtown studio, usually less than one hundred at a time. That is, until the Beastie Boys got their hands on one.

The act of commerce was baked into Andy Warhol's pop art from the start. Throughout his life, Warhol produced over nine thousand paintings and sculptures, nearly twelve thousand drawings, and somewhere around nineteen thousand prints. His artistic priorities lay less with subject matter and more with volume and scale. The famous critic and essayist Louis Menand once described the subjects of pop art not as *objects* but as "advertising, magazine and newspaper photography, packaging, labeling, signage. Pop artists represented the graphic environment in a consumerist world."

Where Warhol took references from mainstream consumerism, T-shirt labels like Stüssy and FUCT borrowed from their own subcultural touchpoints: hip-hop and punk and graffiti and sneakers and weed. Some graphic references stretched aspirationally, like Shawn Stüssy's Chanel and Rolex designs from the eighties. (Although Shawn later downplayed any alignment with the taste of the upper class: "It was just me making fun of luxury. . . . I was having fun.") Stash did not have to wander far to realize the genius in making those Krylon and Rust-O T-shirts. Erik Brunetti carried the tradition of aggressive parody from World Industries and the skateboard industry over to FUCT, taking beloved markers and mucking them up with devilish delight. These guys were next-wave pop artists and appropriationists with a chosen medium of baggy T-shirts and durable plastisol ink.

In early 1992, MTV aired an interview with the buzzed-about Brooklyn rap trio Beastie Boys, whose third album, *Check Your Head*, was due to hit shelves soon. Adam "Ad-Rock" Horovitz sat in the middle of Michael "Mike D" Diamond and Adam "MCA" Yauch. Ad-Rock wore a Not From Concentrate Phillies Blunt T-shirt as the segment aired to millions of viewers. Word only reached Hav-A-Tampa—the company that owned Phillies Blunt—when a twentysomething employee who saw the segment approached a vice president and asked for a T-shirt not knowing it was unofficial merchandise. Gerb, the "business guy" of the GFS trio, found himself on a call with Hav-A-Tampa suits, and they offered a licensing agreement. The three friends had expected a cease and desist, or worse, a lawsuit. Hav-A-Tampa cooked up a win-win situation: The New Yorkers could keep printing the T-shirt, while the big corporation would donate their royalties to the Partnership for a Drug-Free America, earning a tobacco company some rare good press.

Since the seventies, legislation has banned cigarette ads from American TV and radio. A famous musician wearing a T-shirt promoting a tobacco product was a loophole. It was as much a win for Hav-A-Tampa as it was for Not From Concentrate. Soon, musicians of all types started wearing the Phillies Blunt shirts and hats onstage, in music videos, and for magazine photo shoots, from the pot-loving California hip-hop group Cypress Hill, who had a double-platinum-selling album at the time, to the heartthrob singer Marky Mark. *GQ* noted the T-shirt as one of the season's hottest apparel items.

"It totally changed our lives," recalled Futura, who quit his job at Kinko's.

The hype for the shirt even made its way to Japan. Hiroshi Fujiwara was so impressed by GFS and Not From Concentrate that he featured some of their products in his columns in *Popeye* and *Takarajima*, which gave the companies a nice hit of exposure and cachet. "It was super tough to get GFS products here in Tokyo, which just made them more desirable," Nigo said.

They continued to legally slap the Phillies Blunt logo on T-shirts, hoodies, baseball caps, and beanies. The press flocked to these three weed-smoking graffiti guys. Fab 5 Freddy interviewed them on *Yo! MTV Raps*; the group stood next to a rack of their threads in Patricia Field's boutique, which now stocked the entire Not From Concentrate line. In an interview with *New York*, Gerb likened Stash to a stoner Andy Warhol: "I mean, if Andy can take a Brillo box, why can't we take a logo?"

A friend of theirs, Russ Karablin, also found small-scale success in the downtown retail circuit with his own appropriated marijuana-inspired T-shirt, remixing the Adidas Trefoil motif with four additional fronds to look like a cannabis leaf. He released the shirts under his label SSUR and sold the tees to Liquid Sky, Patricia Field, Camella Ehlke's 555 Soul, and eventually, after some persuasion, to James Jebbia's Union. Then Adidas caught word and sent out a cease and desist to every store that sold it, ending Russ's fun.

Gerb, Futura, and Stash had high hopes for their clothing brand. They wanted to take what Stüssy had done for West Coast surfer/skater style and do the same for New York's graffiti and hip-hop look. "Compared to the West Coast, we didn't really have a skateboard culture or a surf culture," Futura recalled. They started to design and plan for a full collection that included trousers, hats, and jackets and branched out into graffiti-inflected accessories like subway car sketch pads and spray-can-nozzle pendants. Unfortunately, the trio couldn't keep up with the volume of Phillies Blunt merch that the market demanded, and knockoffs soon proliferated all over the city and beyond. (One newspaper estimated that around three hundred thousand bogus shirts were in circulation at one point.) They were clueless about how to stop all the bootlegs. Toward the end of 1993, the three friends decided to shutter the label.

"Nobody wanted to buy our other designs that had nothing to do with the Phillies Blunt. It was clear that we put our finger on the pulse of something," Futura said. "Inevitably, the Phillies Blunt was the beginning of the end for us, sadly, because no one cared about anything else we did."

"The truth is the Phillies Blunt T-shirt fucked it up," recalled Stash. "It didn't matter how many other good projects we worked on."

Still, the two graffiti artists-turned-graphic designers knew that these graphic T-shirts they had stumbled upon were something worth pursuing. "We came out with crisper graphics, and our game was better," said Futura. Stash experimented with a short solo endeavor called Subware, in which he printed shirts featuring artwork from names like the legendary PHASE 2, a graffiti pioneer from the Bronx, and KAWS, a baby-faced new designer from New Jersey who was still developing his uniquely cartoonish style. In 1995, Futura and Stash, along with their friend Bleu Valdimer, launched a new collective and label, BSF and Project Dragon.

Around this time, Futura visited Japan on a tour with Mo' Wax, a British record label that he frequently collaborated with, and he met Nigo and his right-hand designer Sk8thing (Shin Nakamura). There was an immediate mutual respect there. Two weeks later, Stash flew to Japan to meet with the distributors who sold Subware to the Japanese market. Before Stash left, Futura gave him a recap of his trip and a list of people to meet: Nigo was one of the first names.

Some twenty-five years after he'd tagged his first train, Futura felt youthful and energized. The excitement of the Phillies Blunt T-shirt and the short but impactful run of GFS had pointed him in the right direction. "It's like everything that happened for me led me off into other avenues of expression and creativity," he said. Futura was surrounded by newness. He kept learning the graphic design programs and felt his career had entered something akin to a second act. His work found a new audience and he forged new friendships outside New York's downtown scene. But one in particular stood above the rest.

"Everything changed when Stash and I met Nigo and Sk8thing," Futura later said. "They had their own streetwear culture up and running with all these different individuals, and we completely plugged in to that."

When it came to graphic T-shirts, Tokyo proved to be a kingmaker. The city possessed the power to turn a New York brand into a covetable fashion label and elevate a humble graffiti writer to a revered graphic designer.

10.

Not Really Underground Anymore

The music paved the way for fashion. It broke out of the inner city and from the underground, from Bronx block parties to the Roxy nightclub, from Brooklyn's St John's Place up to 125th Street in Harlem and back downtown toward the streets of Soho. Then hip-hop's entire package—the sound, the clothes, the aesthetics, the slang—shot across America like a well-styled dart from the tungsten of a rising cultural touchstone formally known as Music Television. By the early nineties, the tough and slouching look of rap was en vogue among young men across the country.

    Much of the MTV generation—a quasi-niche of Generation X defined as twenty-two million young adults in their early twenties, born in the late sixties through the early seventies—flocked to the malls and department stores to fill their closets with the clothes of their favorite rappers. The look was easy enough to replicate. Hip-hop continued to take classic American brands, the kind you found in most suburbs, and dress them to slouchy new heights. A new wave of hip-hop-centric labels popped up. The designer Carl Williams modified baggy denim with Karl Kani; four Black men from Queens founded FUBU, or "For Us, By Us," a streetwise line replete with oversized cuts and vibrant colors; April Walker upgraded her Brooklyn tailor shop into a sporty brand called Walker Wear. Ralph Lauren and Tommy Hilfiger remained sartorial touchstones; youths flocked to the preppy staples, wearing their styles much baggier than their parents ever did. The California rapper then called Snoop Doggy Dogg appeared on *Saturday Night Live* wearing a striped Tommy Hilfiger rugby top, and the very next day it was sold out all across New York City.

Rack-Lo and the original Lo Life Crew, the Polo-obsessed shoplifters from Brooklyn, proved themselves ahead of the trend. In the 1994 music video for Wu-Tang Clan's "Can It Be All So Simple," the influential rapper Raekwon swaggered in a Polo Ralph Lauren windbreaker with bold blocking and the towering words SNOW BEACH across the front. "I was definitely inspired by Lo Lifes . . ." Raekwon later said. British fashion magazine *The Face*, the same title that frequently promoted Stüssy and FUCT, ran a five-page fashion story on the next-generation Lo Life Crew with the headline "B-Boys Go Preppy." The group was no longer written about in the tabloids as smash-and-grab crooks but was proudly presented as bona fide style instigators.

The Stüssy team found itself in a groove of its own, producing one-hundred-piece collections three times a year. Shawn Stüssy and Frank Sinatra held tight to their guiding strategy: Always keep the supply lower than the demand. "It's very important the kids don't see it everywhere," Stüssy's buyer at Nordstrom said at the time. That year, Shawn had so much heat that Tommy Boy Records approached him to design an exclusive Carhartt jacket; the design was so covetable that the record label jumped into the fashion business with its own clothing line. Stüssy's strong association with New York City helped its rap world credibility, even as surfwear's desirability faded in the marketplace. The *Stüssy look* put them outside of the core surf category, an advantage during the nineties.

Surf brands felt the influential force of hip-hop: Quiksilver introduced a collection of street-ready denim clothing; Gotcha reworked the brand's popular "walk shorts" to be baggier and longer so they could be worn elsewhere than the beach. Stüssy did not need to be drastically reconfigured. The brand's collection included droopy khakis, hooded leather jackets, flannels, baggy denim, canvas work jackets, countless baseball caps, and plenty of its trademark graphic T-shirts.

Shawn landed Stüssy another hit with an eight-ball graphic. It was inspired by a $775 jacket introduced by a San Francisco leather boutique that had become a flash point status symbol in the East Coast hip-hop scene. (Reports of wearers being mugged for the specific coat littered the papers.) Harlem's hip-hop haberdasher Dapper Dan created a high-end eight-ball coat that sold for over $1,000. Shawn applied his own eight-ball graphic to T-shirts, hoodies, crewneck sweatshirts, shorts, and hats—offering the phenomenon at a fraction of the price.

The rise of rap's music and fashion happened as MTV exploded in popularity, beaming into more households and becoming the dominant discovery tool that radio once was. (With the key difference of introducing viewers to an artist's image in tandem.) *Yo! MTV Raps* became a mega-hit. The show was still helmed by Fab 5 Freddy—friend of Basquiat, Warhol, Futura, and countless others on the eighties art scene. Fred himself remained an immaculate dresser, with the kind of style you couldn't buy off-the-rack, oscillating through a wardrobe of billowing twill pants, newsboy caps, satin baseball jackets, and accessories like steel-rimmed Jean Paul Gaultier shades and necklaces of wooden beads. His guests dressed in what was being further crystallized as the *hip-hop look*.

Outer layers required The North Face's down puffers and Carhartt duck-canvas jackets. Heavy-duty hooded sweatshirts from Champion. Timberland's six-inch work boots and the retro-cool Clarks Wallabees. Sweaters and rugby tops came from Polo Ralph Lauren and Tommy Hilfiger. Kangol bucket hats and Starter snapback caps. Nike Air Jordans worn off the court as leisurewear. Air Max and Air Force 1 sneakers. Sporty oversized team jerseys or tracksuits from Italian brands like Fila, Kappa, Sergio Tacchini. Jeans were worn supremely baggy, from labels like Karl Kani, Nautica, and Guess. (Tommy Jeans, too.)

It was an evolution of the B-boy style of the seventies, with more menace and bravado as rappers incorporated aesthetic nods to the tough-wearing, utilitarian style preferred by street-level drug dealers. The glossy and acclaimed fashion magazine *Details* called New York rappers one of the biggest fashion influences of the last decade. The look was tailor-made for TV.

MTV was a marketer's wet dream. Innovations in the infrastructure and distribution of cable TV meant the channel was a direct line to practically every teenager in America. MTV broadcast into two hundred and fifty million homes and quickly asserted itself as a mainstay of popular culture; the charismatic hosts and rapid-fire editing made for must-see TV for those under the age of twenty-five. Its capitalistic impact was measurable and profound. In 1993, annual record and music video sales hit an unprecedented $10 billion. MTV eventually delivered a program and a hook for everyone, regardless of musical taste. *Alternative Nation* played alt-rock music videos from Nirvana and Pearl Jam; *Headbangers Ball* focused on heavy metal like Metallica and Pantera; *Club MTV* had VJs broadcasting from a dance club in New York City; and *Yo! MTV Raps* delivered KRS-One, LL Cool J, and Queen Latifah—serving up the attitudes and fashion of hip-hop on a silver platter. The show was so successful that executives bumped it up from a single hour a week to fourteen.

"All of a sudden, millions of suburban kids were seeing rap in their homes for the first time. It went from this cult thing to they put it everywhere they could because of the ratings they were getting," recalled Peter Dougherty, a cocreator of the American *Yo! MTV Raps*. (It had been adapted from MTV Europe.)

The magazine writer John Seabrook explored the long-brewing convergence of advertising with art and music, the shifting hierarchy of culture, and the underground-to-mainstream pipeline in his capstone nineties-zeitgeist book *Nobrow: The Culture of Marketing, the Marketing of Culture*. There are mentions of Andy Warhol's soup cans and other populist art trends, but the author dedicated an entire chapter to the power of peak MTV. Rap proved to be an ideal partner for the platform as it went mainstream, more so than rock. "Like MTV, hip-hop wasn't hung up on the distinction between idealistic and commercial impulses in art . . . a song could be an ad and a pop hit at the same time," he wrote. Even if music videos offered some of the "best visual art on television," Seabrook pointed to an undeniable truth: The videos also acted as ads for the rappers—and by association, the brands they were wearing.

Hip-hop reached stratospheric levels in 1993. *Vibe* later said it was the year that "hip-hop and R&B conquered the world." It did not take long for the fashion industry at large to catch wise to the popularity of inner-city fashion.

The following year, Ralph Lauren put a fresh-faced Jamaican American model named Tyson Beckford in a prominent Polo Sport advertisement shot by ultra-famous photographer Bruce Weber. "Ralph Lauren has used Black models here and there, but nothing has ever been as daringly Black as that Polo ad," the authoritative art curator Thelma Golden said at the time. "Tyson looks like a brother on the block. There is a quality of *ultra-realness* about him." Tommy Hilfiger's brother Andy gave away trunks of clothes to "any rapper with a recording contract."

Beyond Ralph Lauren and Tommy Hilfiger, a new crop of brands founded by Black designers appealed more directly to the deeply hip-hop look. You could trace the lineage to Willi Smith, the pioneering African American designer who founded WilliWear in the late 1970s and became perhaps the most high-profile Black fashion designer of the eighties. Smith designed what the *New York Times* called "inventive low-priced sports clothes that became street classics." The designer collaborated with Keith Haring on a T-shirt, but he also created dazzling deconstructed suits and elaborately patterned jackets. He died in 1987 at the age of thirty-nine. At the time of Smith's death, WilliWear was sold in more than five hundred stores and grossed $25 million in sales annually.

In the early nineties, Russell Simmons's Phat Farm label grew, and newer labels, like FUBU and Mecca USA, proliferated. The standout brand within the category was Cross Colours. It amassed $80 million in sales in its first three years and reached upward of $50 million in 1993 alone before everything came crashing down. The brand unraveled the following year, plagued by fulfillment and cash-flow issues and the loss of a retailer that made about 60 percent of the company's revenue. (The *Los Angeles Times* reported that the brand "all but disintegrated under an ocean of debt" and speculated that a creditor took ownership of the trademark.) "All I can say is we're going forward, and we're going to do it a lot more carefully," said Carl Jones, one of Cross Colours's founders, in an interview at the time. "We know today you're hot, and tomorrow you're dead."

One of the Cross Colours designers, a twenty-six-year-old named Carl Williams, sprang into action. A few years earlier, he had signed a licensing and distribution deal for his Karl Kani label, in which he started selling baggy jeans out of the trunk of his car in Flatbush, Brooklyn. He purchased his trademark back for half a million dollars and threw himself into relaunching the brand on his own. The big jeans gave way to wool shirts, slouchy twill pants, hockey jerseys, and more. The clothes ended up on rappers like Tupac Shakur, LL Cool J, and Big Daddy Kane. Karl Kani was at the forefront of slouchy yet sartorially minded clothes. Carl had been on the ground floor of the mainstream industry, paying attention to the colorful and baggy clothes, and he soon found his label was one of the most successful in the growing category.

"My company and Cross Colours were the only two Black-owned companies [at MAGIC, a biannual trade show in Las Vegas]. We were set up right next to Tommy Hilfiger and Calvin Klein. People were lined up around the corner trying to get into our booth," Carl recalled. "We created such energy that in the years following, they created an *urban* section just because of us."

Most brands that fell under the "urban" umbrella showed their collections at MAGIC, which had been around since 1933. It was a massive industry event but lacked the youthful energy of the Action Sports Retailer show. It attracted over seven thousand brands and ninety thousand buyers with two million square feet of exhibition space. Still, much of that was "balding men hawking pleated khakis and argyle socks." The hip-hop clothes gave it a jolt of buzz.

Retailers called this wave of outsized sportswear, canyon-wide jeans, baggy T-shirts, and hooded sweatshirts "urbanwear." The wide-ranging and largely problematic word was often deployed to other these oversized fashions. What might have been described by fashion executives as "ethnic" or "Black" the decade prior was now relabeled as "urban." It was a clumsy catchall for the fashion establishment to describe this way of dressing—first by Black and brown teenagers in the city, then by white kids in the suburbs.

"We didn't like them calling us *urban*," Daymond John, one of the founders of FUBU, later said. "Why is it urban? Is it because people of color design it, or people of color wear it, or you can buy it where people of color live?"

It was clear that the look was no longer limited to the inner cities, and the fashion establishment finally started to notice the shift in the marketplace. The clothes showed up at Macy's, JC Penney, and Bloomingdale's in suburban shopping malls across the country. Urbanwear was on its way to becoming big business.

This was where the success of FUBU and Karl Kani in the nineties differentiated from that of Willi Smith in the eighties: The more money you made, the more seriously you were taken. The fashion journalist Elena Romero touched on a similar sentiment in her book *Free Stylin': How Hip Hop Changed the Fashion Industry*. "The first germination of urban fashion designs in the 1980s brought really exaggerated fits, colors, and logos, which made industry experts predict the look to be a passing fad," she wrote. "With the second generation of designers in the 1990s, the fashion industry had to recognize the urban brands as legitimate business because of their volume." Trailblazing and cultural influence were one thing; generating extreme commercial success was another.

As these brands expanded and sold hundreds of millions of dollars for chain stores, Stüssy now swirled up in a cross-pollinated marketplace, feeling the forces of a shifting youth fashion landscape. "This is a tough business. It's all variables and no constants," said Frank Sinatra. Tommy Hilfiger and Ralph Lauren had more fashion credibility; Phat Farm, FUBU, and Karl Kani had more rap-world cachet. Still, Stüssy stayed the course; it played to its strengths and kept distribution tight, ever mindful of risking overexposure in the marketplace. However, Shawn and Frank soon learned that some things were out of their control, and one competing brand became their biggest nightmare.

11.

Played Out

Stüssy is irrelevant.

Countless retailers stung Frank Sinatra and Shawn Stüssy with the news. The department stores wanted the Stüssy clothes to be baggier and sportier. The *hip-hop look*. This wasn't exactly a shock to Frank and Shawn; the shift in teenagers' demands became more apparent to their business by the season. That was problem number one. Stüssy's second problem was more precise: a California designer named Massimo "Mossimo" Giannulli, who drained nearly every drop of Stüssy's street credibility like a well-moussed vampire with a wardrobe of shiny suits and a full-time chauffeur.

Mossimo was everything Shawn was not. Mossimo started his namesake label after watching volleyball players on the beach, noticing the logos all over their attire.

Why not sell clothes with my own signature as a logo? he thought.

After fumbling around junior college, the rich California kid sold his Porsche and tricked his father into loaning him $100,000 so he could start his company. (Mossimo once said he convinced his father the money was for university tuition with false report cards and fake bills.) In 1987, he started Mossimo, producing beachwear with a sporty, fashionable twist; his vibrant volleyball shorts and simple T-shirts quickly caught on, and the company hit $1 million in sales within its first year. The clothes looked more suspiciously similar to Stüssy's as seasons passed, even down to the hand-scribbled logo and color palettes. One of Shawn's bestselling designs was the Beach Pant, an easy-wearing chino with a relaxed fit and elastic waistband; Mossimo didn't wait long to add a similar style to his collection.

In 1992, Mossimo galloped toward $23 million in sales, quickly gaining on Stüssy's $40 million. Retailers began to refer to Mossimo as *Stüssimo*. Shawn and Frank held firm to their shared business ethos, limiting how much product they sold despite the increased demand for the brand. Mossimo exploited that principle with aplomb.

"He grew by selling to all the stores that we wouldn't sell to," recalled Frank. "He watered down our look and made our look sort of boring, because now it was everywhere. It was very frustrating to Shawn. . . . [Mossimo] essentially went around in the early nineties and told everybody, *I'm just like Stüssy!*"

"I'm sure there had to be some influence at some point. I'd be lying if I said that there wasn't," Mossimo once admitted. He later said that Shawn's reputation as being "so selective and such a pain in the ass" worked to his advantage.

By 1995, Mossimo had hit $72 million in sales, as Stüssy's slipped to $23 million, and officially became an unavoidable headache for Shawn and Frank. Every season Mossimo sold more clothes, the *Stüssy look* lost more potency. The two companies fought for headlines and rack space, and gossip about the rivalry dominated the industry's insider circle. There was even a point when the two brands exchanged barbs via T-shirt graphics.

Mossimo's arrogance and copycat clothes frustrated the hell out of both Frank and Shawn. Shawn, especially, grew tired of dealing with this bombastic migraine. "[Shawn] was burnt-out. He didn't want to go back to work and do collections. He wanted to hang out and surf," recalled Paul Mittleman, New York's unofficial dot-connector and International Stüssy Tribe member.

"Neither of us wanted to work *that* hard. Shawn wasn't famous for working hard. Shawn was famous for being so talented that it came easy," Frank said. "We were getting all kinds of negative feedback from our accounts, from our friends, saying, Stüssy is not exciting. It's irrelevant. *What are you going to do?* And Shawn wasn't about to change the aesthetic that he was embodying."

The shifting trends in the marketplace—a move toward a deeper hip-hop look, the lookalike competition of Mossimo, and the rise of sporty-casual designerwear—meant that Stüssy would require a higher level of effort to run than in years prior. Retailers asked Frank to tweak designs and styles and produce more trend-driven clothes. Stüssy jeans needed to be bigger, like JNCO jeans. The T-shirts needed to look like the hip-hop ones. The jackets needed to look like Tommy Hilfiger. This is what our customers want, they told him.

Shawn was unwilling to compromise. "If shit didn't sell, Shawn was pretty notorious for saying, *Oh well, if you don't want it, too bad. I'm not making anything else*," recalled one Stüssy employee. At one point, Shawn thought the label might be headed toward closing for good.

Toward the end of 1995, Shawn quit the label he'd started fifteen years before in his tiny shaping studio on Laguna Canyon Road. He sold his stake to Frank—for around $5 million or $6 million, according to former Stüssy employees—and walked away from the company that bore his name. (Frank refused to confirm the exact buyout price except to say $5 million to $6 million was "in the range," adding, "Shawn left at a time when it looked like the company was going out of business.")

The marketplace stomped out Shawn's enthusiasm, and the accidental fashion designer grew out of sync with his team. "A big part of that was my crew of people were not on the same page as me," Shawn later said of his exit. "They didn't see the end of the rainbow like I did. . . . I saw the next phase that wasn't a skateboard or surfboard company." He aspired for Stüssy to be a "proper clothing line" like A.P.C., the willfully timeless French fashion label.

"He felt like nobody appreciated what he saw as compelling fashion," recalled Frank. "Shawn respected me; I respected him. Neither of us went to the mat and said, *It's this way or the highway*. We never had to go there."

Still, the two partners found friction in navigating the balancing act of art and commerce. Shawn refused to compromise, and Frank looked for a flexible middle ground. After all, he was the one in charge of the books. "One of the things that people find very abrasive about me is that I want to control my environment," said Frank. To him, control was a way to mitigate risk and limit failures. "I was perceived to be squashing initiative, to be tamping down creativity, to be too dictatorial, too demanding, when none of that in my mind is true. I'm really just trying to ensure success."

Shawn was gone, with enough cash in the bank not to have to work for the rest of his life. Stüssy had to move forward without him. ("There is no single person that is as good as Shawn was," Frank later said.) As part of his exit package, Frank owned the Stüssy name; Shawn would never be able to use his last name for a clothing brand ever again.

Frank focused on the brand's future and knew some significant changes were in order. The first step was to move the brand onto the standard industry calendar; the company had long released collections only when they were ready. That Stüssy had built up to a $40 million annual brand without adhering to the traditional garment calendar was unheard of.

Frank made a choice to stay within Stüssy's inner circle. Instead of looking to bring in merchandisers or designers from the Orange County surfwear industry, he wanted to draw from people who knew the brand's DNA. It was savvy. James Jebbia mentioned that Paul Mittleman could jump in; Paul was hired as the brand's creative director. The only outsider they brought in was a designer named Nick Bower. He had worked for Gotcha, the surf brand Shawn used to design for, but was also a graduate of Central Saint Martins with stints at Valentino and Versace. He had to be convinced to take the job. "I didn't want the job," recalled Nick. "I was like, *Dude, I'm not going to try and fill Shawn's shoes.*"

Frank and Paul eventually hired a young graphic designer named Kevin Lyons, a recent Rhode Island School of Design graduate. Even with a new team of designers, Shawn's handiwork held a commanding presence within the brand. "We'd have this whole wall with all the designs," Nick said. "And always, the bestsellers were the five that Shawn did when he was still at the company."

As the demand for Stüssy dropped, the brand no longer played coy with fulfillment; if you wanted a Stüssy order, you got it. For the first time in the brand's history, the supply met the demand. There was one thing that Frank knew he needed to change. It was the most extensive edit to the business, and perhaps what would be the label's saving grace. He wanted the brand to turn its back on the American market. This was due not to ego, but to necessity.

"There was no point in chasing American retailers when they

say, *Hey, you know what? People don't ask for it anymore,*" recalled Frank. "And so we basically stopped selling to American stores." The brand remained strong and stable in the international markets; those retailers and customers loved the brand just the same as before. One market in particular stood out as being especially strong.

"Without Japan, Stüssy wouldn't be in business," Paul said.

At that time, the label had upward of twenty Japanese stores, and the Japanese shopper was a *very* loyal customer. The worst of it, all of that swirling uncertainty, seemed to be behind Stüssy. The small team was architecting what the future of Stüssy would look like. The Shawn era was over, and something new was beginning. But one of Stüssy's key New York players had his sights set on a new project to call his own.

Upscale sportswear became retail's money-spinner. It was *the* look of New York, the epicenter of covetable American fashion. The industry-beloved fashion designer Donna Karan introduced DKNY Men, a sub-label of casual sporty clothes with lower prices directed at this younger market. Calvin Klein did the same with CK, a sub-brand built to deliver hip, street-savvy wardrobes. Both collections were hailed as "the saviors of retailing." Tommy Hilfiger's clothes became so widely worn he became simply *Tommy*, in the tradition of one-name American designers like *Ralph* and *Calvin*.

Ralph Lauren's designer sportswear continued to mesmerize rappers and skateboarders alike, not to mention hordes of total squares. In 1993, Ralph opened the first dedicated Polo Sport store on Madison Avenue, across the street from the designer's famed Rhinelander mansion flagship. The two-level expanse with polished cherry floors and white lacquered walls announced that the sporty look was here to stay. The next year, Raekwon gave his Polo down jacket a shoutout on the 1993 Wu-Tang Clan song "C.R.E.A.M.": *a young youth, yo, rockin' the gold tooth, 'lo goose.* (Before Shawn left the company, Stüssy had experimented with a quasi sub-label, Stüssy Sport, inspired by Polo Sport.)

Another distinctly New York trend was how the tough-wearing look of rugged outdoor wear—Timberland, The North Face, Carhartt—gained a stronghold in inner cities and nightclubs alike. The gap between the streets and the boutiques kept shrinking. An article in the *New York Times* highlighted that Carhartt's heavy-duty duck-canvas jackets turned up on the racks at Barneys New York, calling the jacket "a fashion accessory for rappers, club kids, preppie hangers-on, and the otherwise chronically cool." Stüssy simply wasn't as *hard* and didn't bestow the same street cred as a North Face Nuptse or a buttery fresh pair of Timbs. Labels like Karl Kani and FUBU were more accurate to the game than a California brand with origins in surf.

———

James Jebbia made a big move when Shawn soured on his namesake label. Operating Stüssy's SoHo shop, and his friendships with the two owners, gave James a closer view into the company's successes and shortcomings. He invested a lot of his time and energy into the brand, pulling away from Union to focus on Stüssy. The slouching sales and intra-company turmoil had rattled him.

James wasn't going to wait around and leave his livelihood in someone else's hands. He had no doubt that he needed to launch a new business that was his own. In 1994, after months of planning, James launched his newest retail venture: a small skateboard shop on Lafayette Street, just a few blocks from the Union and Stüssy stores.

The idea came from a skater and the manager at Union, Frank Crittenden, whom everyone called Chappy. He told James about the mobs of skateboarders at Washington Square Park and Brooklyn Banks, a downtown skate spot under the Manhattan side of the Brooklyn Bridge. Former Phat Farm designer Eli Morgan Gesner and SHUT Skates founder Rodney Smith had launched Zoo York the year before, giving New York skaters a label to finally call their own. It shot a fresh and palatable energy through the city's beautifully patchwork skate scene.

There is no *real* skate shop in New York, Chappy told him. You need to open one up.

There were plenty of skaters wandering around the nearly empty SoHo streets, though. James had always liked the rebellious spirit of skateboarding and thought he might as well be the person to open one. The space he found was about six hundred square feet, and he paid $2,000 monthly for rent. Lafayette Street was a lonely street not too far from the two major skate spots. He enlisted Chappy, along with a twenty-one-year-old skater named Mathew McGrath he met at ASR in San Diego. Mat quit his job at Deluxe Distribution and moved out east for the job. "We were getting $75 a day as managers and I was working ten-hour days," he recalled. James told Mat that he and Chappy needed to hire "a shop kid."

Just go find a skater that you think is trustworthy, he told him.

James wanted another real skater. He told Mat he never wanted anyone who had worked professional retail experience or any corporate training working for him. "We had a lot of respect for him, but he always kept it real. He was the boss, and you didn't ever question him . . . he was close-mouthed about so much." They hired Giovanni "Gio" Estevez, a well-styled skater and aspiring artist.

The interiors were sparse, with tall SoHo ceilings, walls as white as driven snow and simple plywood shelving and garment racks perched on metal legs. Skate decks hung at the back wall, while T-shirts and hoodies were displayed neatly on the sides. All the merchandise was hidden in the back stockroom. The space in the middle of the store sat empty, like a small pond of varnished hardwood. James wanted skaters to be able to come right in with their boards. It was a bold use of negative space, an unconventional layout for a retail shop that made the store feel akin to an art gallery. In the front window, an installation of six stacked TVs played skate movies and rap videos on an endless loop to the sidewalk outside. "I spent days just sanding stuff and putting the store together while Chappy was at Union. We started ordering stuff and put up the board wall," recalled Mat. "That was all James. He had this incredible vision for the space."

With guidance from Mat and Chappy, James filled the shop with skateboard necessities and standard wares. There were boards, wheels, trucks, baseball caps, T-shirts, jeans, sneakers, and hoodies. Prices ranged from $18 for a T-shirt to $50 for sneakers to $118 for a complete board: the deck, wheels, trucks, bearings, and grip. The shop stocked a curated list of skate brands like Element, Girl, World Industries, and the newly formed Zoo York. It sold classic sneakers like Vans Old Skools and some American workwear like Ben Davis construction jackets. In that first year, business started slow. Sales started off at a few hundred dollars a day; breaking $1,000 was considered "a really good day." James also sold graphic T-shirts branded with the shop's name and logo.

The same simple-looking logo adorned the glass door out front. It was a vibrant glacé red rectangle, with bold white lettering that read SUPREME.

12.

Thrasher Fashion

Somewhere deep in SoHo, between West Broadway and Lafayette Street, James Jebbia parked his black Range Rover between the locations of his three storefronts—Union on Spring, Stüssy on Prince, and now Supreme, at 274 Lafayette. On most days, he'd call his newest shop and chat with Alex Corporan, a suave twentysomething professional skater from Washington Heights who managed the storefront after Chappy and Mat exited. He was nine years James's junior. It was always a quick chat. *How much in sales today? What color sold the best?*

"Once Supreme opened, it was the new clubhouse," Alex said.

James set out for Supreme to be a different skate shop from day one. The New York skater was a different breed of skater, after all. New Yorkers had a fashionable swagger and a unique confidence that came from skating in a city full of seven million people and seven million obstacles. "I was new in town and they all definitely gave me shit for many months," recalled Mat McGrath. "They knew that I had [skate] cred from the West Coast, but in New York you have to earn it."

James presented Supreme's six hundred square feet as a stylish white cube. The back wall displayed some thirty skateboard decks, and the T-shirts were pulled taut, like canvas on stretcher bars. Superfluous objects and decor were stripped away. In this context, everything became a sacred object.

"Skateboard shops were trashed-out spots. They were usually pretty dirty and scroungy and not in the best neighborhoods. They were places that were just completely covered in stickers and broken boards. They were more punk, and Supreme felt like this SoHo fashion boutique," said Aaron Rose, who ran the skater-art crossover Alleged Gallery on the Lower East Side.

The in-house designs marked with the Supreme logo became the shop's calling cards. One featured a black-and-white photo of the titular character from Martin Scorsese's 1976 film *Taxi Driver*, in which a disturbed loner with a thirst for violence moonlights as a New York City cabbie. Another was the "Afro Skater" tee, printed with a photograph smaller than a postcard. The third featured a 1981 painting by Jean-Michel Basquiat known as *Untitled (Skull)*, a deconstructed and sketchy work of a face rendered with abstract lines and shapes (and printed without permission from Basquiat's estate). The fourth was the simplest of them all, later referred to as the "Box Logo" tee: a small red rectangle printed on a white T-shirt.

For these originals, James tapped into his Rolodex of New York City creatives, a small set of graphic artists and graffiti taggers, many of whom also sold their own clothes at Union. Russ Karablin, the designer behind the Adidas weed parody shirt that sold in Union, was tapped for some of the earliest designs. James had approached Futura 2000 for the logo.

"I did some handwritten stuff, and then I suggested a kind of Barbara Kruger messaging. The sort of clean delivery of information with the text and the color blocking," recalled Futura. His other proposed logo design featured SUPREME spelled out in inky, textured, and gritty strokes. But James was immediately drawn to the red-and-white logo.

The Supreme Box Logo played into a shared idea crystallizing across this crop of brands from Los Angeles to New York. It was a spin on appropriation, and the T-shirt was the canvas of choice. Erik Brunetti from FUCT and his parody of the Ford logo, the Phillies Blunt tees by Futura and Stash, Shawn Stüssy with his Chanel-inspired T-shirts. X-Large's Eli Bonerz and Adam Silverman fused the logo of workwear brand Ben Davis with a painting by the Pop Dadaist Steven Gianakos, and Rick Klotz flipped the Tide detergent box for Freshjive, creating an era-defining graphic in the process. These designers were borrowing motifs. Or simply stealing them.

When the first Supreme logo was printed, Barbara Kruger was already art-world famous. In the eighties, the former magazine designer stormed the New York scene with her photomontages—often black-and-white photographs with a red or red-on-white typeface—and quickly rose through the ranks. Her artwork placed her alongside eighties appropriationists of the so-called Pictures Generation: Richard Prince, Louise Lawler, and David Salle. The loose-knit group used image appropriation to examine and question the constitution of American mass media.

The font was a bolded and italicized variant of Futura, a geometric sans-serif typeface released by a German typography foundry in 1927. Futura was ubiquitous in twentieth-century advertising, widely embraced by major brands, corporations, and magazines.

Using Futura within her critiques of commercial culture, Kruger weaponized the font perhaps most synonymous with consumerism. Her color choice was just as deliberate. Red is an emotionally intense and dangerous color that demands attention; designers are taught to use it sparingly, as it can be overwhelming when overused. A 1991 review of Kruger's work described it as "a little like stepping into a roaring furnace that's black and white and red all over—red with anger."

There are no true accidents in art or commerce. By appropriating Kruger's well-known use of color and type, Supreme took the gun and pointed it back in the other direction, selling a winking critique of the commercial and appropriating the appropriator. Supreme was blurring the lines between homage, parody, and outright theft. And it was perfectly legal: No single artist can own a commercial font or a primary color.

Supreme operated as less of a shopping destination in those early years and more of a hang. Loud strains of music, from Slayer to Wu-Tang to Bad Brains to Public Enemy, blared from the speakers. The shop employees burned sticks of Nag Champa incense, masking the back-room smell of sour weed and instead perfuming the space with a spicy, woody resin. Yet, as among kids hanging out behind the handball wall at recess, there was an unspoken code: The front of the shop had to stay tidy. And there was reverence for how James let all the skaters hang out all day, not spending a dime. His employees held a quiet respect for the slightly older British businessman; they quickly came to understand their boss's perfectionist expectations and learned to meticulously refold any T-shirt that was even slightly out of place. "We always kept it beautiful," recalled Alex. "We did our thing in the back room, drinking forties, smoking blunts, whatever. But the shop was pristine."

Once business hours ended and they locked the front door, their crew hung out in the back to kill time before the night started. Some skaters went to the clubs and bars, and others trekked uptown to film footage. (Midtown's architecture provided countless banks and smooth ledges, making an excellent backdrop for transition skating.) At one point, the skaters frequented spots so much that security took notice. Eventually, each building got Rottweilers to chase off the skateboarders. The Supreme crew usually reconvened at Astor Place near the shop at around one a.m.

Business remained slow. "If you came by in those first few years, it was dead," said Alex. If two guys were working a shift, they'd take turns sleeping in the back, because they were usually tired and hungover from partying the night before. James kept behind the scenes. He had wanted the skate shop to be an authentic space and to let the skaters run the storefront as they saw fit.

"James would just do a drive-by . . . looking at the floor, making sure that everything looked good. Meaning you didn't leave it a mess. You saw him just look in, make sure everything's good. And that was it. He stayed away but he was still very hands-on," recalled Aaron "A-Ron" Bondaroff, one of the shop's earliest employees.

Still, James had extremely high standards for the company. "At least three of our friends we hired were fired by James within a week," recalled Alex.

The inner mechanics of running a skateboard company were brand-new to James. "He started to understand how it worked. I told him, 'You got to give stuff away.' Because at Stüssy, he didn't give discounts and he never gave anybody shit for free," recalled Mat McGrath. "I told him that in skateboarding, you give product to cool people and they start repping the brand. That's how the brand gets identified." The company put together an official skate team and, in 1995, released its first skateboarding video, *A Love Supreme*, which starred Peter Bici, Justin Pierce, Giovanni Estevez, Jones Keeffe, and Ryan Hickey. Shot on black-and-white Super 8 film by artist Thomas Campbell, it featured a moody b-roll of the city and a soundtrack not of punk or hip-hop as was the norm, but the jazz of John Coltrane. The result was chaotic, romantic, and, perhaps above all, totally hypnotic. (Although at least one Supreme skater hated the video, later saying the director was "too busy trying to film artsy stuff" instead of focusing on the skatelines.)

The gospel of Supreme started trickling into the world outside of Lafayette Street. The brand's earliest print ads for *Thrasher* were shot by Shadi Perez, featuring lifestyle photography of the skaters as opposed to mid-trick action shots that was typical for the era. James's reference was a 1994 cK One ad staring Kate Moss that was plastered on every bus and phone booth in the city. Others ads nodded to Kruger's work and Warhol's soup cans. Early on, Supreme brought a decidedly art-and-fashion world sensibility to how it projected itself.

"We were the billboards for Supreme," Alex said. "That's just the clothing we had on. We were the hot kids in the club. We were the shit in the street. We were the skateboarders in Supreme like, *Who are these fucking kids wearing this shit?*"

The skaters caught the eye of a wild-haired photographer and filmmaker named Larry Clark, a fiftysomething man armed with a Leica camera and the morals of a teenager. For years, he had been watching the loudmouthed crew of skaters at Washington Square Park. Larry persuaded a cherub-faced film student named Harmony Korine to write a screenplay about the scene. Harmony wrote a script chock-full of profane street talk, explicit sexual situations, and an overall rawness that could only come from a nineteen-year-old who lived it. It was teenage rebellion and leering fantasy with some dramatic Hollywood flair. Much of Supreme's skate team and shop crew were cast in the movie, ranging from lead actors to background parts.

"Justin gets the lead role. Harold [Hunter] was a main guy. Peter's there, I'm there," recalled Alex. "It was New York City skateboarding." The cast rounded itself out with Leo Fitzpatrick, a New Jersey teenager who took the bus into the city to skate; Rosario Dawson, who was cast while sitting on her front stoop; and Chloë Sevigny, a downtown model and buzzed-about "It" girl who had landed a *New Yorker* profile when she was nineteen. No one cast was a professional actor.

The film was released in the summer of 1995, with an NC-17 rating and a storm of controversy that only seemed to build interest and intrigue around the downtown skaters. The film grossed $20 million, with endless ink in national newspapers and magazines sending two brands featured within it—Supreme and Zoo York—out to a much wider audience. One of the label's sponsored skaters, Peter Bici, was approached outside the Supreme shop by a modeling scout who convinced him to audition for a Calvin Klein photo shoot. He booked the gig, a global campaign posing alongside the world-famous Kate Moss. "I went from skateboarding on Lafayette Street in front of the shop to traveling Europe and shooting with Karl Lagerfeld. All while wearing Supreme," said Peter.

The year Supreme opened, it landed in a *New York* magazine feature on chic SoHo shopping, next to A.P.C. and agnès b. The next year, the company popped up in a multipage feature in *Vogue*, in which writer Mary Tannen compared and contrasted a Chanel store on East Fifty-Seventh Street with the Supreme shop downtown. Even as the brand made inroads within the glossier world of fashion and magazines, it held tight to its counterculture ethos. Staff members were known for walking up behind customers and menacingly telling them they could not touch the clothing until they bought it. "We're playing music as loud as hell and running people out if it got too busy," recalled Alex.

Over in Tokyo, Supreme's rising status caught the attention of Kenichi "Ken" Omura, a Japanese businessman who ran a distribution company called OneGram. Ken told James he wanted to export the New York brand to Japan.

13.
An International Machine

Brendon Babenzien and Don Busweiler met as teenagers during the late eighties in Islip on Long Island. Brendon worked at Rick's Action Sports and Surf Shop, a clubby hangout for the town's misfits housed in an elaborate three-story foursquare; Don sold hand-printed PERVERT T-shirts from his backpack to local skaters and surfers in town. Brendon started selling the tees at Rick's, and soon there was a hyperlocal crew of surfers, skaters, and pot smokers running around Islip in Pervert shirts. "We were all looking at what Shawn Stüssy was doing and emulating that," Brendon recalled.

After high school, Don moved to Florida for art school, and by 1993 had leveled up Pervert into a legitimate operation with the help and cash of a partner in Ohio. Don also opened Animal Farm, an eccentric Miami boutique that sold brands like Stüssy, 555 Soul, FUCT, and X-Large. It was a hangout for the amateur skaters and BMX riders, the rave kids and hip-hop heads. After business hours, they'd throw parties in the back room. Pervert grew, expecting to deliver at least $2 million in sales, and Don needed another set of hands. Until then, it was mostly him and Geoff Heath, a self-taught graphic designer with an obsessive knowledge of rap. He also worked the floor at Animal Farm and helped print T-shirts in Don's kitchen. Brendon left New York and joined the two in Miami to work with Pervert.

Pervert scaled up the brand's collections and expanded its reach, selling at industry trade shows and showing up in British and American style magazines. *Rolling Stone* called the label "a line of sportswear for every hip-hop-loving homeboy." The Pervert guys made friends with Los Angeles and New York designers and brand owners like Eric Haze and 555 Soul's Camella Ehlke. "New York's a small place. You end up meeting everybody eventually," recalled Brendon. The brand was distributed throughout the United States, England, and Japan; James Jebbia even stocked the T-shirts at Union. The future of Pervert looked bright. Then Don blindsided his family and friends.

"He threw everything in the ocean and joined a cult," recalled Geoff.

In 1995, Don joined a mysterious religious group called the Brethren. The founder believed that the end of the world was imminent and that the only way to secure a place in heaven was to begin purifying yourself. Members shunned material possessions and forsook their families and friends; they lived essentially as vagrants, dumpster-dove for food, sewed their own clothes, and worked odd jobs to pay expenses.

"Brendon was trying to talk him out of it. Don's mom was going crazy," Geoff said.

"Don was only speaking in biblical terms," Brendon added.

Then, a week after Don announced his plan to join the Brethren, he became a ghost, disappearing from the lives of everyone who knew him.

It was 1995. The other owners and investors of Pervert and

Animal Farm tried to maintain both businesses, but clashed with Geoff and Brendon. "They're not streetwear guys. They just wanted money," Geoff recalled. "That jaded Brendon and me, so we just went off and did our own thing. Pervert just fizzled out." The duo started working with another Miami-based brand, Mankind. The label was stocked in Union, and its owner, Scott Nelson, was already established within James's circle. By then, Geoff and Brendon had already met the Union operator, who was often in Miami to open a new Stüssy store. It was a short-lived endeavor. ("It wasn't going to make money, and James got out of it," said Stüssy owner Frank Sinatra.)

Word reached James that Brendon wanted to move back to New York. The Supreme business was growing, and James needed to bring someone else on board. In 1996, James hired Brendon as the company's first-ever full-time designer.

"He needed someone to help with product development, design, and sourcing. I was just like, *Yeah, whatever, dude, whatever you need, I'll figure it out*," recalled Brendon. "I didn't have enough experience to pull it off, but that wasn't going to stop me."

Something peculiar kept happening at the Supreme store on Lafayette Street. Shop manager Alex Corporan had noticed even more Japanese tourists stopping by than usual. One customer had walked in and tried to buy all four sizes of a single T-shirt design. It wasn't the first time that had happened that week.

No, Alex told him. You can only buy *one*.

Later that day, three other shoppers entered the store, each trying to buy the same graphic tee in multiple sizes. He sold them the T-shirts and watched them walk out the door together. Something was definitely up.

Yo, watch the shop for me! he told his coworker.

Alex grabbed his bike from the back room and walked it out to the street, waiting until the three men were a block away but still in his line of sight. He slowly pedaled in the middle of the street, watching them on the sidewalk until they ducked into the Starbucks on Spring Street. Alex locked his bike outside and paced outside the door, glancing in the massive windows. In the back of the café, he saw a Japanese man orchestrating it all. The man sat at a table with piles of Supreme gear; maybe twenty people surrounded him, and he handed out wallets stuffed with American cash for the "tourists" to use. This had been happening since Supreme first opened, in some form or another. The shop's first manager Mat McGrath remembered the guys from Japanese magazines would come in and take pictures of the shop and the skaters. "After we opened, and they were coming every month and buying tons of shit. James was like, 'You're being too nice to them . . . we don't fuck with those guys, but they can come after hours and we'll sell them what we don't want.'" (In the sixties and seventies, Louis Vuitton encountered a similar situation: Japanese customers traveled to European stores, clearing them out and shipping the product to Tokyo, where the goods sold for up to four times the retail price.)

Supreme was more significant in Japan than in the United States. The Ura-Harajuku scene kickstarted by Hiroshi Fujiwara, Nigo, and crew had given them a full-fisted embrace. Ken Omura told James he wanted to open Supreme stores in Japan. James entered a partnership with Ken's distribution company OneGram to open the brand's first Japanese shop in the Daikanyama neighborhood of Tokyo. They opened a second shop in Osaka; a third soon followed in Fukuoka's shopping district. Ken took the Supreme name and sprinted, opening each shop in quick succession within six months of the last.

The new Japanese stores were a world away from downtown Manhattan, but all were constructed with the design language of the Lafayette Street flagship: stark, gallerylike spaces with hardwood floors and white walls. The T-shirts were displayed neatly on shelves, and American hip-hop and punk rock blasted from stereo systems. Not only did Supreme bring its product to Japan, but the image and attitude came with it. To the Japanese consumer, that was just as important as the clothes.

―――

By the late nineties, Lenny "Futura" McGurr and Josh "Stash" Franklin were cult designers in Japan, their reputations boosted by their friendship with Nigo. The Japanese founder continued to use both New Yorkers to design graphics for A Bathing Ape. When Jun Takahashi moved Undercover out of the shared Nowhere storefront, Nigo turned it into a makeshift art gallery, showing exhibitions from Futura and Stash, and later a younger artist named Brian Donnelly, known as KAWS. Hiroshi Fujiwara hired Futura and Eric Haze to design for his label GOODENOUGH.

"The Japanese crew knew everything about what we were doing," Stash recalled. "The adoption of American street art in Japan definitely came through its commodification. It wasn't infused from the street up. Their introduction to us was the T-shirt. . . . They would finance brands because the business was so big for them, and they could easily advance you. To them, it was nothing, but for us, it made or broke the brand."

The Ura-Harajuku brands had expanded. Nigo opened a second store, Nowhere Limited, that carried the Undercover women's line and sold designs from his New York friends. He also opened the first dedicated A Bathing Ape store in 1997. Shinsuke Takizawa, a former coworker of Hiroshi's at the record label Major Force, started a brand inspired by motorcycle culture and classic American workwear called Neighborhood. Hikaru Iwanaga, who once played in a band with Jun, opened Bounty Hunter, a toy and clothing company that sold artful and offbeat vinyl figurines. Tetsu Nishiyama created WTAPS, a brand inspired by his appreciation of military garments.

Japan also proved the saving grace for Stüssy. After Shawn's departure and the Mossimo fiasco, the brand clawed back its sales, which had been cut nearly in half by the mid-nineties. Only 25 percent of the brand's revenue came from American retailers. "Growth came during the late nineties. We grew from twenty to thirty million," said owner Frank Sinatra. "But all that was the fact that I put Japan on an early calendar, and they could buy more."

James opened Supreme's first office in Tribeca, a twenty-minute walk from the retail store. Brendon set up camp there and worked on his own. James operated out of the Stüssy store on Prince Street; the two met a few times a week to discuss Supreme. Brendon remained in touch with Geoff via phone and fax. In 1998, Supreme hired Geoff for a full-time gig. It was not glamorous. "Just an old abandoned warehouse with me and Brendon sitting in the middle of it," recalled Geoff. The two lived together in Brooklyn, in a tiny apartment with slanted floors, before eventually moving into a three-bedroom spot on the Lower East Side with James's brother Dan. Brendon and Geoff skated through downtown Manhattan to get to work. The label's new Japanese stores demanded more designs with each passing season.

"It felt like it caught fire in 1998," recalled Alex. "At that point, the shop was like eighty percent Japanese customers. They'd take that $28 shirt and turn around and sell it for $120 in Japan."

Brendon focused on the brand's cut-and-sew garments while Geoff handled the graphics. Even with two designers, James was heavily involved with the clothes. He'd taken a hands-off approach with the storefront, giving free rein to the skate kids who worked there. But Supreme's clothes had his thumbprints all over them. He'd come into the office and tell his designers that he wanted to do a trench coat or a heavyweight hoodie. And the rest was up to them.

The vision and design philosophy for Supreme crystallized in James's head early on. He quickly noticed that the skaters at Supreme didn't wear just skate clothes. They'd mix Polo Ralph Lauren, Champion hoodies, and Carhartt jackets—taking inspiration from the baggy fashions of rappers. The majority of the skateboard industry was in California, making skate clothes for California skaters. Those clothes weren't meant for New York's seasons, nor its sense of style. So when Supreme made a sweatshirt, the team used a high-quality, heavyweight sweatshirt blank that could handle a Northeast winter. They used immaculate embroidery: layered stitching and precise thread tension so as not to pucker the fabric.

James noticed the New York skater was extremely particular about his clothing.

Store employees and skaters hanging around would often be asked about forthcoming designs. The skaters became an internal litmus test of whether a product was tough, cool, or otherwise good enough. Skateboarding became a bigger business, too. There were now nine and a half million skateboarders in the United States, and the growing group was expected to spend $838 million dollars on hard goods, clothing, and related accessories.

Supreme was pricier than its competition; A Supreme hoodie retailed for sixty-eight dollars, while other skate brand sweatshirts would be forty-eight. They discovered a customer happily paid the premium because it looked better and lasted longer. There were plenty of domestic manufacturers scattered throughout the New York area. They could get thick, heavyweight sweatshirts made just over the East River in Brooklyn. They could produce baseball caps right in Manhattan. The Supreme designers cold-called manufacturers out of a phone book, made trips to factories out in New Jersey, and bought fabric from wholesalers in the Garment District.

Agustin "Augie" Galan, an employee at Union, had joined the team as the design assistant. James told him he had to start part-time, three days at Union and two days at Supreme. None of them had a background in fashion or production, so everything was learned on the job. They reverse engineered garments to see how they could make them better. "Everybody buys reference samples," said Augie. Supreme referenced *the* reference. "*What is the original that Ralph knocked off?* I'd look for the original. I'd go into the vintage stores. The army-navy stores. I'd see if he replicated it as good as the original, and a lot of times, he might have missed a couple things to cut costs, because he was still a garmento. He was still looking to make money on it."

The vintage clothes always had heavier fabrics and tougher construction. Augie broke the reference down to the components: the fabric, the pocketing, the waist lining, the buttons, even the thread. "I would go down to the yarn, basically." He'd find details that maybe hadn't been replicated and add those back in. The team deconstructed and rebuilt every component at the highest level. "That's how we got this reputation in the early days for making really nice shit."

James wouldn't have it any other way. His standards were impossibly high.

New products required numerous sampling rounds to meet James's demands. While developing a flight jacket, he sent a manufacturer a handwritten note with six magisterial bullet points, calling out that the fabric was too stiff, the label was poorly sewn, and the bottom elastic was awkwardly tight. James ended the note: *I'm not going to compromise on these pieces.*

By 1999, the design team had produced a full range of custom clothing: pants, sweatshirts, crewnecks, hats, backpacks, jackets, jeans, trousers, and shorts. James hired an additional designer named Luke Meier who had formally trained as a tailor in Italy. They felt the brand ramping up and getting bigger, but James kept the financials close. "I don't know exactly how the [Japanese] deal was structured, but I know that we sold them at wholesale, and then James also had some kind of monthly licensing fee. He was getting money two ways," said Augie, who ran all the production. Out of curiosity, Augie added the numbers from the clothing orders across his desk. The company looked to be hovering around $3 million in annual sales.

Even if the New York skater was the litmus test for Supreme's products, Japan was the label's biggest market. The studious Japanese customer appreciated the quality and streetwise authenticity the brand brought to the table. As the nineties burned away and the new millennium approached, James had built Supreme into a underground fashion machine.

Act Two

14.

New Kicks on the Block

Alife opened in the cut of downtown New York City, tucked away in a bargain-bin neighborhood that was not yet fashionable. It was founded by a small clique in their late twenties and early thirties—Rob Cristofaro, Tony Arcabascio, Arnaud Delecolle, Tammy Brainard—as a creative agency, loose art collective, and retail experiment on the Lower East Side. The group formed at their previous day job, working together at the respected, old-hat trade magazine *Sportswear International*. The hours were too long and the paychecks too small, so the four friends struck out on their own. Half of the quartet wanted to open an advertising studio; the other half wanted to open a retail store. The compromise was 178 Orchard Street; it had shop space on the first floor with a small office upstairs. Plus the scrappy upstart couldn't muster the higher rents on the glossier side of Bowery.

Rob grew up in the Bronx; as a high schooler, he was mesmerized by paint-covered subway cars and hip-hop album covers, and he held a New Yorker's loyalty for Timberlands and Air Force 1s into adulthood. Tony was cut from a similar cloth, a tall Italian American guy from Queens with the same interests in graffiti, rap, and wearing the right kicks. Arnaud was a bit spiffier, a fashion journalist from a European family that had imported and manufactured footwear for generations; Tammy had an ambitious attitude and was married to Arnaud. Together, they pooled $60,000 to open Alife, gutting and renovating the 1,400-square-foot space themselves.

Arnaud carried on the family tradition and imported forward-looking footwear: Camper (from Spain), Snipes (Germany), SUBU (Japan), and Gola and Tricker's (Britain). Rob wanted to sell graffiti-approved art supplies and "dope" accessories. He flew to Tokyo with an empty duffel and a pocket stuffed with $3,000 and returned with little toys, lighters, stationery, watches, and other miscellaneous souvenirs. "It was all relatively inexpensive stuff, but stuff that I had never seen in New York at the time," recalled Rob. He also sold graffiti supplies from Krink, a small company founded by a Queens-born writer named Craig "KR" Costello, who mixed homemade ink and assembled paint mops from his nearby apartment. The idea to stock Alife with small-batch and hard-to-find products was clever but came with one major downside. "The store would be full, and then we'd get an influx of customers, and by the end of the month, our store would be completely empty." To help keep the shelves full, Rob printed small runs of Alife T-shirts and sweatshirts.

The agency was the moneymaker that allowed Alife to survive that first year. *Elle* magazine hired them to help launch a more youthful sister title called *Elle Girl*. Alife also started to work on *Mass Appeal*, a rough-hewn graffiti zine that leveled up into an actual magazine. "Whether it was a new product, or new artists, or whatever we were doing, it was funneled into that magazine," said Rob. The practice echoed how Tokyo designers Hiroshi Fujiwara,

Nigo, and Jun Takahashi self-promoted with *Takarajima* and *Asayan* in the nineties.

By 2000, their second year in business, the store was busier, and it was hard to miss these little groups wandering around the store with tiny notebooks in hand, some armed with cameras. "They'd never introduce themselves," recalled Rob. "This was ongoing, and it would happen numerous times a fucking month." One of the Alife guys would strike up a conversation and learn they were from a company like Adidas, Nike, or Levi's. Always a brand with a vested interest in staying hip. Arnaud was working the floor when a group from Nike came in and caught him on a bad day. He was fed up with this. It was the third time that month.

Get the fuck out of here! he barked at them. Come back when you have something to talk about.

The following week, two guys returned—one from Nike and one from their ad agency, Wieden+Kennedy—with a duffel bag in tow, apologizing and asking if they could chat. Rob, Tony, and Arnaud were just about to smoke a joint and invited them upstairs to the studio. As they got stoned together, the Nike guy opened the bag and pulled out a futuristic-looking sneaker, sleek and laceless with strands woven together like a basket made from willows.

This is the Air Woven, he explained.

It didn't even look like a Nike sneaker. Neither of the Alife guys had seen anything like it before.

It hasn't been released yet in America, he continued. We want to launch it with you guys.

The deal that Nike proposed seemed even more surreal. They'd deliver around fifty pairs, and Alife would keep the money from all the sales. No consignment. No wholesale. Nike just wanted them out on the shelves in a cool store, nothing more. Rob, Tony, and

Arnaud told a few friends, and those few friends told a few more. When they opened the store to start selling the Air Wovens, a line of kids had assembled outside. That very same day, the Alife crew decided they needed to open another store as soon as possible.

It would be a dedicated boutique—just for sneakers.

———

In 1991, Robert "Bobbito" Garcia wrote an article for hip-hop magazine *The Source* titled "Confessions of a Sneaker Addict," showcasing his Nike Air Force 1s and Adidas Forums and highlighting how reissued basketball sneakers rose to be *the* en vogue kicks in the inner cities. Bobbito ended his confession with a sneakerhead mantra: "Don't ever be caught out there with a pair of grips that everybody and their mother has." Over a decade later, in 2002, Americans spent more than $15 billion on athletic and "lifestyle" sneakers, nearly 430 million pairs. You now had to work infinitely harder to avoid being caught with the same pair of grips.

Nike looked ahead instead of backward. That same year, the company launched HTM, a sub-label and accelerator group named after three men: Hiroshi Fujiwara, Tokyo's propagator of hype; Tinker Hatfield, who designed the Air Jordan; and Mark Parker, Nike's innovation-driven president (and future CEO). "At the beginning, HTM became an opportunity to add a sense of luxury to sneakers," recalled Hiroshi. The trio sometimes introduced more obscure and eccentric styles like the Air Woven, or revamped a street classic like the Air Force 1, elevating it with premium leather and contrast stitching. "HTM started with the idea of how the three of us could reconstruct a classic sneaker with a new twist to appeal to a different audience," Mark once said. The sneakers no longer had to pledge allegiance to a singular sport or athlete.

Nike also introduced a shadowy and whispered-about Tier 0, or "TZ," program among its global retailers. It looked like an evolution of two programs set by Nike Japan in the nineties, CO.JP and Quick Strike, that started delivering exclusive sneakers and colorways to boutiques. Tier 2 was your run-of-the-mill store, maybe a sporting goods shop that had all the Swoosh staples; Tier 1 was for the smaller and more fashionable boutiques that had access to almost everything. Tier 0 was the upper echelon, completely uncut access to Nike, and it was rumored that only ten stores worldwide had that honor. Alife's name was on that rumored list.

———

Alife Rivington Club was a store without a storefront. There was no signage, and shoppers had to press a barely marked buzzer to be ushered in. The company's success afforded Rob, Tony, and Arnaud a budget of a quarter-million dollars for the build, about four times the budget they'd scraped together for their original Orchard Street spot. The concept was to make the sneaker shop like a mid-century Playboy Club smashed into a Gucci boutique, and it certainly looked the part. Dozens of sneakers gleamed in handsome cherrywood cabinetry, and an Italian crystal chandelier hung from the ceiling. There was a tufted leather couch the length of two ladders, and an entire wall was draped in an opulent ostrich-skin wallpaper. This was a new kind of sneaker store.

"We wanted to create an experience. You'd first walk through this little foyer and then through these huge doors. You'd forget where the hell you were," said Rob.

Alife Rivington Club stocked an elite and eclectic curation of sneakers: a Nike Dunk Premium released in collaboration with Eric Haze, featuring a sleek and monochromatic overspray effect;

the crème de la crème of Air Max silhouettes, the 95—a model especially beloved by Japanese shoppers; and limited-edition Asics runners from the company's just-relaunched Onitsuka Tiger sub-brand. Puma offered exclusive styles to be sold only at the store, and Adidas unlocked its archive for Alife to sell premium versions of vintage styles. Some stock skewed more toward art projects, like Pascal Spengemann's delightfully loopy and unauthorized brand mash-ups, stitching a Nike Swoosh on a pair of Adidas Rod Lavers, priced at $400. The shop also sold the classics, Adidas Superstars and Puma Clydes, two wildly popular styles in the eighties that returned for a second spin.

Rob approached James Jebbia to tell him what they were doing. "I wanted to show him just out of respect," he recalled. "I used to catch him cruising by just to watch what we were doing. So yeah, we were definitely buzzing at that time." It was *all good*, per se, but a slight tension of competition lurked under the surface. "We were an up-and-coming brand that was taking a part of his market."

Over at Supreme, James and his team were also getting in on this emerging sneaker craze. "It was such a crazy transition," recalled Supreme shop manager Alex Corporan. "It was great for the shop, because we made much more money. The clientele went from Japanese customers to everyone in the neighborhood." With the boost from sneakers, Supreme sometimes generated $150,000 in a single day, and it would be almost all in cash. Nike started to supply a steady stream of covetable sneakers to Alife Rivington Club and Supreme as well as Nort 235, a new Lower East Side boutique started by graffiti artist Josh "Stash" Franklin; Prohibit NYC, a store focused on Japanese selvage denim that dabbled in covetable sneakers; and Dave's Quality Meat (DQM), founded by a former pro skater and a former Zoo York employee, which was cleverly designed to look like a butcher shop, winking that they had the *freshest* product. The *New York Times* dubbed this mini-boom, led by Alife, "the rebirth of the New York sneakerhead."

The rebirth of the sneakerhead was not limited to the Big Apple. In Los Angeles, Stüssy Union manager Eddie Cruz partnered with James Bond to open Undefeated, a wood-paneled boutique rumored to have Nike Tier 0 status; in London, International Stüssy Tribe members Michael Kopelman and Marc "Fraser" Cooke opened a sneaker shop called Footpatrol; in Amsterdam, two fervent sneaker hunters, Edson Sabajo and Guillaume "Gee" Schmidt, opened Patta; and among Tokyo's countless sneaker shops, the shining star was Atmos, founded by Hommyo Hidefumi, who got his start flipping retro American sneakers in Japan for ten times what he paid for them.

Nike wasn't the only major brand knocking on Alife's unmarked doors. Levi's tapped them to produce a limited-edition collection of 501 denim for New York Fashion Week. The Alife logo was placed on the iconic Levi's patch, the first co-brand in the storied jean maker's 150 years of existence. Levi's gave Alife $250,000 to build an installation; they remodeled the entire Orchard Street store beyond recognition, in a stark white with heavenly light beams and an ethereal stairway. Alife still went over budget, putting $10,000 of their own money into it; Rob, Tony, and Arnaud were better at generating hype than profit. "We were making money but kept investing it back into the company. If we could do a thing for fifty thousand dollars, we'd do it for ninety thousand," recalled Tony. "All we wanted to do was make noise."

The shop also served as a launchpad for downtown artists of all stripes: graffiti writers, painters, and photographers. Alife teamed up with famed art dealer Jeffrey Deitch on a joint exhibition featuring work from Barry McGee, Craig "KR" Costello, Eric Haze, Brian "KAWS" Donnelly, Mark Gonzales, Ryan McGinness, Geoff McFetridge, Todd James, and Shepard Fairey, among others. The exhibition's promotional poster featured a flip on Warhol's Campbell's soup can. "We were always putting people on a platform. And then these other people, smart people who were watching, began to tap into it," recalled Rob. (Deitch Projects and other established SoHo art galleries poached artists who had shown in scrappy shows in Alife's Orchard Street shop by offering bigger budgets and establishment cachet.)

Still, Alife's most immense reputation was that of a bona fide sneaker store, the spot for kingpin collectors. In 2003, *New York* bestowed the shop with its coveted "Best of New York" award, and the *New York Times* later proclaimed them "the original purveyors of high sneaker culture." Kalman Ruttenstein, Bloomingdale's mountainous fashion director, called the shop nearly every Friday morning to see if any worthwhile sneakers had arrived in size twelve. Everyone wanted a piece of Alife Rivington Club.

On a tropical Thursday afternoon in August 2003, a sprawling power outage brought New York City largely to a standstill. Tony was working out of the Orchard Street studio when the lights went out, so he locked up and called it a day. He walked to Max Fish, a nearby Lower East Side watering hole frequented by the skate and graffiti crowd; they were giving away free beer before it spoiled. After darkness crept over the city, a friend ran over and told Tony that the Rivington Street shop was being broken into. Tony headed over; it was only five blocks away. He arrived to the storefront's fireproof door bent off the hinges like it was flimsy sheet metal. He tiptoed inside. "I knew by just touching around that [the shop] was fucked up," Tony recalled. Once he realized the looters had left, he stepped outside and waited on the sidewalk, trying to think of his next move. "All of a sudden, I see these kids and they start walking past me."

Yo, where the fuck you going? he asked.

Going to get sneakers, one replied.

Tony told them he owned the store.

You ain't the fucking owner, another snarled back.

But the mini mob turned around and walked away, disappearing into the eerie darkness. Then Tony heard beer bottles whizzing in the air and smashing on the concrete. The kids were trying to push him away from the front of the store so they could get back inside. They eventually succeeded.

In the daylight, the damage became more evident. The level of looting was insignificant compared to the city's infamous 1977 blackout. There were around 56 break-ins identified as looting—a fraction compared to the 1,600 of 1977, where looters roamed the streets with couches, TVs, electronics, and armfuls of clothing. The mayor and police widely praised the city as "orderly, behaved" afterward, but that was little comfort to one corner of the city. In downtown New York, the looters focused on stealing sneakers instead of TVs. ("With Lights Out, Looters Set Sights on Sneaker Shops" read one newspaper headline.) At Stash's Nort 235, someone attempted (but failed) to cut through the padlocks; another would-be looter smashed a window at Prohibit before being chased away by a neighbor. Other downtown shoe stores and multiple Foot Lockers across the city were burglarized. But Alife Rivington Club got hit the worst.

A band of young men cleared out most of their inventory, even ransacking the basement. The store was wrecked: missing sneakers, structural damage, and at least seventeen stitches—one employee, Keefe, and Tony's girlfriend, Jennifer, each got smashed in the face with forty-ounce bottles in the chaos of the night. An oversight in Alife's insurance policy meant they got nothing for the theft and damage, but luckily, friends and brands like Adidas and Nike pitched in to help. Still, it was tough to keep working. "We almost didn't reopen. I'd see some kid wearing some shit that I knew only my store had," recalled Tony. He'd think to himself, *Were you one of the dicks that was in there that night?*

The Alife crew continued to innovate—with brand collaborations and art installations so focused on the cutting edge that they learned being rich in buzz wasn't the same as cash. Alife had to figure out how to turn all the fanfare and accolades into profits.

A ten-minute walk west to SoHo, the designer who got her start selling handsewn 555 SOUL caps and T-shirts in a raggedy Lower East Side store over a decade ago had upgraded to the slicker and more legitimate Lafayette Street. She was dealing with a different kind of problem.

Her brand had gotten *too* big. The money changed everything—and she didn't like it.

15.

Triple Five Sold

Camella Ehlke was already fed up with her business partner. The Triple Five Soul label was bigger than ever. It was 2004, and her clothes were sold in over three hundred stores, including fashion royalty Bloomingdale's, the hip chain retailer Urban Outfitters, and the exceedingly influential Fred Segal. The brand hovered around $38 million in annual sales. Yet Camella was whiplashed by the growth and as miserable as ever. Some days, the money didn't even feel worth it.

Everything changed in 1996 when she partnered with Troy Morehouse, a New York fashion executive who had worked with several downtown shops and labels, including Russell Simmons's Phat Farm. Camella met Troy at a factory in Chinatown; they befriended each other after he sold her unused Phat Farm fabric for her 555 Soul designs. Troy invited her to his studio space in Long Island City. He was a queer man from Canada, handsome and charismatic; he liked to party but could otherwise be quiet and introverted. She liked that Troy was younger and hipper than the usual garmento. His space operated more as a mini-manufacturer than an art studio. He had employees, and there were sewing machines, steam irons, embroidery machines, and enough fabric to rival some of Camella's New Jersey suppliers. He floated the idea of working together.

Camella kept having to turn down orders or downsize them. Retailers asked for one thousand units of a certain style, and she simply didn't have enough cash to front for production. Her factories extended her credit, but then if a retailer was late or missed a payment, the ripple effect was a headache. It took a toll on her. Camella had slowly accepted that if she didn't get help, her 555 Soul project was unlikely to last. She owed her Chinatown factory $200,000 and another $30,000 to a New Jersey fabric supplier. No matter how many hours Camella worked, the designer couldn't shake the feeling that her business was falling behind.

Troy was calm and put-together.

"He stepped to me because he knew I was in over my head. My business was growing so fast. I was one girl doing everything," she recalled. "I started getting really in debt, so it made sense for me to take on a partner that was going to inject some capital and then help me manage the production, because I was doing the production all myself and running the store. . . . I mean, it basically was a one-man show."

She sold 50 percent of the company to Troy when the label was hovering around $1 million in annual sales. It felt like she had little choice; the brand grew, and she kept running into walls. The change was immediate. Troy injected major cash into the business to pay off her debts and took over her production. The brand's name went from 555 Soul to Triple Five Soul because they couldn't trademark the "555" part. In their new office in Williamsburg, Brooklyn, Camella had a two-hundred-foot wall of closets to keep reference materials and racks of samples. In 1996, the tiny Ludlow storefront upgraded to a bigger spot on Lafayette Street in SoHo, less than two hundred feet from Supreme. Two months after they shook hands, the new partners were on a flight to Las Vegas to attend MAGIC, the men's fashion trade show where all the "urban" brands went. Troy really wanted to insert Triple Five Soul into the booming category.

"He pushed me into going to MAGIC right away, which was a shock to my system and my friends and community. All of a sudden, it became this bigger commercial brand," recalled Camella. "I was one of the first ones to take the leap to go to MAGIC to do the trade shows, and I was *a sellout.*"

The "urban" category surged throughout the late nineties and into the early aughts, expanding the market size to $58 billion by 2002. Ecko, the mall-friendly brand started by a "boyish white guy" from suburban New Jersey, sat at the top of the mountain, reaching $600 million in annual sales. Then came FUBU, which hit yearly sales of $350 million. Jay-Z and Damon Dash's Rocawear became a major player, as did Sean "Puffy" Combs and his Sean John label. Russell Simmons eventually sold Phat Farm and his newer women's line Baby Phat for $140 million to one of the country's largest clothing producers. *Vibe* magazine ran a feature on seven brands "changing fashion" by tapping into "hip-hop culture" and the "urban lifestyle": Karl Kani, FUBU, Phat Farm, Triple Five Soul, PNB Nation, Bushi, and Enyce. The big and baggy look was officially big business.

Even into the early aughts, *sellout* remained an epithet in the underground, especially among the graffiti writers and skaters who hung out south of Houston Street. Going to corporate trade shows or selling to chain retailers remained verboten. "That's *disgusting*. You never do that to a brand. A brand didn't do that back then. You can't sell out," recalled an early Supreme employee. "You can't be wanting to be successful. If you go for the fucking success, it's not authentic."

Authenticity remained a badge of honor, even if that purist line of thinking peaked in the nineties. This was a significant idea through all facets of creative and underground culture, a holdover from the nineties and a cornerstone of Generation X. It became a foundational operating ethos for these *underground fashion* brands; they held tight to this thinking even as the world changed at a faster clip. Chuck Klosterman, the music writer turned cultural scholar of Gen X phenomena, cut to the concept's core in *The Nineties: A Book*. "The key to that coolness was disinterest in conventional success. The nineties were not an age for the aspirant. The worst thing you could be was a sellout." But the vulgarity of selling out held true into the new millennium. Success and money weren't cool, at least for the time being.

Triple Five Soul was a natural fit for the "urban" category, even if the brand was born from the downtown cohort who valued creativity over capitalism. Camilla's designs featured boxy, simple silhouettes with bold colors, and rappers like Mos Def and Pos from De La Soul had worn the label for years. Camella noticed she was not marked with the same "urban" label ascribed to some of her peers. "I bet because we were white, we passed in the sense where we were *streetwear*, she said. "[At MAGIC], they didn't throw us in the room with all the other Black brands, which was really fucked-up and noticeable." The corporate trade show was where the brand landed its biggest retail accounts. Her downtown friends always asked her, *Why are you selling out to all these stores?*

Selling out wasn't any of Troy's concern; he brought in a distributor, and they moved production to China. Triple Five Soul finally fulfilled orders in units of thousands with ease. No more begging factories on Ludlow and Orchard Streets for credit extensions. The brand also joined Stüssy, Supreme, and X-Large in Japan. First came a flagship store in Tokyo, then Osaka, and finally Fukuoka; all opened within a two-year stretch. Troy wanted to make Triple Five Soul a global powerhouse, as big as it could be.

"It was full-force. *Open a big office, go to all the trade shows, make full-on collections.* It became formal," recalled Camella. "It happened so fast I couldn't even catch my breath."

As the label grew, Camella did her best to maintain the community feel of her original Ludlow store. She'd have friends over at the office to hang out—musicians, DJs, graffiti artists—and then walk them down to the warehouse to let them pick whatever new threads they wanted. Her vision for the brand's future included more community spaces to hang out in; she wanted to open a café and a record shop. She pictured it in her head: Triple Five Café, Triple Five Sounds, Triple Five Home. Camella wanted to do more than make baggy pants and T-shirts.

Troy wasn't here to hang out and make arty clothes or build a lifestyle; he'd bought half of her company to make money. This division bubbled up into a more extensive fracture within the company culture. Troy let Camella "roam free"—until sales reached $10 million. Then he turned colder, stricter, and more mysterious. Any rogue ideas she mentioned were promptly stomped out.

"I had people on my side that were maintaining the energy and ethos of the brand, while Troy had his team," she recalled. "His team of sales and merchandisers would try to influence the design. It just got too hard for me, too toxic and too difficult." She discovered Troy had secret design meetings with only the sales staff, bringing in a pair of G-Star jeans and requesting that they make a similar pair. It became a business of knocking off other popular products in the marketplace. "He started making executive creative decisions, and that really bothered me. Not because I have an ego—it's because the taste level was so watered down and embarrassing."

Camella had become frustrated and tired, though. And suspicious.

She had started to notice that Troy was drinking earlier and earlier in the evening. It wasn't uncommon to see him sitting next to a vodka-filled carafe at night, slowly sipping from a glass tumbler. Sometimes it started as early as the late afternoon. "I knew things were going on with him, and I knew money was being filtered in his direction, but part of me didn't even really care to argue it and fight it," she said. "I made a deal with the devil, but it was fine. . . . I rolled my eyes, took a deep breath, and just went with it."

Larger suspicions started to arise. They stored the cash in a safe in the company's headquarters. Only she and Troy had the combination. Camella opened the safe after a massive sample sale and noticed that $100,000 was missing. She caught him trying to manipulate Japanese distributors. He once made an offhand comment about having their China factory buy out her ownership so she would no longer be an owner. Then she discovered he'd signed with a Canadian licensor behind her back and kept all the money from the deal for himself.

"Did he get me to the next level? Yeah. Did he do it fast? Yeah," Camella later wondered. "I don't know if it's right or wrong."

It took her seven years to grow Triple Five Soul into a million-dollar label; Troy only needed four years to turn that $1 million into $38 million. Right or wrong, one thing was clear: Camella no longer recognized Triple Five Soul and dreaded going into the office. "Money had become the driver, and it started losing its soul," she said. It was no longer her sitting in her small studio sewing until her hands were numb, blasting *The Low End Theory* and smoking weed with friends as they covered fabric with aerosol paint. She found the brand to be a toxic presence in her life.

Troy wanted to sell the business to get more capital. He talked to Marc Ecko's company and Rocawear founder Damon Dash. He looped Camella into these conversations. "That's when I got the idea, *I am just out of here. I can't do this*," she said. They went back and forth on numbers for her exit; she eventually sold her remaining stake for $3 million. Camella felt it was an unfair deal and she should have held out for more, but she was also desperate to close this chapter, move on with her life, and never speak to Troy again.

Camella thought back to when she knew every number and inch and fabric scrap of her brand. When Triple Five Soul was still 555 Soul and she stored the shop's cash in a Phillies Blunt box. When Pos from De La Soul wore her hat on the cover of downtown's style bible, *Paper* magazine. Camella thought of the vibrant red-orange door at the Ludlow Street storefront, her apartment in the back tucked away behind a curtain. She remembered, right before she partnered with Troy, how she would drive from the city to the New Jersey fabric warehouses, the freshest ninety-minute mixtape cassette from G-Bo The Pro & DJ Rei Double R playing on her car stereo. She'd leave in the late morning, often tired out from the night before, and by the evening, she'd be back on Ludlow Street. It was nonstop, the humming of her sewing machine and the ambition in her head. She missed that—when things were simpler, and the stakes were lower. There was less money, but there was still plenty of honest and artistic work to be done.

16.

Slouching Toward Bowery

All Aaron "A-Ron" Bondaroff ever wanted was a *fucking Andy Warhol loft*. But it was no longer the sixties, so he set up shop in an ample studio apartment on Bowery and East Third Street. It was the mid-aughts, and the rent was only $500. He nicknamed it the Baby Loft. A-Ron had been slouching toward Bowery since he was a teenager. Without James Jebbia and Supreme, he might never have gotten to the Baby Loft.

A-Ron was the fifth employee at 274 Lafayette Street, after Chappy, Gio, Mat, and Pooky. The Baby Loft was a fourteen-minute walk to Supreme's triplex offices on Wooster Street, and it only took nine minutes to walk from there to the Lafayette storefront where he had spent most of the late nineties. A-Ron had dropped out of high school at fifteen, and he'd take the train into the city every day and just *float around*. "I was just trying to understand how to find my way . . . I just knew there was another life out there in downtown New York," he recalled.

One afternoon in 1993, when he was sixteen or seventeen, he strolled into Union. He never had money to buy anything but still liked to look, thumbing through the cotton T-shirts from CONART,

Not From Concentrate, Freshjive, and Pervert. Most brands included a sticker on the hang tag; A-Ron decided to steal one. Before he put it in his pocket, he felt someone lurking over him.

What are you doing there, man? asked Chappy, the shop's manager. He let the teenager keep the sticker and told him to get lost with a winking smile.

A-Ron eventually landed a job working the floor at Stüssy's Prince Street shop. On his second day at work, Paul Mittleman—the man who introduced Shawn Stüssy to James and who was now Stüssy's creative director—stopped by to tell A-Ron that he wanted to throw him in some print ads. Later in the week, a Dutchman with a camera named Ari Marcopoulos rolled through and plucked him from the shop, and they ran around downtown with some skaters. The shop was soon plastered with A-Ron's face. "You walk into Stüssy, every photo is basically of me," he recalled. When the Japanese tourists noticed it was him on the walls, they asked him for pictures and autographs.

Supreme was considerably less busy than Stüssy and only staffed by two guys. If a delivery came, they'd have to lock the front door to deal with it. They'd often call A-Ron at Stüssy and have him come over to help with the shipment, and they'd end up hanging out. "I always had weed on me," he said. "My dad was a weed dealer growing up." Sometimes they'd ring A-Ron over, and there wouldn't be a delivery.

"You're getting high. You're hanging out on your day off at another shop. If you work at Union, on your day off, you're at Supreme in the front. If you're not at Supreme, you're riding a bike around, and you're going to check out all the other shops. It's just this network that we had," A-Ron recalled. Another stop was at 262 Mott Street, an 1850s armory turned warehouse space where

Russ Karablin operated SSUR and Futura and Stash had a studio together.

Paul and James started sending A-Ron worldwide on Stüssy and Supreme's dime. They flew him out to Laguna Beach for a photo shoot. When A-Ron heard about the ASR trade show and told them he wanted to go, they sent him, and James ensured his rental car was "the newest, biggest Cadillac." A-Ron linked up with former New Yorkers who were now living there: Harold Hunter, Justin Pierce, Dave "Weirdo Dave" Sandey, and Jefferson Pang. Supreme sent him to Japan, sometimes four times a year, to shoot editorials for magazines like *Relax*, *Smart*, *Honeyee*, and *Asayan*. Eventually, Supreme started to pay for A-Ron's cell phone plan.

Within the Jebbia-built world of Union, Stüssy, and Supreme, the new skate shop was the most coveted place to be. Union was tiny and central enough that people constantly came in and out, asking for favors. It was also the smallest store, a claustrophobic shop in which to work an eight-hour shift. "It felt like a fishbowl," recalled Augie Galan, who started on the floor at Union before moving to Supreme's design team. "There was no privacy. There was a full wall of glass windows and doors so everyone could see you." Over at Stüssy, James always worked in the upper mezzanine; a quick turn of the shoulder was all it took for him to check up on the staff. "The ultimate graduation was getting to Supreme," recalled A-Ron. "If you could hang there and get accepted, then you're going to get your master's."

A-Ron was loud, fast, and winsome, always chasing the setting sun. With a mop of curly chestnut hair, he spoke with a full and scratchy voice that carried at least half a city block. His energized charisma spilled onto whoever he was talking to. But if you got him one-on-one, he'd downshift slightly, revealing a soulful and intelligent kid. One day, he was sent from Stüssy to Supreme to help with something and never went back. A-Ron was the youngest of the Supreme crew. "The skate guys protected me. They gave me a ring, they gave me this affiliation, and they gave me this kind of style that was so authentic anywhere in the world," he said. "The skaters that came before me were true artists and cultural pioneers."

The back of the shop remained an anything-goes clubhouse hang, stocked with weed and forties and personalities the size of moons. Nag Champa still perfumed the air. Some employees had no qualms about getting physical with annoying shoppers—it could be a shove for shouting over the sneaker line or grabbing another by the neck from behind the counter after they were mouthing off. They'd swap a Supreme tee for a Dean & DeLuca sandwich or a quarter-bag. There were larger transactions: trading T-shirts or the access to skirt the store's "only one" policy for new Air Jordans, TVs, laptops, or sometimes just cold, hard cash. (Supreme's long-standing policy limited customers to buying only one style of each product.) "Everyone was reselling," recalled a former Supreme employee. Even the big boss wasn't above leveraging the brand's international demand. "James would take advantage of it every once in a while if we were really stuck with stuff," said the brand's designer Geoff Heath. "Make a deal with one of these guys and backdoor some inventory of a bunch of pants that didn't sell." James still drove by in the mornings to check the floor, ensuring everything looked up to his standard. As long as the shop was neat, it was all good. The unspoken exchange of 274 Lafayette Street remained: The skaters respected the shop, keeping it tidy, and James let them run the roost. Although, an early employee was caught embezzling money from the shop, and promptly fired after James caught wise. "It was way more elaborate than reselling. That's all I'll say," recalled one staffer.

The design team—Brendon Babenzien, Geoff Heath, and Augie Galan—all worked out of Supreme's nearby office and didn't run in the same circle as the guys at the shop did. It was almost like they were two separate worlds. Some of the store staff recalled only seeing James at the shop a few times a year. At one point, someone asked A-Ron if he wanted to learn about the design and production side of the business. "I remember Augie saying to me, 'Don't you want to learn how this shit goes down?' I was like, *Fuck that. No, I'm good.* I'm in the front. I'm chilling. I'm traveling the world. What are you talking about?"

Still, even trips to Tokyo and rented Cadillacs became routine. A-Ron grew bored of hanging out on the bench, drinking the same forty-ounce and smoking the same blunt, talking the same shit with the same skaters. That's when he started to notice a new cast of characters roaming around SoHo.

The first time the graffiti writer Kunle Martins showed up at Supreme, the shop guys ran him out. "I remember he came by as a runaway kid to the shop, and everybody was like, *What is this fucking weirdo-looking dude doing here? Get him out of here*, and they chased him out. But I remembered him." Kunle was hard to miss—big, tall, aggressive, and openly gay, he wore insanely baggy pants with legs as wide as sleeping bags. His EARSNOT tag popped up everywhere, and he ran around downtown with a group of messy-looking art school kids: Ryan McGinley, Dan Colen, Dash Snow, Nate Lowman, and others. A-Ron saw them out at night, and they seemed to be having insane amounts of fun. *Who are these fucking weirdo characters*, he wondered. He started to talk to them and found them as creative and compelling as they looked.

They sometimes rolled twenty-five deep, in a rowdy crew they branded IRAK, and started to show up in New York's media and art-world circles. *Vice* magazine once described them as "always on the verge of losing their lives." Dash, Ryan, and Dan landed on a *New York* cover titled "Warhol's Children," proclaiming the trio was doing "their decadent best to prove that downtown lives on." These guys were taggers, painters, sculptors, and photographers who lived and breathed their art. A post-9/11 micro-generation and micro-school of downtown artists. They embraced A-Ron, showing him arthouse indie films and eccentric European fashion magazines. A-Ron got to the point where he just wanted to hang out all day. The city was bigger than the back room of Supreme, and he wanted to wander this strange new world below Houston Street. Not just with the skaters, but also the artists and the weirdos. He went to James with a proposal.

I don't want to work in the shop anymore, A-Ron told him. I'm an asset, so I feel like I want to stay on payroll. But I want to hit the streets all day.

James agreed, a platinum vote of confidence.

The legal capacity of Deitch Projects on Wooster Street, a garage-esque art gallery, was about two hundred people. Still, one thousand crowded the space on a cold December evening in 2002. Artwork from KAWS, Todd James, Larry Clark, Martha Cooper, Dash Snow, Futura, Shepard Fairey, and others were displayed. A-Ron was both the MC and the night's agent of chaos. The downtown skaters had infiltrated the art world, or vice versa.

James and A-Ron printed stickers that said CORPORATE GALLERY'S BULLSHIT ATTEMPT TO REPRESENT THE DOWNTOWN SCENE. A-Ron recruited younger kids to throw the stickers. "I didn't understand the gallery scene. All I knew was that I was gonna go in and cause some chaos," said A-Ron. The fire marshal was called because of overcapacity. "A-Ron comes up and punches me in the gut. Then chaos really ensued," Jeffrey Deitch recalled in an interview. Someone from IRAK got up in Jeffrey's face, and at least one skater poured beer over the powerful dealer's head, dirtying some of the nearby artwork that was for sale.

At the same time, Alife took over Deitch Projects' second location for a complementary installation, the walls mounted with shiny skate decks, stickers, sneakers, toy figurines, and a bottle of Krink graffiti ink. The Alife guys felt as if the big-time gallerist had forced their hand. "He was watching our curation, and he liked what we were doing," recalled Rob Cristofaro, one of Alife's founders. "He would approach the people we were working with and then give his platform." Rob fronted a few thousand dollars to mount small shows for graffiti artists; Jeffrey's offer for an exhibition with Deitch Projects could come with a six-figure budget. "Everyone was jumping into the street art look. Everyone wanted to tap into that because it gave them street cred," said Alife cofounder Tony Arcabascio. "It made them cool."

———

James gave A-Ron an office across from his own at Supreme's Wooster Street headquarters. "I had a corporate credit card, which is wild. What I did on that credit card was pretty wild. James gave us the fucking long-ass leash," recalled A-Ron. "We were taken care of, but we also took care of Supreme at the same time." James trusted A-Ron's opinion on things. *How would you style this? What do you think of this design?* He operated as sort of a silent brand director to support James. "A-Ron was like Malcolm McLaren," recalled a former Supreme employee. "He was in the streets, and he was meeting everybody that was doing something new and interesting. He kept James more or less informed about what was happening. He brought so much to that organization in the form of talent, graphic people, and artists. A-Ron was like the true New York thing. New York street culture is built by people like that."

"Aaron is part of the original crew who basically set the tone and image," James told the website The Brilliance! in a 2005 article about A-Ron. "There's mutual respect and friendship between us."

From his office, A-Ron worked with the brand's new graphic designer Eric Elms, a former studio assistant to Shepard Fairey and KAWS, on Supreme's magazine, which published issues for the Japanese market. A-Ron got Dan Colen to design a skateboard deck for the brand. When *Dune*, a Japanese magazine, approached the brand to shoot an editorial, A-Ron told them to fly out Ryan McGinley as the photographer. That same year, Ryan became the youngest artist to ever receive a solo exhibition at the Whitney Museum of American Art. That was how A-Ron operated; it had become his job to know the next thing before everyone else did.

Supreme's in-house skateboard decks took on the role of canvases. The brand tapped downtown artists like Ryan McGinness, KAWS, and Dan Colen before branching out to Russian conceptualist Andrei Molodkin, Queens-born multi-hyphenate Rammellzee, photographer and *Kids* director Larry Clark, and Peter Saville, the British graphic designer most famous for producing Joy Division's *Unknown Pleasures* cover. As Ryan McGinness later put it, Products were the new art.

Eventually, A-Ron wanted to strike out on his own with a brand. He had been printing small-run T-shirts with aNYthing, or A New York Thing, since 2002. A longtime friend had reached out, telling him he had just received some money from his father. The two friends wanted to scale up aNYthing and open a storefront *deep* downtown, on Hester Street in Chinatown. And with the help of another friend, Samuel Spitzer, he'd launch a proper website for aNYthing.

A-Ron stocked the storefront with an eclectic mix of goods. Supreme had produced shoes with the Irish company Padmore & Barnes that were sitting on the shelves; James told A-Ron to grab a bunch to sell. Dan Colen gave him some off-kilter sculptures that worked as uncomfortable, cool-looking benches. Dan, Weirdo Dave, and Neck Face produced zines for the shelves. He filled the rest of the store with books from Jack Kerouac and Allen Ginsberg, CDs, jewelry, and vintage clothes.

A-Ron was a darling of the press. They called him "the cap-wearing Pied Piper of underground cool" and "one of those individuals who embodies a scene." He was a raconteur who never ran out of snappy quotes. "I'm so downtown, I don't go above Delancey," he told the *New York Times Magazine* in a feature titled "The Brand Underground." The article dove into how the younger generation's mode of cultural expression was not just through art, music, or literature, but now included T-shirts, products, and brands. In addition to featuring A-Ron and aNYthing, the article dedicated much ink to a buzzy, internet-driven new label from Los Angeles called The Hundreds. These new types of brands were opening online stores on their websites and starting blogs that posted pictures of the carefree, well-styled people that populated their world. (aNYthing's blog was called The Glob.) Kids reading online felt like they were in on the action; it was a new way to sell T-shirts.

James Jebbia took notice of the aNYthing website and emailed the man who built it.

Hi Sam. Saw Aaron's website. Thought it looked real good. Let me know when I can expect to see something for Supreme.

17.

Internet Magazines

Not too far from his apartment in Boston, Jeff Carvalho discovered a Japanese convenience store. Most people shopped there for snacks and beverages that you couldn't find elsewhere, but when Jeff walked in, he immediately eyed a newsstand in front that was stacked with Japanese magazines. Jeff bought the latest issue of *Popeye* and asked the clerk at the cash register if it would be possible to order some other titles he didn't see. *Men's Non-No, Free & Easy, Huge.* Or *Relax, Smart, Honeyee, Asayan.* He returned to the store a few weeks later and left with a paper bag full of Japanese magazines.

    Jeff trekked to the nearest Kinko's and posted up at one of the computers, flipping through each magazine and marking the pages with images that caught his eye. The Japanese market was frequently "ahead" of the rest of the world, and the foreign periodicals were often stacked with unreleased T-shirts and sneakers months before they hit the American and European markets. Jeff cut out each product image, often smaller than a Post-it note, and scanned it to his zip-drive disk. Once he returned to his apartment, he powered up his computer, uploaded the images, and started to type. When everything was done, there was a new blog post on Highsnobiety, the website he'd teamed up with in 2007.

Highsnobiety was founded two years earlier by a well-spoken Swiss guy named David Fischer, who had just graduated from business school. As a teenager, David was heavily influenced by America's music and clothing. "I wore a lot of Stüssy and Tommy Hilfiger," he recalled, before diving one level deeper and discovering FUCT and X-Large and then Tokyo's A Bathing Ape. David immersed himself in this world of graphic T-shirts and sneakers and started publishing short articles on Blogspot. Soon, David was blogging about Krink and Alife collaborative T-shirts, Futura-designed Nike Dunks, and Sugar Cane & Co. denim. By the time David launched the proper Highsnobiety website, he was posting throughout the day, using every free hour he had. "David was an animal. He knew all of the Japanese websites to find stuff. He'd go deep into a link and check that shit fifteen times a day," recalled Jeff.

David made a few hundred dollars a month by selling advertising space for display banners through Google's AdSense. He realized he was building a business and decided he would do it full-time, giving himself a deadline of two years to see if he could turn this into a career. Suddenly the blog was making a thousand dollars a month, and the advertising money kept growing.

David had a few people writing for Highsnobiety scattered across the globe, and they did their best to churn out fifty to sixty posts a day. The website never asked for money from any of the brands it featured; they were doing it because they felt a duty to the emerging audience. To David, running Highsnobiety was an act of service. He was connecting like-minded people with objects he loved and spreading the work of these talented designers. "I was working fourteen hours a day to make sure that our audience was always ahead of the curve," he recalled. At one point, before he started to bring on freelance writers, David was clocking an average of forty articles a day.

Some brands welcomed the free press, and others were pissed off by it. David and Jeff carried on regardless. Highsnobiety blog posts often showcased products to the public that were meant to stay behind closed doors: those scans from the Japanese magazines. A rogue quality assurance picture of a new sneaker might be posted on an obscure message board; Highsnobiety found it and posted about it. Friends emailed stealth pictures from booths at the MAGIC and Action Sports Retailer trade shows. The brand owners didn't want their customers to see something six months before it was supposed to be released. It would be stale, old news by the time it finally hit shelves. Only wholesalers and store buyers were supposed to see the goods this early on, not the internet.

"The Alifes and the Supremes didn't have the most positive view of the blog," David recalled. "It was a little bit like, *Don't tell anybody about us. We don't want everyone to know.*"

The same year that David started Highsnobiety, halfway across the world in Vancouver, a college student named Kevin Ma launched his blog, Hypebeast. Like David and Jeff, Kevin was obsessive about sneakers. Before Hypebeast and Highsnobiety became must-read web destinations, it was all about online forums: NikeTalk, BapeTalk, Superfuture. Kevin spent his days lurking on NikeTalk, where he cribbed his new site's name. "Hypebeast"—slang for a trend-chaser, a consumer of status who followed the hype wherever it went—was the go-to insult on the forums. When Kevin graduated, he moved to Hong Kong and took a finance job, and practically sprang out of the office to return home to his computer.

"I really loved what I was doing. I would blog until the middle of the night, then go to sleep, and repeat," Kevin said. Every week, he'd check the viewer tracker. In a few months, it went from hundreds to thousands of readers. The more he posted, the more traffic Hypebeast got. "There were other websites doing this kind of stuff before us. But I think the thing with those websites is that they were not updated enough. When we came in, blogging was starting to take off. . . . It was much easier to share information. You just click a button, publish, and done."

A 2005 column in *Wired* proclaimed, "Like it or not, blogs have legs." The authoritative technology writer Adam L. Penenberg explained, "We are in the midst of a new kind of internet boom, thanks in large part to this weblog phenomenon . . . it's a revolution in the dissemination of intellectual capital." He likened the blogging revolution to the democratic participation of open-source code and an era of the internet where information became currency. Internet users could soon find blogs and message forums for every niche of culture you imagined. At the same time, across much of America, broadband replaced dial-up as the primary method of internet access. Households went from intermittently connected to always on, just as the rudimentary internet of plain text became stylized and image-driven.

More blogs popped up every year. *Complex*, the bimonthly magazine founded by Marc Ecko, launched an online network in 2007 that included websites like Nice Kicks and Slamxhype in addition to the flagship site. In Chicago, Benjamin Edgar and Chuck Anderson emailed links and images to each other with some quick opinions attached; they decided to turn those emails into The Brilliance!, a blog that skewed quite peculiar and individualistic: An interview with Futura or an entry about a KAWS collaboration appeared alongside posts about cult-loved metalcore bands and $100,000 watches. A new T-shirt brand from Los Angeles called The Hundreds started blogging. It was a real-time diary, as the designer Bobby Kim gave readers an inside look at starting a brand. Justin R. Saunders, a part-time art teacher in Montreal, brought a more visual approach to blogging, posting sprawling batches of images without text on his blog JJJJound. Even the rising rapper Kanye West launched a blog where he posted visuals and wrote about Japanese brands BAPE and Neighborhood alongside fashion labels like Maison Martin Margiela and Goyard. Kanye also "reblogged" Highsnobiety and Hypebeast with the frequency of a diehard reader.

NikeTalk and Superfuture launched in 1999 on a gawky and sluggish iteration of the internet, fundamentally different than that of Highsnobiety and Hypebeast. A Canadian computer programmer named Nelson Cabral started NikeTalk (NT) as a message board for sneaker collectors. Within a few days of launching, there were already hundreds of users, and by the mid-aughts, as the new "sneakerhead" phenomenon grew, it boasted over fifty thousand members. Users checked the forum feverishly for the latest news on Nike releases, traded tips on cleaning sneakers, and generally talked shit. (There was at least one ruthless thread about a member's jeans being too tight.)

"Your presence online was through the forums. There wasn't really any other way to have a presence digitally at that point in time," recalled Dennis Todisco, then a college student and an avid poster on NikeTalk. "It was just real people connecting. We were just trying to navigate this uncharted space of streetwear and sneakers."

However, the main reason sneakerheads converged on NT was for the most essential element of their collecting: the drop date. That detail usually came from a boutique employee or industry insider, often obscured by an indecipherable username. (Some retail employees would later be fired for sharing such information on the forum.) Those were the brass tacks Highsnobiety or Hypebeast scooped and posted on its website.

Superfuture focused more on fashion and shopping, boasting a glossary of 3,500 boutiques in over a hundred cities. It was founded by a former industrial designer turned magazine art director, Wayne Berkowitz. All the internet chatter drove guys into stores and increased sales in these boutiques, even if the website's founder wrestled with what he had created. "At some point, having too much traffic might work against Superfuture, as becoming mainstream would defeat the original purpose of making it," Wayne once said.

Both forums had cultivated an audience of thousands of graphic T-shirt and sneaker loyalists who became dedicated Highsnobiety and Hypebeast readers. Hypebeast focused more on sneakers than Highsnobiety; Kevin launched a forum section, which started to take off in 2006, and switched to the vBulletin platform the following year. The Hypebeast forums had become a central digital hub, with sub-forums like Nike Chat, Sneaker Chat, Fashion & Shopping Chat, and Toys & Art Chat. At Highsnobiety, David and Jeff upgraded from scanning photos from magazines to writing and producing their own features. David's first big assignment came when he secured an interview with the team at Colette, the influential Parisian boutique run by Sarah Andelman. More and more

Highsnobiety articles started to feature original photography and narrative storytelling, much closer to a legacy publication. Soon, the brands that once shunned them had begun to change their stance on being featured on a blog.

"It quite quickly changed. I think it was a combination of, quite frankly, the 2008 recession," David explained. "So I think some of the brands suddenly started having a significantly harder time. And only then they were like, *Well, I guess I don't mind the free promotion.*"

Both publications made significant progress in the media landscape as the younger, faster, and more streetwise alternative to legacy men's titles like *GQ* and *Esquire*. "Very slowly, brands didn't see us as a hindrance that was detrimental to marketing plans," Jeff said. "They essentially had no choice but to start working with us, because things were being leaked from factories and trade shows. The photos were still coming up." The pages of Highsnobiety and Hypebeast were like the shelves at Alife Rivington Club: The major sneaker brands wanted their products there. As more teenagers logged on to the internet, it replaced magazines and TV as a discovery tool for new music and fashion. Blogs rose as MTV simultaneously pivoted from music videos to reality programming. (By 2008, the network was down to just three hours of music videos a day, a cliff-dive for a network that launched as a twenty-four-hour platform for music videos.) As the expression went: Video killed the radio star, and then the internet killed the video star.

Still, even as it became apparent that this Web 2.0 version of the internet was destined to be a dominant cultural force, not every brand felt beholden to it. "Sometimes people just don't like outsiders, and it's a symptom of being in a closed loop a little bit," said Jeff. To Jeff, what he was doing wasn't much different than the hand-hemmed zines he used to buy. Sure, the websites were making some money from the banner ads, but so were the brands. It was a win-win, in his mind. Kevin and Hypebeast wrestled with similar hostility.

"I think there is some pushback from the so-called OG guys about this . . . but sharing is cool," Kevin later said. "What if I lived in the middle of nowhere—not in Paris, not in Tokyo, not in New York—how would I ever learn about this cool stuff?"

Highsnobiety and Hypebeast *were* a Paris and a Tokyo and a New York to which every suburban American kid with an internet connection had access. With just a few clicks, you could see what sneakers and T-shirts were being worn on the streets of SoHo or Harajuku. David and Jeff managed a freelance network of writers in Berlin and London; Kevin did from Hong Kong and Tokyo. Both online magazines kept New York writers on their rosters. The two websites generated millions of page views monthly and received phone calls from the biggest footwear companies in the world. The advertising money kept growing, and no one had to destroy Japanese magazines for sneaker photos anymore. This nascent industry now had its own fashion media that was quicker and more plugged-in than the old guard of printed legacy titles.

18.

Sneaker Frenzy

Jeff Ng trudged north on Orchard Street until he spotted a crowd of a hundred bundled-up people crushed together on the sidewalk, spilling out onto the street, and blocking the entrance to his store, Reed Space.

He had woken up that morning in February 2005, and it felt like any other bone-chilling day that month, other than it was release day for a new Nike sneaker he designed. There had been a couple of sneakerheads who had lined up outside of his shop. One kid on Sunday night turned into a handful on Monday; by Tuesday, the night before the shoe was set to drop, there were no more than a dozen guys huddled outside the shop when Jeff closed up for the night. He didn't think much of it; he bought them a pizza. His shop had been open for four years, and like Alife Rivington Club or Nort 235, Reed Space had dealt with overnight lines for sneakers a few times before.

As he approached his store around ten, he noticed police barricades and black SWAT vans parked diagonally to block the stretch of the street. He kept going about thirty more feet before he realized all the commotion was for his store. For the sneaker he'd designed.

He was grabbing his keys from his pocket when a uniformed officer barked at him, each question and command coming quicker than the last: Do you work here? Are you the owner? What the hell is going on? There are too many people on this block.

Yeah, that's me, Jeff answered. We're selling a new sneaker today.

That can't be true. What are you *actually* doing here?

No, I swear, replied Jeff. We're just selling sneakers. It's a Nike.

The cop still looked suspicious of something more, so Jeff let him and his partner into the shop and walked them down to the basement to show them the stacks of Nike boxes. Both cops looked stunned to find out the restless male mob was just there for shoes.

Okay, okay, the main cop said. *Whatever.* You have to bring order to this right now.

Jeff had no idea how he was going to do that. Only 150 pairs of this sneaker existed in the world. It was a limited-edition Nike SB Dunk Low Pro, designed as part of the Swoosh's "City" series alongside sneakers paying tribute to London, Paris, and Tokyo.

The company had tasked Jeff with designing the New York entry under Staple Design, the clothing brand and design studio he'd founded in the late nineties, selling his earliest T-shirt designs at Camella Ehlke's Triple Five Soul and James Jebbia's Union. When Jeff found the Orchard Street storefront, he saw it was large enough to tuck his studio operations in the back and open a retail space in the front. The monthly rent price was daunting—$8,000, four times what he'd paid for his first office space farther downtown. At the time, he was curious to see if other New York brand owners might open shops, like Scott Sasso from 10.Deep or Aaron LaCrate of Milkcrate Athletics, but he made the leap himself. "I have a bit of a gambler's mentality where I'm sort of willing to just go all in on something that I believe in. . . . I kind of felt like I couldn't wait for anybody else," recalled Jeff. "There was Triple Five Soul and Union, and that was pretty much it." Reed Space opened as a stylized boutique that sold streetwear, art magazines, collectibles, accessories, and sneakers. It was such an eclectic mix that when shoppers came in, the first question they asked was *What kind of store is this?*

Someone had gotten a pair of Jeff's Nike early and already listed it on eBay for $1,000, which cranked up anticipation for the release. Reed Space got thirty pairs, as did other shops across the city: Supreme and Rival in SoHo, Nort on the Lower East Side, and KCDC in Williamsburg.

"After sitting around and thinking for a while about what represented New York the best, the pigeon kept coming up," Jeff said. "It just doesn't give a crap . . . and I think that personifies New York."

The front of the line started to jostle and shove to secure their positions, with some grabbing on to the cold metal of the front gate, which hadn't yet been lifted. Everything Jeff and the police said to the crowd only seemed to piss them off more. They told the latter half of the line to leave; waiting was pointless because there were only enough sneakers for the first two dozen people. No one moved an inch. More cops showed up by the hour. A fistfight broke out, and one person was thrown in handcuffs, but no arrests were made. The line took almost four hours to thin out and resemble some sense of order. Jeff and his staff finally lifted the metal gate just before two in the afternoon.

It was around this time that they noticed baseball bats and large knives scattered on the sidewalk and lurking in the gutters. They also saw some shady characters idling at the top and bottom of the block, trying to stay out of sight of the police. The cops told Jeff that these guys were probably waiting to mug the kids for their sneakers as they walked away, so a plan to shield the customers was hatched. Reed Space had a rear entryway that spat onto Allen Street; the NYPD made a few phone calls, and soon a string of yellow taxicabs lined up out back. One by one, they let customers inside the store, rang them up for the $300 sneakers, threw the box in a bag, and then escorted them out into a waiting cab. Within the hour, all the sneakers were sold.

The Nike Dunk debuted in 1985, the same year as Michael Jordan's rookie season and when the Air Jordan 1 hit the shelves. The Dunk was designed as a high-top basketball sneaker, and the company envisioned that the on-court shoe would be worn mainly by college basketball players, promoting it via the "Be True to Your School" campaign, offering the silhouette in team colors from various American universities. The marketing worked initially, and then—like many of Nike's basketball sneakers—the Dunk was eclipsed by the Air Jordan's ardent popularity. It faded into the background until the mid-nineties, when skateboarders discovered it in discount bins. The design offered the cushioning, support, and traction needed for the sport; Nike had accidentally designed a stellar skate shoe.

This happened when Nike aggressively pushed to get into skateboarding, as street skating expanded the sport into a suburban after-school activity. The brand promoted longtime employee Sandy Bodecker as the new general manager of its flailing skateboarding division. In the late nineties, Nike released skate-specific sneakers with names like "the Choad" alongside cheesy advertisements starring the pro skater (and future *Jackass* star) Bam Margera. Skaters hated the shoes and the ads. Sandy was wise that the Dunk was organically loved by skaters. Nike retooled the silhouette as the SB Dunk, tweaking the original design to include a plush padded tongue, thicker shoelaces, and a grippier outsole—all revisions to adapt to the wear and tear of skateboarding. Sandy recruited four respected skaters—Reese Forbes; Gino Iannucci, an original member of Supreme's skate team; Richard Mulder; and Daniel Supasiriratana, aka Danny Supa—as the new faces of Nike Skateboarding and gave them each their own Dunk colorway. Former Phat Farm designer Alyasha Owerka-Moore designed the first collaborative Dunk, the Alphanumeric Dunk Low, which was released in January 2001; the following year brought the four skater-designed sneakers as well as collaborations with Zoo York, Chocolate Skateboards, and Supreme. (Not long after, both Futura and Stash were tapped to each design their iterations of the Dunk.)

Supreme's Dunk was the first-ever Nike sneaker to feature the iconic Air Jordan elephant print. The shoe was so hyped that it was the first time customers had lined up outside of Supreme before the doors opened. "We got to hire our friends to be at the door as security," recalled Supreme's shop manager, Alex Corporan. "It started with the Danny Supa Dunk and the Zoo York Dunk. It was like someone hit a switch."

The morning after the release of Staple's Pigeon Dunk, Jeff woke up, threw on his puffiest winter coat and winter stompers, and walked down to the bodega at the end of the block. The neighborhood had snapped back to normal. No more hordes of sneakerheads, no more cops, no more SWAT vans. Jeff wanted to pick up a copy of the *New York Post*. A reporter was running around in the crowd yesterday. She had interviewed him, and he was curious if the story had been printed already.

It was a coincidence that a reporter was on the scene as it unfolded in real time. Rachel Sklar, a buttoned-up Canadian with wavy brown hair and a warm smile, had just moved to the Lower East Side a few days earlier. She was hanging out at her friend's apartment on Orchard Street into the night's later hours. When she left the apartment at one a.m. to walk to her new place a couple of blocks away, she noticed a few young men lined up by a closed storefront. It was, at most, 19°F outside.

What are you guys waiting for? she shouted out.

Sneakers! someone yelled back.

Her journalist intuition clicked. This line wasn't for a designer fashion piece from a SoHo boutique, but *sneakers* on the gritty Lower East Side? Rachel had worked the city beat for the *New York Times* for years and knew teenagers waiting in raw February weather for rare kicks in an offbeat neighborhood was enough of a hook. The following morning, she fired up her laptop to see if any outlet was interested in the story; an editor at the *Post* responded to her first and told her to write it. When Rachel walked to Reed Space the morning of the release, she entered the same surprising chaos as Jeff. Her story escalated—from a local human-interest piece on young men with a niche hobby waiting in biting cold to the story of a downtown rumble over sneakers emblazoned with a pigeon. She grabbed quotes from Jeff, his shop manager, customers in line, and the cops, then returned home to write about how tempers flared when a line of sneakerheads turned into an unruly crowd that descended into a mini riot, all in the hope of getting their hands on a pair of rare Nikes. She filed her story and didn't think too much of it.

At the corner bodega, Jeff picked up the *New York Post*. He didn't even need to open it—there it was, right on the cover: a picture of the sneaker he designed, next to the headline "Sneaker Frenzy: Hot Shoe Sparks Ruckus." The article appeared on page 7 under the different, all-caps headline "SNEAKER RIOT" and a photo of the parka-clad mosh pit outside Reed Space with at least seven NYPD officers looking on. When Rachel went out to pick up a copy, she was just as surprised to find it on the cover, that her neighborhood-level story had bubbled up into something more significant. Scans of the newspaper cover started circulating on the NikeTalk and Hypebeast forums. Sneakerheads across the globe were soon talking and blogging about it.

Later that afternoon, the head of Nike New York called Jeff. She was angry, venting about how the botched release made for terrible optics and how it made the company look bad. "She sounded really, really mad," said Jeff. "But then her assistant calls me right after, and she's like, *Jeff, between you and me, she's really not mad. She's actually stoked. She just had to say that for formality. She's actually having me run to every newsstand in the city and buy as many copies of the newspaper as possible for her archive and to send to executives.*"

The aftermath of that frigid February day confirmed the importance to Nike of this new wave of sneaker boutiques and kicked off a year of other frantic Dunk releases, including one designed to look like Neapolitan ice cream and another like a Tiffany & Co. jewelry box. This was different than the Air Jordan; these customers weren't buying into an athlete, but rather into the idea behind the shoe and its limitedness. The *Post* cover pushed a hyperlocal sneaker story from a downtown sensation to a citywide one, and thanks to the internet, it became known across the globe.

Jeff later appeared on the evening edition of *CBS News*. "If Rachel Sklar was not on Orchard Street, the whole mythology of the Pigeon Dunk might be different now," he recalled. "That newspaper cover is so tied to the actual shoe."

The mob at Reed Space announced to the outside world that this new wave of clothing designers was producing covetable fashion. People were willing to brave the bitter cold to get those T-shirts, hoodies, and sneakers. The month after the "SNEAKER RIOT" story, the *Post* published a larger report about the New York City sneaker craze, listing a roster of the hottest downtown sneaker shops: A Bathing Ape, Alife, Dave's Quality Meat, Nom de Guerre, Supreme. To the mainstream, the idea of men lusting after shoes remained difficult to grasp, so an editor at *Complex* offered a contemporary analogy: "Guys go crazy for sneakers in the way that girls go crazy for Manolo Blahniks."

19.

Frontin'

Nigo knew Pharrell before Pharrell knew Nigo.

Ever since the Japanese designer and A Bathing Ape (BAPE) founder heard "Superthug" by the Queens rapper Noreaga, he raved to friends about the track's off-kilter beat. It was produced by the Neptunes, a duo of relatively unknown guys in their mid-twenties from Virginia. Nigo was drawn to Pharrell Williams, the unofficial charismatic leader with an excellent sense of style—he wore a wide-ranging assemblage of American fashions including varsity jackets, skateboard graphic T-shirts, fitted baseball caps, camouflage cargo pants, and dressy sneakers.

Nigo's obsession with American fashion and popular culture had not waned with age. Now in his thirties, with the same round and boyish face, he held a teenage obsession with the country's fashion and music. He'd discuss these things on the phone with Toby Feltwell, a British A&R rep from Mo' Wax and XL Recordings he had befriended in Tokyo. The two friends mailed each other magazines and videotapes and even planned a New York trip together; Nigo told him they had to make a stop in the Diamond District to see a man called Jacob the Jeweler he had read about in *The Source*. Pharrell used Jacob, so he must be good.

Jacob was the best hip-hop jeweler in New York, which is to say the best hip-hop jeweler in the world. When Nigo and Toby showed up to Jacob the Jeweler's Diamond Quasar booth, a counter nestled inside the Kaplan Diamond Exchange at Forty-Seventh Street, they spotted the unmissable Biz Markie. Nigo left empty-handed that time, but on his next trip he purchased a chain, and then things quickly escalated. Nigo would show up with a folder of reference pictures of Pharrell's jewelry, asking Jacob to make similar pieces for him. The next time Pharrell stopped in, the jeweler told him about this stylish Japanese guy who was coming in and wanting to spend good money on versions inspired by his stuff. "He was afraid to ask me to meet Pharrell," Jacob recalled. "I knew he was dying to meet Pharrell."

In the decade since Nigo launched A Bathing Ape from the small Nowhere storefront alongside Jun Takahashi's Undercover, it had exploded in popularity. Nigo was a micro-celebrity in his own right, no longer in the shadow of his former mentor Hiroshi Fujiwara. (The two remained great friends and still worked together.) Nigo appeared on the cover of men's magazines was rumored to be the "richest designer in Tokyo." BAPE hovered between $15 million and $20 million in sales annually and had nineteen stores across Japan. The number could have been much higher, but Nigo kept his production numbers deliberately tight.

There was an organic connection between the Pharrell and Nigo camps, and when the American producer was in Japan for a N.E.R.D. concert, they finally met. Pharrell needed a recording studio and Nigo offered up his, located in the BAPE offices. (In 2000, the designer produced and released an album called *Ape*

Sounds.) Toby told Pharrell and his crew that after they were done for the day, they should stop by Nigo's house for dinner.

Toby split his time between Tokyo and London as he finished law school. He worked as one of Nigo's advisors and was primarily responsible for navigating international deals and markets. But that night at dinner, Toby's job was translator. Pharrell told the table how he had grown frustrated with the clothing label he was trying to start. It was called Billionaire Boys Club, but he kept hitting dead ends with the logo; he worked with some of the best American graphic designers and yet none of them delivered on what he had in his head. Toby nodded along, turning to Nigo to translate. It was clear to everyone that they would soon be in some sort of business together.

Pharrell had a DJ gig booked later that night, so he and his team left for the venue. Toby looped in Shin "Sk8thing" Nakamura, still the group's go-to graphic designer. Shin had designed the BAPE logo that was now worth millions. "I felt supremely confident that Shin would be able to do exactly what Pharrell was looking for," Toby recalled. A few hours later, Toby printed out Shin's logo concepts into a binder and headed out to the venue to show Pharrell. He pulled out printouts of four graphics, one of which showed an astronaut's head with a *B* on his helmet. It was stark and looked as if it had been done with a block print instead of Adobe Illustrator. Pharrell lit up when he saw it; he finally had his Billionaire Boys Club logo.

Later that evening, when it was just Toby and Nigo, Toby asked if Nigo was sure he wanted to take this on. He was already extremely busy with A Bathing Ape.

Yes, I'm good, he told Toby. Zero hesitation in his voice.

Toby sensed that his friend was bored with BAPE. Perhaps Nigo felt as if the company had reached its apex. He had just launched a massive collaboration with Pepsi that thrust millions of soda cans covered in the brand's signature camouflage into Japanese households. A collaborative project with a rising American rapper and producer sounded like a new challenge. Toby also sensed his friend felt a deep kinship with Pharrell.

In 2003, Pharrell Williams dropped his debut solo single, "Frontin'," which also featured the mega-famous Jay-Z. With a single music video, Pharrell introduced America to Billionaire Boys Club, or BBC, and his friend named Nigo. Pharrell sauntered around a house party inside a Miami mansion full of red Solo cups and pretty girls, and a halfpipe full of skaters—a curveball for a mainstream hip-hop video. He wore a black Billionaire Boys Club T-shirt; Nigo appeared wearing a shirt and cap from A Bathing Ape. The song and video were a smash, peaking at number five on the *Billboard* Hot 100 chart. Pharrell's cosign of Nigo sent BAPE's full-zippered hoodies and caps into hip-hop videos everywhere: Lil Wayne, Kanye West, Big Sean. A Bathing Ape had finally landed in America in a big new way.

Marc Jacobs, the bold young American designer who was once fired from Perry Ellis for a divisive 1992 "grunge" collection with $300 silk flannels, was now the creative director at Louis Vuitton. Under his tenure at the French house, he often looked in unexpected places for collaborations, including with Japanese artist Takashi Murakami, New York artist-appropriationist Richard Prince, and Stephen Sprouse, a bleeding-edge "punk couture" designer who had mixed New York's uptown and downtown worlds since the eighties. Marc spun up these outsider influences within the

French luxury house, releasing artist-edition bags and accessories: Sprouse's frantic scribbled handwriting, Murakami's candy-colored monogram, and Prince's joke-printed design with the LV logo partly blanked out. At the time, the legendary fashion critic Cathy Horyn wrote that Marc's methods and success "seem to conflict with the old values and assumptions in the industry." The more rules he broke, the better the work was received. Marc brought a brash American and Warholian sensibility to luxury fashion.

Toward the end of 2003, Marc met Pharrell, who had been photographed wearing an LV wallet called the Wapity clipped on to the belt loop of his pants as an accessory. Marc, a devoted shopper of celebrity culture, had seen photos of the music producer in supremely stylish sunglasses. When the two connected, Pharrell told him that Nigo was the one who made the glasses. Soon Marc asked the two friends to design a collection of sunglasses for Louis Vuitton; the result was full of bright colors and metallic details, priced between $300 and $500 a pair. The standout pair was the Millionaires, a chunky look-at-me silhouette with gold trim on the label's monogram logo, the perfect complement to the flashy chains and boisterous prints that held a constant presence in Pharrell's and Nigo's personal wardrobes. Among the intended audience, it was a hit. A review in the *Times* noted the eyewear was "Vuitton's latest co-operation between art and commerce."

The thin boundary between fine art and fashion, between the street and the runway, eroded further each year.

There wasn't enough time to set up Billionaire Boys Club as a standalone operation, so Nigo and Toby first ran everything through Nigo's parent company Nowhere. (An American company would be set up later.) Pharrell's business and operational counterparts came from his music team: Robert Walker, his longtime manager and a cofounder of the Star Trak Entertainment record label; Loïc Villepontoux, another face on the management team; and Phillip Leeds, a tour manager and producer. "We all come from the music industry. We're not in the fashion clothing business. So we really deferred to Nigo and Toby," recalled Phillip.

The brand also turned out to have wide appeal. Pharrell's music meant the hip-hop scene and its devotees paid immediate attention. Nigo's status as a cult-loved Japanese designer added intrigue. And the fashion establishment embraced BBC right away. The dazzling André Leon Talley of *Vogue* wore the label during the 2010 New York Fashion Week, and Chanel designer Karl Lagerfeld was photographed wearing a BBC jacket in *Harper's Bazaar*. Couple that with the Louis Vuitton Millionaires sunglasses, and the design duo had earned some bona fide luxury fashion stripes. It showed up within the label's pricing.

Billionaire Boys Club occupied a relatively new space within the marketplace. The price points were aspirational for their demographic: eighty dollars for a T-shirt, when most brands sold them for thirty or forty at most. Everything was being produced in Japan by Nigo's factories, so the wholesale price of goods had to be higher when it landed stateside. The early stockists included vaunted names like Barneys New York, Union, and the Parisian boutique Colette.

The winter after the brand's second season, the team was stuck with a surplus of clothes—brand-new and still packaged in plastic—that hadn't sold. It was a bitingly cold day, and Phillip, his friend Jay "Icepick" Jackson, and others waited outside on the downtown sidewalk. Earlier in the day, they'd texted and called every stylish friend they could think of to come get laced up with as much gear as they could carry. Hoodies, T-shirts, hats, you name it. Anything that was left over was going to get ripped into oblivion. Phillip had hired a shredding truck, and it was on the way. Once it showed up, they started to toss in the leftovers, only to discover the shredders melted the plastic bags. The crew had to remove their gloves, shivering in their North Face jackets and Timberland boots, to take the clothes out of the bags and throw items into the machine one by one. By the end of the day, the leftover BBC stock was cotton shrapnel, and no one could feel their fingers.

"I don't know whose idea it was or where this philosophy came from, but we knew that Louis Vuitton destroyed goods," Phillip recalled. "It was tragic. But we destroyed it because we didn't want it discounted. It was worth the loss to keep the brand hot."

Toby continued to act as the bridge between Nigo and Pharrell. "I was completely in the loop. I was translating every conversation." Since the "Frontin'" video, BAPE had risen to an omnipresence in American hip-hop and streetwear. It reached a peak of around $70 million in 2006, but commanded a much larger market share. "The perception of what we were doing was way, way higher than the actual volume of sales," recalled Toby. That was thanks to the prolific counterfeiters. He guessed that there was likely five times the amount of fake BAPE—$350 million—in circulation at one point. The bootleggers were the ones flooding the market, not Nigo. They shut down factories in China and once seized two shipping containers of footwear that had arrived at a port in Miami. "We did what we could, but you quickly realized that it's fairly pointless."

At one point Toby and Nigo stayed with Pharrell in Virginia to work on the clothes, and Pharrell was always quick to offer up his connections in America if Toby and Nigo ever needed help with anything. "It was this two-way street. The partnership worked extremely well," Toby recalled. "I think the key to all of this is that these two people, and by extension these two groups of people, really trusted each other's taste." They decided their next goal was to open a store in New York.

In November 2007, they opened the Billionaire Boys Club & ICECREAM store. The first floor was for the ICECREAM sublabel, stocked with flashy sneakers displayed in ice cream tubs, with prices from $80 to $180; a rainbow assortment of $80 T-shirts hung on the walls. Hoodies with the "all-over print." A glow-in-the-dark staircase led shoppers upstairs to the second floor to browse the slightly calmer Billionaire Boys Club clothes, where the art and furniture included a photographic print of the moon and a couch shaped like an ice cream sandwich. It was an intricate and expensive build-out. The Japanese design firm they used insisted on flying in steel beams from Japan.

Building the too-expensive store caused BBC America to fall into debt with BBC Japan. And then the 2007–2008 financial crisis hit, and the Japanese yen surged as the American dollar slipped. The amount BBC America owed its Japanese counterpart increased in a short period of time. They had been working on opening another store in Los Angeles but kept hitting delays with a troublesome landlord and construction difficulties. (They ended up in arbitration with the landlord.) The plan was to open in LA in 2007, but it took until until 2008, in the middle of the economic crisis. "It was a nightmare," recalled Toby.

A Bathing Ape was having its own financial troubles, too. The company had expanded its employee base and storefronts, along with the overhead to match. The Japanese tax system nudges owners to reinvest their net profits in their businesses instead of paying themselves a large dividend, which would be heavily taxed. "The system almost encourages you to spend more money," said Toby. "As the company's growing, the costs grow. It's all good, but there's no room for sales to come down." So BAPE's philosophy was to spend and grow, which created a fragile system extremely vulnerable to downturns in profits or unexpected expenses. (Like slowing sales or lavish store build-outs.) By 2007, Nigo's parent company, Nowhere, had posted a loss of nearly $2.8 million for the year: it had a loss of $1.3 million the next.

In early 2011, the Hong Kong–based retail group I.T Ltd. announced it had bought 90 percent of Nowhere, which included A Bathing Ape, for approximately $2.8 million. It agreed to take on Nowhere's nearly $53 million in outstanding bank loans and storefront leases and implemented a cost-saving restructure. As part of the deal, Nigo would stay on as creative director for two more years. The designer disputed the debt in the press but conceded that the buyout was the best option. He didn't want to file for bankruptcy or damage the brand. "I spent twenty years building it up, so it would be a real shame for it to disappear. I wanted the brand to survive, so the main thing was thinking what to do about that." Now Nigo also wanted out of Billionaire Boys Club. "I think Nigo just wanted to take a total break for a minute," said Toby.

Some on the Billionaire Boys Club team also realized that they had been given a false sense of success; they hit the market right as this Technicolor graphic-heavy look was at the peak of desirability. There was nowhere for sales to go but down. The BBC America team looked for a domestic partner to buy Nigo out. It meant a lot of meetings with "American garmentos and clothing fashion people that gave us all the heebie-jeebies." Then Pharrell and Jay-Z spoke.

The two had such a great music relationship that it sounded like a good idea for them to partner up through Iconix Brand Group, the company that had purchased Jay-Z's Rocawear a few years prior. Iconix owned brands like Mossimo, Ecko, and Joe Boxer and had as much fashion cachet as a ragpicker. But BBC had little choice.

Iconix planned to flood the market with Billionaire Boys Club, announcing they were projecting $30 million in annual sales for 2013, more than double the brand's previous peak of $12 million. But Iconix dealt in volume; the factories they worked with had much higher minimums than those BBC had previously worked with. "It really cheapened the whole thing," recalled Phillip. "They had a whole different outlook toward it and didn't care so much about maintaining the standards that we had held so high. When we first started, we approached our business like we were Louis Vuitton, and our stuff was worth more than gold. And if it didn't sell, we destroyed it. Iconix will take anything. They'll take their gold, and put it in the Burlington Coat Factory."

Nigo had already started his next project, Human Made, inspired by American vintage and chock-full of woolen blazers, cargo jackets, sturdy plaid shirts, and classic-looking denim. Pharrell put an even deeper focus on his music. Later in the year, he was set to release two new songs he worked on: One was called "Blurred Lines" and the other "Happy." Those records would catapult Pharrell into the stratosphere, opening more of fashion's doors for him than he could have ever imagined.

20.

Cross-Promotion

Nicholas Tershay caused a stir at Nike. He'd posted a picture of the sneaker collaboration he'd designed on his MySpace profile, and the company wasn't happy about it. It was 2005, and the shoe wouldn't hit shelves until much later in the year. Everyone came running to Hunter Muraira, Nike Skateboarding's team manager and the architect of the project. *What the hell is going on? Why did Nick post this? Can you tell him to take it down?* It was too late; the sneaker forums and blogs had already scooped it up. Diamond Supply Co. had started as a skateboarding company, and now the small-time brand was responsible for one of the most sought-after Nike sneakers of the year.

"I grew up as a skateboarder, but I was into clothes. In the early nineties, I was really into the whole Nautica, Polo, Tommy Hilfiger craze," Nick said. "Once I got off my board, I'd put on my Jordans, and I'd be on the bus in my Jordans and my skate shoes would be in my backpack because I wanted to be fresh."

Diamond's path to designing a buzzed-about Nike sneaker was slow and steady. Nick started the company in 1998 when he was in his mid-twenties and lived in San Francisco. A lifelong skater, he originally planned to produce a new type of skateboard bolt. But when the mechanics proved impossible, he produced standard bolts—and printed Diamond Supply Co. T-shirts, hoodies, and baseball caps. Nick gave the gear to his friends who were professional skaters, and the Diamond logo popped up in skateboarding videos and magazines alike. The first stores that Nick sold to were FTC, a core skate shop in the city's historic Haight-Ashbury district, and Supreme in New York. The T-shirts sold well, and Nick scored a Japanese distribution deal. Nick had a tenacious work ethic; his boss at FTC, Kent Uyehara, helped him score a Japanese distribution deal. In addition to the Diamond tees, he worked at FTC and Nordstrom, sold weed, and hustled as a barber, cutting hair out of his home. For two years, he ran the company out of his Divisadero Street apartment until Mike Carroll, a pro skater who owned Girl Skateboards, approached him about distributing Diamond. The only catch was Nick needed to move to Los Angeles, so he arrived in LA in 2000 with his entire life packed into a U-Haul trailer. There was no office for him at Girl's headquarters in Torrance, California, but they gave him a "little desk" in the shipping area of the warehouse. It made Diamond feel legitimate, surrounded by industrial metal shelving and cardboard boxes as far as the eye could see.

Diamond plugged into Girl's existing framework of distribution and sales, although Nick still had to fund everything himself. The brand was an easy sell for the sales reps, because it was nearly impossible to open a copy of *Thrasher* or *Transworld Skateboarding* without seeing a pro skater in a Diamond T-shirt. But Nick felt stuck; he didn't have the cash to cover larger orders that came in. He'd have to wait for the retailers to pay Girl before the money finally came his way. Everything was always sold out, and months went by where the brand had zero inventory. "People just thought it was a hard-to-get, limited-edition company . . . It wasn't on purpose," Nick said. For years, it felt like Diamond was destined to remain a small-time label for good.

Hunter had originally reached out to Girl's team manager Sam Smyth to collaborate on a Nike SB Dunk sneaker. The company was planning a big push for the shoe. Sam mentioned to Nick that he was probably going to pass, because he didn't think the bosses would be too happy about the idea. (They ran their own skate shoe company called Lakai.)

Well, if Girl doesn't do it, see if I can make a Diamond one, he asked Sam.

Nick already knew what he wanted his sneaker to look like. He'd previously printed a Diamond T-shirt that featured a luxurious robin's-egg blue synonymous with Tiffany; it had been an immediate hit within Diamond's circle. "I feel that maybe a lot of it had to do with that it was such an original colorway that nobody ever used . . . everyone was tripping on it," Nick recalled. He carried the color over to his Dunk design: a black leather sneaker with vibrant blue-green paneling and a glittering silver Swoosh. The next day Hunter emailed Sam to say that Nike wanted to move forward with Nick's Diamond Dunk.

The first sneaker sample was underwhelming; the color wasn't right, and the Swoosh was a dull gray. It needed to look more expensive. Nick pushed them to redo it, telling Nike the blue needed to be closer to Tiffany's iconic shade, and also told them to add a crocodile-embossed texture to the black leather and make the Swoosh as shiny as chrome. Nike sent over a revised sample, and it was perfect.

The same day Nick received the revised sneaker, he posted a

picture on his MySpace profile to show his friends. In the photo, he wore a T-shirt with the Diamond logo printed in the Tiffany-esque color and was holding the robin's-egg blue sneaker in his hand. Within a week, all corners of Nick's social circle—from skaters to sneakerheads—started to hit him up about it. Nick assumed they had just seen it on MySpace.

Nah, dude, his friend told him. It's all over the internet.

———

The forums and online magazines dedicated to sneakers and streetwear expanded in readership. In addition to NikeTalk and Superfuture, Nice Kicks and Sole Collector had their own forums; there was an invite-only forum for Supreme fans called Strictly Supreme, and BAPE loyalists converged on BapeTalk. The Hypebeast forums became more active. Then came the missing piece of this new digital ecosystem: an e-commerce website called Karmaloop that became more popular by the year. It outpaced another site called Digital Gravel, and became the default destination to buy from the crop of brands that populated the webpages of Hypebeast, Highsnobiety, and *Complex*.

Greg Selkoe launched Karmaloop from the basement of his parents' house on a leafy street in Boston's Jamaica Plain neighborhood. The idea was to bring the T-shirts to the kids in the suburbs who couldn't shop in Lower Manhattan or on Fairfax Avenue in LA; Karmaloop delivered the T-shirt right to your door. Greg was a tenacious entrepreneur, armed with an Ivy League degree and full of can't-lose ambition. He devised an innovative digital street team for Karmaloop: Members registered and were given a unique shopping code to share with friends in exchange for discounts and free clothing.

One of these reps was Dennis Todisco, then a young college student in Boston and an avid poster on the NikeTalk and Hypebeast forums. "That's how we got all of our info. That's how you found out about what Dunks were dropping. It just made it feel even more inner-circle. If you knew, you knew," recalled Dennis. He found the forums a great place to promote his Karmaloop rep code, too. It was common for users to post asking for help identifying certain designs. "Someone would ask where to get this T-shirt that Mos Def wore, and I'd tell them it's actually a Triple Five Soul shirt," he recalled. Dennis would include his unique 20-percent-off code and was soon earning hundreds of dollars in free clothes every month.

By 2008, Karmaloop had generated $40 million in sales, and the street-team sales reps drove 15 percent of Karmaloop's total revenue. Dennis became one of the company's top-earning sales reps, so Greg hired him full-time. The press described Karmaloop's customers as "alpha consumers," using a term coined by consultant Michael J. Wolf in 1999 to describe the kids who "feel the first vibrations of the explosion and transmit them to the rest of the culture." At thirty-three, Greg was named one of *Entrepreneur* magazine's "Young Millionaires." Karmaloop looked unstoppable. Upward of one million people visited the website every month, and selling T-shirts online appeared to be the future of this still-forming industry.

———

Nick had never heard of Sole Collector's ISS (In Style Shoes) forum and was only vaguely familiar with NikeTalk. He pulled up the two forums, and there was already a two-hundred-page thread of users frothing over Diamond's "Tiffany" Dunk. Within the month, Nick became an instant sneaker celebrity. Hypebeast posted the shoe and even reported when the sneaker started showing up in European boutiques, which had an earlier release schedule than the American market. "What bugged people out is that I made it look all luxury with the croc skin and the silver Swoosh. It was, like, the most luxury-looking shoe at the time," said Nick.

His friend who worked at Nike told him that Tinker Hatfield, perhaps the brand's most famous designer, gave a presentation on marketing, and the backdrop of the entire meeting was Nick holding the Dunk, pulled directly from Nick's MySpace page. The massive company was studying how Nick and his small skateboard brand had managed to create such intense excitement. "I started building a fan base on MySpace. I was posting pictures of my product and everyone—all my peers from every company, every single person was like, 'What are you doing? This is so lame.' People were making fun of me. People didn't understand it," Nick said. But the designer soon learned that this online community translated into a very IRL thing. "I'd come to New York and kids were just stopping me on the street and asking me for my autograph, and the shoe hadn't even dropped yet." And the part that surprised Nick the most? The kids weren't even skaters—they were sneakerheads. By the time the "Tiffany Dunk" came out, there were thousands of forum posts and it sold out within the day. It made so much industry noise the sneaker landed on the radar of Tiffany & Co., who sent Nick a cease and desist.

The attention from the Nike surged the demand for Diamond nationwide, and Nick felt on the verge of leveling up from a skate company to a clothing brand. Within Girl's distribution, Diamond hovered around $2 million to $3 million in annual sales, but he knew he could grow more with the right partner. More kids than ever wanted the T-shirts, and new retailers were constantly reaching out. There was just one problem: "I still couldn't make any more tees. I still didn't have the money," Nick said. Around this time, he noticed labels like Freshjive and X-Large were charging $30 for tees, while most skateboard brands priced theirs at $20. He wanted Diamond in that top tier—he went to Girl and said he needed help and wanted to raise his prices. "They were like, 'No, you're not.' So I told them, 'I'm out of here.' I knew I [had to] go do this the way that I wanted to do it." After six years at Girl, Nick struck out on his own.

Go have fun selling *thirty-dollar* T-shirts, dude, the head sales rep at Girl told him.

When Nick raised the price of his T-shirts, he found that it made the brand feel more premium, like a luxury shirt. The skate shops said the same thing to him. Even at the new higher price, they still couldn't keep them in stock. He met Bobby Kim, a cofounder of The Hundreds, who introduced him to Hypebeast forums. You should go on forums, Bobby told him. There are a ton of Diamond fans on there.

In 2006, Nick opened the first Diamond Supply Co. store on Fairfax Avenue, joining Supreme, The Hundreds, pro skater Sal Barbier's SLB boutique, and the sneaker shop Flight Club. Most of these shops were on the "400" block, which had earned a reputation as the epicenter of streetwear in Los Angeles. On opening day, there was a line of three hundred kids waiting down the block.

Nick started to post all his new designs on the forums, and he created an official Diamond Supply Co. thread. Kids were asking when he was dropping new T-shirts, where they could buy them. "I didn't sleep much. I was either designing or posting designs on the forums and talking to these kids twenty-four hours a day.

I built a community on [the Hypebeast forums], NikeTalk, and SoleCollector." To them, he became known as "Nicky Diamonds." He launched a Diamond webstore and started to do these quick-fire product releases to play into his growing online fan base. "I realized early that I didn't [have to] wait a month for a magazine to come out, or wait six months for the design to hit stores," Nick said. He would add his latest T-shirts to the Diamond website and then promote them on the forums. "I'd have the printer print them and then we'd ship them to people. I was doing it like once a week."

Since Nick had opened the Fairfax store, his ambition and appetite never slowed. The Fairfax store legitimized the brand and he started selling to Greg Selkoe and Karmaloop. Nick did collaborations with rappers like Raekwon and Rick Ross, which boosted Diamond's popularity among the hip-hop set. (At one point, a young Tyler, the Creator also worked in the Fairfax store, packing boxes in the back.) He landed a bestselling T-shirt, flipping the logo of the Misfits by giving a gold grill to the horror-punk band's iconic Crimson Ghost skull.

As Diamond grew, Nick's supply-and-demand problem only became more exasperating. Nick knew he could sell ten times as much if he could solve the massive gaps in his production. Everything was in place to take Diamond to the next level. He sold at Karmaloop and the mall retail chain Zumiez, but when they tried to place larger orders, Nick didn't have the capital to fulfill them. Nick kept up his posts on the Hypebeast forum, which remained his biggest asset. "Those forums were monumental for Diamond because we built a community of kids that would buy all of our shit, selling it out, and that just made Diamond seem like it was insane," recalled Nick. "Other brands would be like, 'How do you do it?' And I just said, 'I talk to the kids. I have a community.'"

The Diamond Supply Co. thread on the Hypebeast forums was by far the biggest and most active. He was still all demand and no supply.

In 2007, a year after Nick left Girl, the company's major breakthrough finally came when he struck an unconventional arrangement with a new printer. The company agreed to front all of the production costs—the blank T-shirts, the ink, the labor—if they collected payment directly from Diamond's retailers. Then, after costs were covered, they'd pay out to Nick.

"All of a sudden, I could fulfill the demand," he recalled. "I went from $3 million in sales to $15 million in one year."

Nick was just getting started.

21.
The Next Level

It took Samuel Spitzer five months to convince James Jebbia to launch a simple website for Supreme. "Everyone was resistant at the company, because they thought [the internet] would ruin their business," Sam recalled. Supremenewyork.com launched in April 2006. The site only contained the Box Logo and a single form field to input an email address to receive updates from the brand. It took another two years before James allowed an online shop to be added.

Sam's family moved to New York from Romania when he was twelve, and as a teenager he watched public access TV, in particular *Rappin' with the Rickster*, a show stacked with cameos from rappers, skaters, graffiti writers, and more, hosted by the wisecracking photographer Ricky Powell. "I see [Futura] on there with Ricky listening to music and smoking weed and whatnot," recalled Sam. "I was like, *What is this?* I was fascinated." While Sam's friends were being filmed by Larry Clark for *Kids* in 1994, he headed to Harvard to attend a summer program for gifted high schoolers. The next year, he registered his own domain, Splay.com, via a fax machine. By nineteen, he'd built a website for Futura 2000 and taught the graffiti artist, two decades his senior, how to update it. "Some kids would make zines; I just made websites," Sam said. It was Futura who introduced him to James and another early client: Mo' Wax Records. He graduated from Brown University, attended postgraduate programs at MIT, and worked as a digital designer with the famed Dutch architect Rem Koolhaas, launching the web identity for the Italian fashion house Prada. James offered Sam part ownership of Supreme's online venture and a partial stake in the overall brand. He told him to go design and develop an e-commerce platform—under Sam's development firm Splay, but Supreme would get to use it.

By the time the website launched, Supreme had grown to approximately $20 million in annual sales. "The main growth happened between 2002 and 2006. We were probably at $10 million in 2002 and it grew by millions every year . . . it was gradual but always growing," recalled Supreme's production manager Augie Galan.

Japan's reverence for Supreme deepened, and the country remained a major pillar of the brand's growth. It was the Japanese magazines—*Smart, Relax, Cool Trans*—that photographed and editorialized Supreme's products. The partnership with Ken Omura and his distribution company OneGram continued to pay big dividends. In 2006, the company added a fourth Japanese store in Tokyo's Harajuku neighborhood, and in 2008, they added another in Nagoya. Ken stopped by Supreme's Wooster Street offices with a greater frequency than in the brand's earlier days. "He'd come once a year just to physically look at samples, to talk about what was missing in the Japanese market, and what we might want to make specifically for the Japanese market," Augie said.

Supreme's American team remained small and scrappy. James and his longtime accountant, Onna Lee, sat on one side of the

Wooster Street offices while the design team worked toward the back. The mid-aughts brought a shuffling to the core group. Brendon Babenzien returned after a stint running a prep-inspired label he'd founded called Noah. Geoff Heath, the primary graphic designer, left in 2004 after butting heads with James. Augie departed in 2006, and Aaron "A-Ron" Bondaroff was off running aNYthing, though he remained close with James and the Supreme universe.

Ricky Saiz, an aspiring director and shop employee at Union, was brought to Supreme by James because of his personal style. Erin Magee, a twenty-three-year-old designer, joined after being poached from the British sportswear brand Umbro. Two former Bay Area skaters named Billy Teichen and Kyle Demers, who came from HUF's inner circle, joined the team. Most notably, Angelo Baque was hired as Supreme's first brand director, a title that spanned marketing, art direction, and styling. He was the guy in charge of Supreme's overall image.

"I was scared shitless, because there was no predecessor. There was no one that actually worked in the office that basically was set up to be James's eyes and ears and his right hand," recalled Angelo. "It was very much sink-or-swim the first year."

A charismatic kid who grew up in Queens, born to immigrant parents from Ecuador, Angelo had cycled through magazine internships and retail jobs while also studying at the School of Visual Arts until the tuition became too expensive. Jeff Ng of Staple Design and Reed Space acted as a mentor and landed Angelo a brisk interview with James for a job at the original Stüssy boutique. "He just looked me up and down, looked at my outfit," Angelo said. "He was like, *All right . . . I want you to be in front of the store tomorrow at nine o'clock in the morning.*" He eventually left Stüssy to focus on his brand, Absurd, and work at Nom de Guerre, a high-concept Manhattan boutique that sold sleek and artful menswear, expensive hoodies, and expensive sneakers. "Everybody was battling Supreme. Supreme had the illest fucking graphics back then. Alife. A-Ron with aNYthing. Everybody. It was such a great moment to have a T-shirt brand. There were also a lot of wack ones. But if you were good, you were respected. That's how you'd be able to get your street cred." Everyone used the same screenprinter, Rich DiBernardo's Prographix, who printed for everyone from 555 Soul and Futura to Supreme and Alife. Angelo had been working at Nom de Guerre for three years when his friend told him that James wanted to talk to him.

"*Oi, I heard you're not making any money over there.* That was his opening line," recalled Angelo when James asked if he wanted to work for Supreme. "It's like getting a call from George Steinbrenner: *Hey, you ready to come to the majors and play for the Yankees?* Yeah, get me the fuck out of the bush league."

By 2008, Supreme had added an online store, including a specialized version for the Japanese market. As the look of web design evolved—less negative space and wider imagery—Supreme's website stayed locked into the initial framework it had launched with. The fuller website possessed the neat minimalism of Dieter Rams matched with a new-wave typographer's willingness to flout well-worn design conventions. The result was a website with a specific flow that users had to learn, just like stepping into one of the stores. The brand posted images of product flat-lays and hoodies and jackets hanging from floating metal racks. On the homepage, there was a neat grid of ultra-cropped product photos, little slivers of Supreme products. The idea was to mimic one jacket next to another, a shirt next to another shirt, just as a shopper experienced it in the Supreme stores.

The lookbooks were launched in Japanese magazines like *Relax*, *Smart*, and *Cool Trans*. At first, the American photographers they hired weren't as skilled as the ones in Japanese magazines. James convinced his partner Ken Omura to pay for photography to happen in Japan, to provide New York with imagery to use on the website. The brand published *Supreme* magazine, with text in both English and Japanese, exclusively for Japan. Its products were shown alongside styled editorials and interviews with Shawn Stüssy, Malcolm McLaren, Richard Prince, RZA, Peter Saville, Takashi Murakami.

By 2010, Supreme's audience knew they could now go straight to the source to see photos and imagery. Before the Supreme website launched, images of Supreme's clothes were photos poorly shot on mid-aughts digital cameras that customers posted on eBay and message boards, or low-quality scans from Japanese magazines. The brand introduced a specific cadence, too. First, a COMING SOON announcement with a teaser image; then, weeks later, a full unveiling of all the products alongside an editorial lookbook. And then, every Thursday at eleven a.m., a slow trickle of the collection would be made available in the online shop in fragments. It was an atypical format for a company to release its products.

The shiny new website gave James and his team greater control of the brand's image. And Thursday's digital drop became essential viewing in the Supreme universe.

At the time, Tyler Gregory Okonma—Tyler, the Creator—had every misfit in America under the age of twenty-five in the palm of his hand. The great American pastime of rock music continued to wane in cultural influence; rappers were the new rock stars, and

Tyler, the Creator was unmissable. As part of a juvenile, outlandish, and foul-mouthed crew from Los Angeles called Odd Future—Odd Future Wolf Gang Kill Them All in full—Tyler was the group's principal provocateur, a lanky blabbermouth with a megawatt smile and undeniable star quality. The rowdy crew hung out on Fairfax Avenue, befriending pro skater Jason Dill and Supreme's Los Angeles store manager Javier Nunez, and pushed toward a breakthrough that came in 2011 with "Yonkers," a single from Tyler's major-label debut, when he was just nineteen years old.

The music video was hellish: A cockroach crawls over his hands; he eats it, then vomits. Tyler spat out the opening line, *I'm a fucking walking paradox / No I'm not*, as the camera's focus deliberately wavered, adding to the effect of a fever dream. It only made the Supreme Box Logo hat on his head pop out even more. It ends with a noose and a stool being kicked.

It was the start of the streaming era; YouTube was the new MTV, and "Yonkers" ricocheted across the music blogosphere and message boards. Tyler won the 2011 MTV Video Music Award for Best New Artist, and he took the stage with a leopard-print Supreme hat on his head. "I've been wearing this Supreme hat for a month," Tyler told *GQ* the following year, in a conversation with writer Glenn O'Brien about the pair's cross-generational love of the brand. The Supreme hat was to Tyler what a ratty flannel was to Kurt Cobain. The new-media rap star turned the Supreme logo into a symbol of youthful rebellion, slowly wedging the brand into popular culture.

Before he became famous, Tyler was a regular poster on the Hypebeast and BapeTalk forums. He promoted his first album, *Bastard*, with a thread titled "18yearKid raps and produces his shit. Bape and Ice Cream quotes." Elsewhere on the forum, he posted looking to buy specific, older Billionaire Boys Club pieces. "There's this site called Hypebeast, I'd post on the forums there, and they always showed us a lot of love," he said in an early interview. "I kinda feel like without them, we wouldn't even be where we're at now. . . . No one else would fuck with us."

One commenter later described Tyler as "the first internet hypebeast kid that got that famous."

Supreme's fashion continued to sharpen.

Brendon and Ricky traveled to fabric shows in Japan and France, sourcing patterns and materials that caught their eye. There were contemporary items like rigid slim jeans and polka-dot flannel shirts, American classics like navy peacoats and fisherman sweaters, and the more outré fashions like bright-red coach jackets lined with leopard print and faux snakeskin caps. The graphic T-shirts and heavy hooded sweatshirts remained an anchor of each collection. At the same time, Supreme's headwear program became a staple: corduroy bucket hats, velour trapper hats, beanies knitted with showy patterns, and plenty of five-panel camp hats. Angelo's travels also informed his styling and branding. He'd take note of Parisian teenagers wearing Air Max 98s with tracksuits and little Gucci bags or bring home a sheepskin bomber jacket from a London flea market. He'd tell James, *I see this happening in the street. We need to adapt to that real quick and add it to the collection.*

The styling was unusual and elevated, unlike anything else in the menswear space. "We would have these meetings where James, myself, and Angelo would just look at the board of designs and talk about all the different possibilities," recalled Brendon. The Americana of a nineties J.Crew catalog mixed with a dose of Studio 54 and a Japanese contemporariness. "We were really looking at the history of New York and downtown and the art world. People were wearing sport coats and people were wearing topcoats and people were wearing nice clothes. They're still artists. They're still interesting and fun. Not everything has to be a T-shirt and a hoodie, right?"

The brand worked with raw, unfiltered photographers like Ari Marcopoulos, Terry Richardson, and Kenneth Cappello. Supreme's clothes still got the full editorial treatment in Japanese magazines, but the in-house lookbook became the main event. One of their skaters, Jason Dill—a natural in front of the camera, with honeyed hair, stubble, and soulful eyes—became the brand's de facto model. Dill had been a pro skater since he was a teenager, riding for the influential Alien Workshop, with his part in the company's 2000 film *Photosynthesis* establishing him as an offbeat and original skater. In the upcoming seasons, Supreme tapped other team skaters for the high-profile lookbook gig: Lucien Clarke, Sage Elsesser, Sean Pablo, and Tyshawn Jones. A-Ron appeared less frequently as he focused on building his own world off the Bowery, no longer Supreme's most famous son.

In 2011, James and the team collaborated on the label's first suit with Adam Kimmel, a rising American fashion designer Bergdorf Goodman called "the future of menswear." The idea was to make a casual suit for skaters, which resulted in a beautiful two-button suit, cut faintly slim with simple details and made of fine-wale corduroy from Italy. Notably, Supreme democratized the price, selling the suit for $538, less than half the price of a mainline Adam Kimmel suit.

Supreme hit its stride as a master of the collaboration. This stretch brought a flurry of official projects with high-profile artists:

Damien Hirst's famous *Spot* paintings appeared on skate decks and T-shirts, as did the old-master surrealism of George Condo, joining a growing list that included Jeff Koons, Christopher Wool, and Richard Prince. It worked with musicians across genres: the Clash and Bad Brains, Public Enemy and Three 6 Mafia, John Coltrane and Miles Davis. The brand also established ongoing collaborations with clothing companies (The North Face, Timberland, Vans), popular American brands (*Playboy*, Budweiser), and ones more specific to its downtown world (*Thrasher*, Rust-Oleum).

That same year, photographer Terry Richardson shot Lady Gaga, who had the third-bestselling album of the entire year, for a Supreme ad campaign. "That was insane," recalled Brendon. "There were five tables of products for that shoot, more things than you could ever imagine to choose from, and we ended up shooting her in a Box Logo T-shirt." She was the buzziest name in a growing list that, over the years, included Raekwon, Mike Tyson, and Lou Reed. All of this was featured in a thick and glossy monograph published by Rizzoli, the Italian purveyor of high-end coffee table books.

By 2012, James had added new Supreme shops in London and Tokyo (the city's third outpost), bringing the global total to nine. The brand photographed the British supermodel Kate Moss for its spring/summer campaign, blanketing New York in wheat-pasted posters. By now, the shops had earned a reputation for their steel-wool staff, surly skaters hired from within the brand's social circle. At the original Lafayette Street store, shoppers lined up overnight, often by the hundreds, ahead of the product's release every Thursday morning—known as "drop day" in the vernacular of its savviest customers. The website sold through all of its product stock within minutes of being refreshed with the wares. Some hot-ticket items like Box Logo T-shirts and especially covetable collaborations sold out within seconds; on the secondary market, products commanded up to four times the retail price.

It was as A-Ron wrote in the foreword of Supreme's three-hundred-page tome for Rizzoli: "We made the rules and ran a business that was very successful. People were addicted to the clothes like a drug."

22.

RSWD

As Bobby Kim turned the corner onto Rosewood Avenue, he saw Ben Shenassafar pacing outside of The Hundreds's LA clubhouse.

Fuck! Ben yelled out. What do we do?

The two friends and business partners were in for a long day. A big appointment was set with their Canadian distributor for the afternoon, and another retailer was also in town. But first, Bobby and Ben had to fix a more pressing problem. They had accidentally oversold hoodies to hundreds of customers.

It was back in 2006, when The Hundreds was barely three years old; Ben and Bobby only just started being able to pay their bills from it. The brand didn't have a professional e-commerce website. Even as their sales slowly grew, it felt more like an art project than a legitimate business—until now.

The "Paisley" hoodie was their first certifiable hit.

Inspired by the classic bandanna print, the black zip-up hooded sweatshirt turned repeating buta droplets into an ornate fashion object. It both played into and subverted the all-over print trend that was dominating the current marketplace. Nigo's A Bathing Ape popularized hooded sweatshirts with massive colorful prints in the American streetwear landscape; he and Pharrell carried the style over to Billionaire Boys Club, too. Designer Jonas Bevacqua and his massively popular brand LRG, or Lifted Research Group, earned a bestseller with the "Dead Serious" hoodie, a vibrant red sweatshirt covered in a sprawling skeleton print sold in malls nationwide. The Hundreds's Paisley hoodie was a highly desaturated riff on that.

The brand's website mainly served as Bobby's blog, a place for him to document his daily life and encounters with other creatives. The Hundreds embraced the internet early; most brands didn't have websites or a daily feed of updates and images. Many people, especially the downtown New York guys, thought it was corny. When it came time to sell the Paisley hoodie online, Bobby jerry-built a makeshift landing page with some rudimentary code and PayPal's e-commerce function. It wasn't perfect, it looked wonky, and you couldn't manage inventory, but it would at least let customers order online. That morning in their tiny office space on Rosewood, Bobby scrolled through their PayPal transactions with Ben looking over his shoulder. They had woefully underestimated the number of people who wanted to buy the sweatshirts and would have to refund nearly half of the orders. There was never a question about printing *more* hoodies to meet the demand and pocket more cash. "We didn't make any more because that was the attitude of the era," recalled Bobby. "This was the amount we made; it was finite. If you didn't get it, shame on you."

After all the necessary refunds were issued, they tallied up the numbers. The two friends were gobsmacked. With the single design, The Hundreds now had $100,000 in its bank account, the number floating on the screen like it had been granted by a genie.

There was no hesitation about what they would do with the money.

We're going to turn this into a store now, Ben told Bobby. Our store.

The two twenty-six-year-olds had been renting 7909 Rosewood in the Fairfax District of central Los Angeles for the past year. Ben and Bobby had met in graduate school at Loyola Law and had much in common; each was raised in immigrant households with a ravenous appreciation for American pop culture, sneakers, graphic T-shirts, and hip-hop. They were also opposites in the same number of ways. Bobby was a Korean American kid who grew up loving comic books, skateboarding, and punk rock. Ben was the eldest son from a Persian American family who loved basketball and flashier fashion; he'd sometimes show up to class in haute Diesel jeans and shiny Gucci shades. Ben and Bobby bonded over the shared experience of being first-generation kids and the pressures that came along with it. They also bonded over Nike Dunks and Supreme tees.

The move to Rosewood gave them a boost of confidence, and it didn't take long for the tiny office to turn into an unofficial clubhouse. Most days, they were joined by Scott Litel, an energetic kid with messy hair and a scruffy beard whom everyone called Scotty iLL. Scotty was their designated sales manager and hype man, a devoted street-teamer who posted stickers and flyers before Ben and Bobby put him on payroll.

Opening a store on Rosewood delivered a sense of concreteness. The Hundreds was here: You could touch the T-shirts and knock on the wood. The brand didn't just exist online; they soon sold nearly $3,000 worth of T-shirts daily. "It felt like I was on top of the world. The idea of forging your own universe in the world," Bobby said.

Even though The Hundreds had earned a reputation as one of the first internet-era brands with a blog, the two founders knew that the right attitude and shop experience was irreplaceable within streetwear's DNA. On a trip to New York years earlier, Bobby visited the Alife and Rivington Club shops, and remembered seeing cofounders Rob Cristofaro and Tony Arcabascio working from their upstairs studio. "Rob was one of my north stars, still is. Alife was this fortress," Bobby recalled. Even as a young brand owner, he understood the magic and the power of the presence of a physical store. Since the start, The Hundreds knew the importance of optics. The very first store they sold to was the hip fashion boutique Fred Segal. Ben and Bobby immediately devised a plan to make an impression with the shop's buyer. They'd make Fred Segal sell out of The Hundreds by giving friends and family some cash and sending them in to buy their T-shirts. Bobby's girlfriend went in one day, then a few days later it was Ben's brother. "It was our first door, and selling at Fred Segal was the biggest deal in the world," said Ben. "We did whatever we had to do to make [ourselves] seem bigger than we were. . . . We would play that game with them, and we had to in a way."

By the end of 2007, The Hundreds and its first store on Rosewood had brought in nearly $2 million in sales. Ben and Bobby were already dreaming about opening their second.

Fairfax Avenue was not an obvious choice for a retail shop when James Jebbia opened the Supreme store in 2004. The rent was cheaper than on more established streets like La Brea or Melrose. Over on La Brea, Union Los Angeles was still in business, now owned by Chris Gibbs, the onetime manager of the original

New York outpost; nearby, the former Union staffer Eddie Cruz ran the sneaker-shop-turned-brand Undefeated. There was also Brooklyn Projects on Melrose, run by former MTV VJ and East Coast native Dom DeLuca. But Fairfax increasingly felt like the spot to be.

After Supreme, other shops started to pop up around the block: Reserve was an indie bookstore that later became the flagship for Rick Klotz's Freshjive; the professional skater Sal Barbier opened SLB, a shop that sold an eclectic mix of workwear and skateboard gear; plus the sneaker shop Flight Club. After The Hundreds opened its doors, Alife, Hall of Fame, Diamond Supply Co., HUF, and Crooks & Castles joined the block within a few years. A new world was being built in a sleepy corner of Central Los Angeles, otherwise filled with Jewish retail stores and delis that were slowly closing down. It became a shopping destination and a local hangout. It didn't take long before Japanese tour buses started to drop off visitors at Fairfax, the tourists hoping to return home with Supreme T-shirts and rare American sneakers.

———

All it took was a day trip to San Francisco to spark the idea of building a The Hundreds store there. Bobby and Ben traveled north in an old, clunky Ford Explorer to participate in a warehouse sale. They had sold out of stock by the early afternoon. They made a few more visits to find a space they liked: at Post and Taylor Streets, on the border of the touristy Union Square. The space was previously a wholesale uniform shop, but it was double the size of their first store. The duo decided to spare no expense when it came to the remodel. Inspired by *2001: A Space Odyssey* and *The Goonies*, the shop felt like a theme park ride. The high-gloss floors gave the illusion of rolling black water and a central showcase was rigged with hidden lighting so it appeared to float through the space. The Hundreds San Francisco opened its doors in March 2008.

The brand continued to explode, holding a regular presence on the streetwear blogs, with one of the top threads on the Hypebeast forums. Bobby was a determined and ferocious designer. If he thought a graphic was an eight, he'd tear it up just to try and make it a ten. They released a high-profile collaboration with Disney that reimagined the Lost Boys from *Peter Pan*. They found another hit with New Era baseball caps (POST and RSWD) that paid homage to vintage Polo Ralph Lauren lettering. The former Phat Farm designer Alyasha Owerka-Moore took Bobby on his first trip to China to visit manufacturers, giving the younger designer an advanced grasp on the custom garment process, pushing the brand's cut-and-sew pieces to new levels. The company went from employing three people to fourteen, and sales grew to nearly $5 million by the end of 2008.

The Hundreds carried on with their internet hijinks. Bobby blogged almost every day, roiling brand owners and industry players along the way. An incident involving another Los Angeles brand and a sticker war likely escalated into the windows on Bobby's car being smashed in. "That generation was fighting over these internet territories, which was just crazy," recalled one designer who came up in the nineties New York scene. Season after season, the brand grew. They introduced their own sneaker program in 2009. At one Agenda trade show, they covered up their entire booth so that only buyers with appointments could see the collection. The Hundreds was full of these types of marketing stunts. And it was working. Between that and an ever-expanding product lineup, The

Hundreds made a lot of noise and did it swiftly. That year, the brand landed a profile in the *Los Angeles Times*, titled "Hip Apparel Brand Wants to Sell Without Selling Out."

Greg Selkoe's Karmaloop steadily rose in tandem with brands like Diamond Supply Co. and The Hundreds. Each year, Greg and his team convinced more and more brands to join their digital shelves. The e-commerce website was massively popular and offered consistent sales and broader visibility. Karmaloop already sold a roster of The Hundreds's contemporaries: Crooks & Castles, a flashy Los Angeles brand founded by Dennis Calvero and Robert Panlilio; Obey, a company born from the graphics of street artist Shepard Fairey; Black Scale, a San Francisco label heavy with gothic imagery started by former HUF employee Michael "Mega" Yabut and Alfred De Tagle. Greg had long wanted to sell The Hundreds; Ben and Bobby had always told him no. They liked Greg, but their brand had plenty of buzz on its own, and staying small was part of their ethos. "Karmaloop, to us, was symbolic of this transition of streetwear from the underground to the mainstream," Bobby said.

Eventually, Karmaloop and The Hundreds landed on a "starter order" of $300,000, and some buyers flew from Boston to Los Angeles to finalize the insertion order, the last step of the deal.

The Hundreds backed out two days before the order was supposed to leave the Los Angeles warehouse. Ben and Bobby, but mainly Bobby, had gotten cold feet. "It just wasn't sitting right in my gut," he recalled. "It's not like the customers would have cared. Maybe there'd be a few kids who would grumble about you selling to Karmaloop. No one cared as much as we did. But this is what it's like when you run a brand—you overthink everything, and things are more serious to you than anybody else."

That is how The Hundreds operated—on instinct and gut feelings. They were serious and playful, old-school and new-school. By 2010, The Hundreds had hit $17 million in sales, and Ben and Bobby wanted to open a store in the city that birthed so many of the brands they admired. The Hundreds New York was up next.

23.

Most Official Bitch

Leah McSweeney had a meeting on the sixty-sixth floor of the Empire State Building. She wore a Ralph Lauren cashmere sweater and black silk trousers with her trusty Chanel ballet flats. Her blond hair was straight and neat. Leah looked official. This meeting could change her life.

She was there to meet with FUBU, the onetime powerhouse sportswear "urban" brand that peaked at $350 million in sales in the late nineties. It was 2008, and in the recent past the company had overplayed its hand, flooding the market with inventory to the point where the brand had become a staple of the discount bin. The brand's founder, Daymond John, summed up its fall from trendiness: "Once you hit markdown bins, it's tough to climb out, because you've lost the sense that your clothes are fresh and vibrant." The company pivoted by pushing FUBU to the international market and hunting license deals with promising new brands for its portfolio to sell stateside.

Leah's brand Married to the Mob (MTTM) had pulled in nearly half a million dollars that year, and FUBU was interested.

Leah came up with the idea for Married to the Mob—colloquially known as MOB, an acronym for Most Official Bitches—in 2004 with a friend, Sharon Coyne, as the two sipped frozen margaritas on an East Village stoop during a sweltering summer afternoon. Leah was impressed by aNYthing and SSUR. It also felt like every dude under the age of thirty had his own T-shirt brand. None of her female friends did, though. "The goal was never money back then," she said. "It was just to express ourselves." The duo decided to produce a collection of four designs, printed on women's-cut T-shirts from American Apparel.

Alife was the first store to sell MTTM. Leah had two friends who worked at Union in SoHo, and she often hung there. She had befriended co-owner Mary Ann Fusco and decided she'd just bring in the T-shirts to show her. One of the shirts featured a red rectangle with white Futura-font text that read SUPREME BITCH. It was an obvious flip on the Supreme logo. Mary Ann loved it. She walked Leah over to Supreme's Wooster Street offices to show James Jebbia and told her to wait downstairs. A few minutes later she came back down.

James thinks it's really cute, she said. We're going to sell it.

The coveted and influential Union cosign was Leah's.

The FUBU meeting helped her believe that her brand was growing. The company still felt small to her. Leah was in her mid-twenties, a new mother, and ran MTTM out of her apartment, but she thought it could be huge. It was the growth she was most proud of: the label had just hit $400,000 in annual sales. The year before, sales were $200,000, up from $100,000 a year prior. She was confident she could hit $1 million the next year.

Leah came prepared. She had all these numbers printed out in a presentation. She brought the legal documentation showing that she owned the Married to the Mob trademark. The proper paperwork was key when getting a licensing deal. She also brought her press book, including write-ups in *Vogue* and *Elle*.

The magazines loved Leah. She was a downtown party girl with dirty-blond hair and a mischievous smile. When it came to storytelling, she was a firehose, spitting out the type of stories you lean in closer to hear: about getting wasted and dancing on tables and how she and her friends fought anyone who gave them dirty looks. In 2002, when Leah was twenty, she stepped in when a friend was getting handcuffed by the police. A sergeant grabbed her by the ponytail and smashed her face into a subway grate with such force that it knocked out two of her teeth. She received a $75,000 settlement from the NYPD that she used to start MTTM. All of these stories and her bad-girl persona swirled into the label's lore.

"Girls don't want to wear some bullshit brand . . . they want the best," she was fond of saying. "People can come out with a clothing line, but it's a waste of time if there is no message or authenticity behind it."

Leah went on to tell the FUBU executives how she'd grown up in the city, shopping on Lafayette Street and listening to Lil' Kim. She went through the story about getting assaulted by the cop, how Married to the Mob was pretty much the only female-led brand in the streetwear game. The label was all about being unapologetically yourself, she told them. She sensed her pitch was working; she moved on to the collaborations she already had under her belt.

In 2008, Leah had designed a Dunk High for Nike that was inspired by Chanel, a black-and-white sneaker with tweed, patent leather, and gold. She wanted to do something "high-low," like she saw on the New York streets. The same year, Sarah Andelman from the influential Parisian boutique Colette picked Leah to design a

Reebok sneaker. The result was a shiny white shoe adorned with a collage of MTTM's "Lipstick" logo. She told them she worked with artists, too. The $150 bikinis she made with KAWS, now an established name among the "street artist" set, sold out immediately in New York, Paris, and Tokyo. The room nodded along.

She looked to finish strong. Married to the Mob was already being sold in fifty of the hottest boutiques across the globe, she said. The credibility was there; she just needed to expand. She told them she wanted to be the next Kimora Lee Simmons, the model-turned-designer and face of Baby Phat. Then the meeting wrapped up, and Leah returned to her less corporate life downtown.

By that evening, an offer letter from FUBU had arrived. She'd have to give up equity in the label and a percentage of the sales; in return, MTTM would have access to their production, distribution, and marketing channels. They'd also give her an annual salary starting at $250,000. More money if sales exceeded expectations. A quarter of a million dollars a year. She thought that was pretty official.

This is going to change Mob, she told her boyfriend, Rob Cristofaro, that night at their Tribeca apartment. If I don't do this, I might regret it forever.

Rob, twelve years her senior, was a designer and cofounder of Alife. Leah's friend Nikki worked at Alife's shop on Orchard Street, and Leah saw Rob whenever she visited the store. She thought he was handsome and liked his sly smile; the two started dating and soon moved in together. He helped her with the earliest MTTM graphics. They worked together, Leah firing out ideas while Rob pushed pixels to bring his girlfriend's vision to life. The year before Leah's FUBU meeting, she got pregnant. It wasn't planned, but the couple embraced it, and when Leah gave birth, they were both in awe of their daughter.

Trust your gut, Rob told her.

There was no questioning it. Leah had to take the deal.

With a few exceptions, what became codified as streetwear had long been a bona fide boys' club. April Walker founded her trailblazing brand Walkerwear back in 1987. In the mid-nineties, Sonic Youth's Kim Gordon founded X-Girl with her friend Daisy von Furth, who worked at X-Large. It was worn by the likes of Chloë Sevigny and Sofia Coppola—who eventually launched her own short-lived brand called Milk Fed, with designs by Geoff McFetridge—but mostly shuttered by the end of the nineties. By the mid-aughts, Leah only had a few contemporaries, most scattered across the globe. Supreme designer Erin Magee had MadeMe; Laura Fama and Ashley Jones launched Dimepiece; Lanie Alabanza-Barcena, a designer with stints at a post–Camella Ehlke Triple Five Soul and Rocawear, founded HLZBLZ (pronounced "hell's belles"). Over in England, the Italian-born designer Sofia Prantera cut her teeth at Slam City Skates in London and later started a label called Silas with Russell Waterman. There were some others here and there, but it was mostly a lot of dudes.

Some brands had attempted to tap into the women's market, often with little success. In the early nineties, Stüssy launched a short-lived women's line called Stüssy Sista Gear. The Hundreds tried something similar in 2006 with Tens by The Hundreds. And there were the corporate threads of Baby Phat and Ecko Red. Leah was never quite sure if it was a good or bad thing that MTTM was largely alone in the marketplace.

In 2012, wheat-pasted posters of supermodel Kate Moss in a Supreme T-shirt and leopard-print coat—her famous pouty lips and the brand's increasingly famous Box Logo—appeared all over downtown New York. There were often blank spots on the walls where posters had been carefully removed, and eBay was soon littered with the stolen, wrinkled posters. Leah was amid her own MTTM campaign around the city, which she dubbed "Bitchisms," inspired by art-world star Jenny Holzer's *Truisms*. The slogans were set in a bold and curvy typeface, and the posters featured slogans like *Men are the new women*, *Don't be scared to be a bitch*, and *Good dick will imprison you*.

A wall on Spring at Crosby Street, around the corner from the iconic French brasserie Balthazar, was a sought-after and highly visible spot. Supreme plastered its Kate Moss posters there; then Leah posted over those with her own. "Me and Supreme were having a war going over each other," she recalled. "It was costing me a fortune, but it was so much fun."

Leah's licensing deal with FUBU ended the year prior, and she regained full ownership of Married to the Mob and its profits. "They thought I was going to be a cash cow. I thought I was going to be, too," she said. "I thought I was going to have a pink private jet and be the next Kimora Lee Simmons, and then the economy crashed." She missed the swanky Midtown office space, but MTTM's sales were nearly as strong as they had always been, at about $1.5 million a year. The independence gave her more creative freedom. The pop superstar Rihanna had become a loyal wearer, frequently photographed in Leah's designs, boosting sales along the way.

As Leah began her workday, now working out of a tiny office she rented, an email came through. It was a cease and desist from Supreme's lawyers that demanded Married to the Mob stop selling its Supreme Bitch design immediately.

Leah was pissed. She and James Jebbia were not close, but they shared several mutual friends. Leah felt he could have gotten her phone number or email and reached out directly. After all, he had approved the design himself. To have a lawyer send a warning on official letterhead felt cold and unnecessary. The letter also requested that Leah provide an itemized list of her orders and sales featuring the design. When she consulted her attorney later in the day, he advised her to file a trademark for "Supreme Bitch." So she did.

It turned out to be unintentional fuel to the fire. Two months later, the situation escalated dramatically. Supreme filed a lawsuit against Leah for $10 million and demanded she remove the offending items from retailers. The lawsuit acknowledged that James had initially approved the design, but noted he "thought it was just going to be a one-off" and how it now appeared on hats, T-shirts, towels, mugs, mousepads. It also accused Leah of "trying to build her whole brand by piggybacking off Supreme." The usual streetwear blogs wrote about the ordeal heavily, and coverage eventually bubbled into *New York* magazine and trade titles like *California Apparel News*.

"I made so much less money than my male counterparts. They wanted to see how much money I had made? I'm only at $1.5 million at my peak, and you're bothering *me*?" she recalled.

Leah posted a statement on the MTTM website that she titled "Supreme Bitchiness." She wrote, "As some of you may have heard, Supreme is suing me for ten million dollars. . . . I don't think Supreme should be able to squash free speech or my right to utilize parody in my design aesthetic." The letter ended with her trademark attitude: "This isn't a fight I went out looking for, but I have no choice other than to fight back. Because right now, it's about more than just a T-shirt!" Norman Siegel, a renowned civil liberties lawyer, signed on as Leah's cocounsel alongside a New York firm specializing in trademark law.

This wasn't all about free speech or ego. There was money at stake. Leah was about to finalize wholesale orders with Urban Outfitters and Karmaloop for over a million dollars total, which would have been a massive and much-needed influx of cash. But both retailers canceled orders after being threatened with litigation from Supreme's lawyers. Media interest in the lawsuit ramped up. "I can't help but think that I'm being silenced by Supreme with this lawsuit. I don't have a quarter of a million dollars to litigate this case, and they know that," Leah told *New York*.

Her team's defense was simple: Her creativity, a form of parody, was protected under the First Amendment. They aimed to strengthen their argument by showing the misogyny in the industry niche and establishing how parody was a common practice among these brands. Her counterclaim pointed to a 2003 Supreme calendar shot by photographer Terry Richardson, and a salacious interview he'd given *Vice* about it. It also mentioned numerous parody designs Supreme had produced over the years, including riffs on the *New Yorker* mascot and the Coca-Cola logo. James's legal team hit back by showing a T-shirt printed with a photo of Leah in a hot-pink bikini, suggestively posing against a man in a gorilla suit, as well as her WILL FUCK FOR CHANEL T-shirt design, among others, and asserted that these "plainly degrade and marginalize women rather than send a feminist message." Both sides kept throwing mud at each other, seeing what stuck. It poked a hole in the projected nonchalance that Supreme had spent almost two decades cultivating.

The lawsuit came to an end before it escalated any further. A friend of Leah's reached out to a "friend of someone who worked [at Supreme]," and they settled it out of court in the summer of 2013. The condition was that Leah stop selling the Supreme Bitch design set with the Box Logo aesthetic. James was defending his brand; Supreme was a big business now, no longer limited to downtown New York, and he had his livelihood and that of his employees to protect. Leah, by her own admission, should never have filed for that trademark and knew she was being hotheaded by refusing to back down from a legal fight.

The silver lining to the press and attention of the lawsuit was that it woke a sleeping giant. Barbara Kruger, the legendary artist and designer who inspired Supreme's Box Logo, acknowledged the use of her artwork in this commercial apparel space for the first time, addressing both parties: "What a ridiculous clusterfuck of totally uncool jokers."

24.

The Hundreds Is Huge

Months after the opening of the New York shop came the Santa Monica Hundreds store, a corner over from the Third Street Promenade and sharing an alley with Fred Segal. With four storefronts, The Hundreds could afford to be picky with stockists. "We came from the school of Supreme, SSUR, and A New York Thing," said Bobby Kim. "If a store doesn't feel authentic, we're not going to sell to them." He remembered walking the floor at MAGIC one year with SSUR designer Russ Karablin as the two passed the gigantic booth of a crossover brand that sold fiercely to the malls and peaked at $150 million in annual sales in the mid-aughts. There were probably forty guys dressed head to toe in the brand's gaudy clothes along with chains and sunglasses. That's the worst thing that could happen to your brand, Russ whispered to Bobby.

The Hundreds wanted to stay small, to sell to core shops and to stay independent—even if that meant leaving millions on the table. But Bobby felt as if The Hundreds had hit a ceiling. "There are only so many streetwear stores in the world, only so much shelf space on those stores' shelves." They had four stores and a solid network of boutiques across the globe. But how does a rising brand stay rising when it hits a ceiling?

Ben Shenassafar and Bobby first broke their self-imposed "hard-line, restrictive sales doctrine" with Active Ride Shop, selling to the retail chain of skate stores that had been founded in 1989. It was the first chain The Hundreds ever sold to. Active had around thirty stores across Southern California, from the coastal suburbs to cities deep in the valley. It felt like a half step between shopping in a core skate store and the mall. Like skate shops across the country, the Nike SB Dunk craze brought in a new type of customer: the non-skater sneakerhead. The shops expanded to stock T-shirts from the brands to keep them there.

Bobby updated the blog like he was addicted to it, posting two or three times a day, throwing up photos of whoever rolled by the office or daily happenings in the Fairfax neighborhood. It quickly found a following, with people across the globe discovering it from Hypebeast and its growing forums. If you were a sneaker-obsessed teenager in Tokyo or Toledo and wanted to know what happened in the Los Angeles scene that day, you read Bobby's blog. At their first Agenda trade show, Bobby and Ben sat behind a folding table from morning until night for three days. No one wrote a single order. Fast-forward a few years, and the Hundreds booth had appointments booked for every working hour of the convention, with two domestic sales reps and one international.

"Even at the tables, there would be three or four appointments booked at the same time," recalled Bobby. "You remember those days. There'd be like ten buyers sitting around—it looked like an auction house with sales guys holding up shirts and hats and people being like, 'Oh, what's the name of that one?' And writing thousands of dollars of orders, hundreds of thousands of orders. I remember the first Agenda where it was rumored Scott Sasso at 10.Deep had booked a million dollars, and we couldn't believe it. That was something to aspire for."

Between booking new shops at Agenda, their deal with Active, expanding international accounts, and their four flagship stores, The Hundreds was firing on all cylinders. Bobby's blog generated millions of hits. "When you have momentum in this game, it's very easy to make money, you barely have to try. . . . But if you want to sustain, you have to turn it into a business with infrastructure, and you have to be a boss," Bobby said. They were legitimate now, no longer two kids in their twenties running around an alley off of Fairfax.

"Our focus had slowly evolved from being cool to being profitable."

Founded by Aaron Levant in 2003, Agenda reshaped the teenage and young adult apparel industry for an entire generation. Aaron was a former graffiti-writing kid and general troublemaker from Agoura Hills, California, who was kicked out of high school and never returned. Instead, he started working with Luis Pulido at GAT as the brand reinvented itself as Grn Apple Tree in the early aughts. Aaron's earliest Agenda shows started scrappy; his venues included Thai restaurants, obscure warehouses, and parking lots near the Action Sports Retailer (ASR) show to siphon off its attendees. He wasn't the first to try and spin up an outsider trade show; in the early nineties, the short-lived 432F Clothing Show became a place for alternative brands that didn't quite fit in with surf and skate. (555 Soul, GFS/Not From Concentrate, Pervert, CONART, and Eric Haze's namesake label all held booths at 432F.) But Agenda quickly earned industry buzz as the up-and-coming "streetwear and fashion" trade show, making serious inroads into the action sports category. "ASR was so mad that we were taking all their customers, they went and rented this building [we used] for a three-year lease just so we couldn't use it," recalled Aaron. "And they locked up everything else in the city." In 2009, after years of operating as an unauthorized satellite show to ASR, Aaron wanted to become the main event. He broke away entirely and relocated from San Diego to Orange County. The move landed Hurley and Nike booths at Agenda for the first time. Soon, other industry giants like Quiksilver, Volcom, and Vans joined. It became his biggest show, with hundreds of brands and almost four thousand attendees. He decided that, moving forward, Agenda would be held in January and July, just slightly ahead of ASR's February and September shows. At one point, ASR executives offered him $200,000 to buy Agenda and fold it into their show. By then, Aaron was making millions a year in profit for himself. He declined. "I was digging the ditch for ASR."

Aaron worried the big names might result in pushback from his core brands—The Hundreds, Diamond Supply Co., Crooks & Castles, Black Scale, HUF, and Obey were all early to embrace Agenda—as his trade show leveled up, but he also knew that many of them were doing well in the surf and skate market. He promised to help position their brands as potential crossover labels for shops looking for more specialty pieces. This new wave of streetwear appealed to the youth at large, winning over a bigger, cross-cultural demographic than the more segmented categories of surf, skate, and "urban" before it. By the end of 2010, ASR announced it was calling it quits after nearly thirty years in business. Two years later, Agenda landed in Long Beach with 235,000 square feet, more than double the space from the previous year.

Aaron's trade show was no longer the outsider; it was now the industry standard.

Ben called a meeting with Bobby and some of the other department heads. By now, The Hundreds had moved to a warehouse space in downtown Los Angeles, no longer headquartered in the tiny studio above their Rosewood store. As the brand grew, so did their overhead: from a couple hundred square feet to seventeen thousand, from five employees to fifty.

No matter where I turn, I end up back at the mall, Ben told the room.

It was the only way to break through that ceiling they kept hitting.

"Zumiez had been knocking on the door for years before we opened them up. It wasn't something that I really wanted to do either, but we just felt in order for us to continue to grow that that was just the next step," recalled Ben. It was easy enough to find the logic to do it, though. Both Ben and Bobby grew up in the suburbs of sprawling Los Angeles, where it could be a desert when it came to streetwear boutiques and skate shops. But every mall had a Zumiez. Most of their contemporaries were already there: Crooks & Castles, Diamond Supply Co., Married to the Mob, Obey, and REBEL8, a San Francisco brand run by Josh "Joshy D" Drapiewski that featured the artwork of illustrator and tattoo artist Mike "Mike Giant" LeSage.

Ben and Bobby figured it would be okay if they did it on their own terms. It was a push-and-pull: The mall chain wanted orders for three hundred doors and Ben countered with fifty, saying that if it worked out, they could explore one hundred. Within a few years, The Hundreds had moved into over three hundred stores, and it accounted for about 20 percent of their total annual sales. "It very easily could have been fifty percent, and our business could have been not double, but definitely quite a bit bigger," recalled Ben. "At the end of the day, Bobby and I don't love selling to stores like Zumiez. But in order for us to continue to grow, that was the next step. There are times where you have to work with the necessary evil. It always felt uncomfortable, but we felt like we needed to be there. All of our friends got fully in bed with them, fully made all the money they could and fully abused the relationship. Bobby and I were always one foot in, one foot out, and we would never let Zumiez have all the doors they wanted."

The Hundreds looked unstoppable. They demoed the Rosewood store and connected it to the storefronts on each side, tripling its size. The stores in San Francisco and New York and Santa Monica were profitable. The move into the mall had worked. The Hundreds had hit a new peak: $22 million in sales. But on the outside, they looked much bigger.

"I don't know if that's a streetwear thing and it's just the image and the hype have always outsized us, or it was just the way that we marketed ourselves, as we'd always say, *The Hundreds is huge*, and we presented really well. . . . Some people thought we were a hundred-million-dollar company," Bobby said.

Those optics, while a snappy marketing tool, came with a hit to the brand's street credibility. "I would walk by Supreme, and I would feel like the Hundreds guy," recalled a former staffer at the Rosewood shop. "It was a little more commercial. I think the time that I got there was the tail end of it being *the shit*, basically."

This was when a query came in from a well-known designer and his team. The designer was interested in learning more about Ben and Bobby's label. He saw untapped potential. Maybe he would even consider buying it.

The designer was Tommy Hilfiger.

25.

Diamond Life

Nick Tershay was now a man with million-dollar checks arriving like clockwork. Sometimes a single check totaled three million. With his new production partner, the business of Diamond Supply Co. had found its way into a new era. Sales swelled from $15 million to a towering $50 million. The old days of not having enough cash to cover larger orders were officially behind him. It was time to build. In 2012, Nick opened a massive Diamond headquarters complete with a twenty-three-thousand-square-foot warehouse for inventory and shipping, as well as a skate park in the back. Then came new Diamond stores in San Francisco and New York, and always, the Fairfax shop, still booming and at the center of it all.

As the company grew, Nick remained focused on the power of a digital community. Now there were Twitter and Instagram to contend with, and he built out a marketing team to stay ahead of the curve. An early hire was Brock "Brocky Marciano" Korsan, a former college radio DJ who worked with a few up-and-coming rappers, among them Kendrick Lamar and Schoolboy Q. Nick hired Dennis Todisco, who had spent the last five years at Karmaloop, advancing from intern to the director of lifestyle marketing. (The two befriended each other through the Hypebeast forums.) Dennis watched the e-commerce retailer rise to a giant, selling T-shirts and hoodies and caps from over one hundred and sixty brands. Dennis's savvy for new-media marketing and Brock's hip-hop connections turned Diamond hotter and more popular by the season. The brand's thread on the Hypebeast forums was by far the biggest and most active; both Nick and Dennis posted throughout the day, interacting with fans and teasing out upcoming projects and designs. Diamond had broken outside of skateboarding, releasing collaborations with rising names in hip-hop like Wiz Khalifa, Big Sean, Mac Miller, and Curren$y. "The whole music industry at the time really grasped onto Diamond just 'cause of the name. All these rappers were fucking with it," Nick recalled. Even Rhianna was photographed wearing a Diamond sweatshirt.

The company also collaborated with brands on both coasts: The Hundreds and Crooks & Castles in California, and 10.Deep and Mighty Healthy out in New York. He teamed up with a friend, the celebrity jeweler Ben "Ben Baller" Yang, on blinged-out T-shirt graphics and gold-dipped Diamond jewelry. But beyond the forums and the celebrities and the collaborations, the biggest factor in driving Diamond's growth was the American mall. Nick sold to two massive retail chains: PacSun and Zumiez. You could walk into almost any mall in America and buy a Diamond T-shirt.

If your brand had boldly printed graphic T-shirts, and you were a label that was covered on Hypebeast or Highsnobiety, or sold by Karmaloop, your demand surged. (PacSun adapted to the times by poaching several employees from Karmaloop.) At the American mall, you could now buy the likes of 10.Deep, The Hundreds, Crooks & Castles, HUF, and Obey. Some brands kept distribution tighter, limiting the number of doors they'd sell to;

others, like Diamond, delivered product far and wide. It was a plastisol gold rush.

"It became a machine. Less art-driven, more transactional, more commercial," recalled The Hundreds cofounder Bobby Kim. "People were getting famous. People were getting rich."

"A lot of the brands from our era were able to get there quicker because we had a blueprint for it," said Hanni El Khatib, the musician and long-running creative director at HUF. "We were trying to protect this thing, too. We wanted to be known and be big, but we still wanted it to be rare."

Each year, Zumiez hosted its Zumiez 100K event, where the retailer invited its top salespeople and managers to a ski resort in Colorado. Employees who sold six figures of merchandise scored an invite. Booze flowed freely; there were raffles, poker tables, and even baby Bengal tigers. Performers included Lil Wayne, Pharrell, and Skrillex; action sports stars like Tony Hawk, Rob Dyrdek, and Nyjah Huston stopped by. One year, a twenty-two-year-old sales associate won the top prize for selling $600,000, and Zumiez sent him home with a brand-new Dodge Charger.

The Zumiez 100K became the industry's epicenter, a showy symbol of the money this generation of brands was bringing in; the crowd could swell to over one thousand attendees, and all the brand owners made the trip. Nick from Diamond, Ben and Bobby from The Hundreds, Leah from Married to the Mob, Shepard from Obey, Dennis from Crooks & Castles, Joshy D from REBEL8, and on and on. The brand owners were often treated with the same fanfare as the professional athletes. Social media had turned the designers into micro-celebrities, known by their brands: "Nicky Diamonds" and "Bobby Hundreds." On Instagram, Nick led the pack with 600,000 followers. Bobby had 160,000 in addition to his widely read blog. The cachet even extended to these brand's employees. Corey Populus began working for Diamond when he was just a nineteen-year-old who skated and posted on the Hypebeast and NikeTalk forums. He helped Nick pack orders but eventually landed on the floor at the Fairfax store. "Being a sales associate at Diamond was being a celebrity in itself. . . . This was around the time that Instagram and Twitter were blowing up, and we would build massive followings just from being at the store."

The name for the company that made Nicky Diamonds into a multimillionaire came to him back in the nineties, when he was only twenty-four. He and a friend were driving around the Tenderloin—then a seedy San Francisco neighborhood on the southern slope of Nob Hill, full of addicts and cheap motels—when the song "Smooth Operator" by Nigerian British pop star Sade played on the radio. Her low, soulful alto crooned over the car's speakers: *Diamond life, lover boy.* He remembered his eyes scanning the trashed-out streets and thinking, *I'm going to live that diamond life one day.*

The year 2013 was huge for Diamond, with the brand hitting a peak of $92 million in annual sales, with nearly one hundred and fifty employees.

Nick was undoubtedly living a diamond life. That year, he woke up on his thirty-ninth birthday in the mood to celebrate; he wanted to treat himself to a Ferrari. Nick took in the view of the smoggy Hollywood Hills from his bed, got up and dressed, and headed to the Beverly Hills dealership. At first, the salesman looked him up and down—at his jeans, T-shirt, and sneakers—practically wincing, keeping him at arm's length as they walked around the showroom. His attitude flipped when Nick showed his bank statement, and within the hour, the Diamond designer drove off the lot in the latest Ferrari 458 in a sleek midnight black. But the $250,000 Italian sports car wasn't flashy enough; black was too plain a color. He drove to a high-end car shop on Melrose and had his new ride wrapped in the same color as the Tiffany-inspired blue from his Nike SB Dunk.

"I specifically remember the day that Nick got a Ferrari and pulled up in front of the shop. I remember when he got a Rolls-Royce. It was insane . . . It's hard to fathom that somebody selling hoodies and T-shirts with no college degree could live like that," recalled Corey.

Within a calendar year, Nick bought two Rolls-Royces, a Range Rover, a Mercedes S550, and an assortment of vintage Chevys. But the head-turning blue Ferrari was his calling card, often parked outside the Diamond shop. He bought a striking contemporary home worth almost $7 million, four stories that cascaded down the hills of Hollywood, and filled it with Louis Vuitton luggage, Rolex watches, limited-edition Bearbrick figures, and art by everyone from KAWS to Keith Haring. All of this was displayed on his Instagram for the world to see.

Nicky Diamonds was living the diamond life, and it only made his T-shirts more covetable to his fans. The kids wanted to live that diamond life, too.

Two mall retailers—PacSun and Zumiez—had long supplied the youthful masses with apparel. Both stores were usually placed inside malls or shopping centers and targeted consumers ages twelve to twenty-four. Zumiez was founded in Washington in 1978 by two former JCPenney employees. By the early nineties, it had narrowed its buying strategy to chase what was most popular then:

surf and skate. It took a pumping of private equity money in 2002 and continued to scale up. PacSun's origins were as a small surf shop that opened in 1980 and expanded throughout the following decades as the surfer look went global. In 1998, PacSun launched d.e.m.o., a hip-hop-themed chain that sold Rocawear, Baby Phat, and Ecko and rose to 154 stores before shuttering in 2008. "The urban consumer was no longer interested in wearing the loose-fitting clothes that typically characterized urban fashions. Skate-influenced streetwear looks became more popular," read a report in *California Apparel News* at the time.

Both chains were major players within the mainstream retail space, an edgier alternative to Abercrombie & Fitch and American Eagle. Zumiez had more than five hundred stores nationwide; PacSun had expanded to nearly one thousand. By the mid-2010s, the two retailers were chasing the latest marketplace trend. They found it at Aaron Levant's Agenda trade show, which plugged these once-underground brands—Diamond, Crooks & Castles, The Hundreds, Obey, and the like—into the mainstream mall.

"We became the broker to present the new version of apparel and what was cool to the mass market," said Aaron. "At one point, we had two thousand brands . . . but I'd place Obey and The Hundreds or Crooks or whatever the hot brands at the time would be in the front. You'd have to walk to the back to get to Billabong or Quicksilver. So, when buyers from Macy's, Zumiez, or PacSun walked in, we changed the dynamic of how those people perceived brands. We changed the assortments on the retail floors. We became a big part. We became an authority." Even Aaron's business was boosted by streetwear's invasion of the mall; he sold a controlling stake in his Agenda trade show to Reed Exhibitions in 2012 for $40 million.

"Diamond Life," or #diamondlife, became the brand's calling card. Nick's designs leaned into a luxurious and sometimes illicit lifestyle, with nods to luxury and weed in equal measure. His graphics skewed straightforward: flat vector graphics often studded with simple motifs, neat typography, and phrases like THE WORLD IS YOURS and GET YOUR SHINE ON. There was still plenty of robin's-egg blue across the collections, plus nods to brands like Comme des Garçons PLAY and Rolex. For a T-shirt brand, Nick had managed to infuse a sense of aspirational luxury that separated Diamond within the marketplace full of graphic tees.

For all of his adult life, Nick had lived off a couple thousand dollars a month. Now he was rich—fabulously, absurdly rich. "I was just making millions of dollars and spending millions of dollars at the same time.... I grew up in a group home. I dropped out of high school. I never cared about money. I was never raised to understand money. I had no guidance . . . I didn't know what to do with it. So I was, like, *What do I do with all this money? I guess I just spend it*," Nick said. "All I knew is that I was a skateboarder and I wanted to fucking make shit. The whole money part was an afterthought." Nick liked to party, and he paid for everything and everyone, ordering bottles without an ounce of hesitation. Almost always Dom Pérignon Luminous, at over $1,000 per bottle. "We'd go out to a club and just fucking spend $50,000 like was nothing. We would do it every night," Nick recalled. Private jets to Vegas to party. There was one year when he spent $3 million on clubbing alone.

"It got to the point where streetwear money saw something they never saw before," Ben Baller later told *Complex*. "[Nick] bought me a Ferrari and the pink slip was in the glove box."

One PacSun buyer recalled the sheer volume of SKUs, or stock-keeping units, within the Diamond line sheets; the designs were simple but offered on T-shirts, windbreakers, hoodies, crewnecks, polos, hats, beanies, sneakers, socks. "I would literally do two hundred pieces a season while other people's lines were like twenty pieces a season," Nick said. During Diamond's peak years, he estimated PacSun was selling between $10 million and $15 million while Zumiez sold $35 million every year. "They told me that that's the biggest they've ever done with any brand." Diamond was explicitly mentioned on a PacSun earnings call as a top driver for growth in the men's category, along with another era-defining brand called Crooks & Castles.

Crooks & Castles (Crooks) held a bold and unmistakable presence within the marketplace. Nick was good friends with the label's founders, Dennis Calvero and Robert Panlilio. (They were in a car club together.) Crooks's founders and core team had been in the industry since the nineties, with stints at Ecko, Mecca, and FUBU. The brand came out of the gates with a bang, and Dennis and Rob pushed and pulled against their own demand. Earlier in the brand's trajectory, they declined Greg Selkoe's offer to sell on Karmaloop. Undeterred, the boisterous CEO found a way to purchase directly from the brand's Canadian distributor. "They went fucking berserk trying to stop us," recalled Greg. "We had this big showdown. . . . But we walked away saying, *Let's really build something big together.*" Crooks became one of Karmaloop's bestselling brands, generating millions of dollars annually. The brand built an image of a streets-to-luxury story on pillars of "hustle, loyalty, and rebellion" with T-shirts printed with slogans like EVERY DAY IS PAY DAY and COCAINE & CAVIAR. "The crooks symbolized starting at the bottom and eventually working your way up to having a castle," Dennis once said. Crooks's graphics often appropriated imagery, imbuing it with sinister undertones: the Versace medusa head with a bandit's bandanna over its face, Mickey Mouse's iconic cartoon hands in the gesture of a handgun, Andy Warhol's soup can reimagined as a grenade. Industry insiders estimated Crooks & Castles's yearly sales to be around $15 million at its peak.

Like Zumiez and PacSun, Karmaloop was another kingmaker of the era, reaching its peak in annual sales of $127 million around this time. The company earned a reputation as the deep-pocketed wild boys of Agenda and MAGIC. "Money was just pouring in from them . . . Those guys were throwing the best parties in Vegas. Everyone was doing a bunch of blow," recalled one brand owner. "It was very much, you had to go to the Karmaloop parties." The digital retailer proved to be massively impactful for the midsized and smaller labels as well. "At the height of Mishka, we were doing like eight or nine million dollars a year, and two million of it was from Karmaloop," said Gregory Rivera, a cofounder of the playful New York label. "That's almost a quarter of your business."

One evening in 2013, Agenda founder Aaron Levant gathered a hundred owners, reps, and buyers for dinner at an upscale Brazilian steakhouse, including Stüssy's VP of sales Scott Terpstra, Dennis and Rob from Crooks & Castles, Ben and Bobby from The Hundreds, and Nick from Diamond. After drinks had arrived, but before the platters of perfectly grilled filet mignon and picanha hit the table, Aaron tapped his glass with his knife. He thanked everyone at the table for their support of Agenda over the years. Together, they had knocked the old-guard ASR out of business. Next, he said, they'd come for MAGIC in Las Vegas. He announced that Agenda Vegas was in the works. It was a war captain rallying the troops. He had made them rich, and they'd follow him to wherever it led.

When kids bought a Diamond T-shirt, they were buying into the luxurious image projected on Nick's Instagram feed: the cars, the clothes, the bottles. Many brand owners later recalled Diamond as an anomaly, this skate brand that vaulted into a lifestyle and streetwear juggernaut, the most commercial brand of its class. "It was all community," said Nick. "Community is what made Diamond bigger than everything else." Nick could finally enjoy the fruits of his labor. He had come from nothing and worked for it. The youth fashion market had always moved in cycles, and the spotlight looked to finally be on his class of brands. Diamond Supply Co., The Hundreds, Crooks & Castles, Obey, Black Scale, and HUF. The West Coasters and their sold-at-the-mall strand of streetwear had snatched the crown from downtown New York.

It was their moment in the sun, and it felt like it'd shine on them forever.

Act Three

26.

Fifty Racks

The Mercer Hotel was Kanye West's home away from home. The four-star SoHo landmark had long been one of the rapper's go-to spots when he was in New York City. It's where he and Jay-Z famously recorded their hit collaborative album, the bombastic and luxurious *Watch the Throne*. The six-story brick fortress held a long-standing reputation as a celebrity hideaway in the scrum of downtown Manhattan. It was where Kanye took most of his meetings.

Jim Moore, the long-standing and influential *GQ* fashion editor, popped out of a black town car on the cobblestoned corner of Mercer and Prince. Jim walked into the Christian Liaigre–designed lobby, breezing past the warm expensive lighting and the rich mahogany bookshelves. This wasn't his first time at the Mercer. The elevator opened to Kanye's floor, and a handler ushered Jim into the room. It was 2014, and Kanye's *GQ* cover shoot was just weeks away. The two men needed to finalize outfits for the hip-hop superstar to wear. Both were also excited to gab about their mutual favorite pastime, fashion.

For this shoot, I really want to do one color, Jim told Kanye. *One* color, he repeated. Head to toe.

Jim straightened the display board he'd brought so it stood at attention. It featured twenty-five outfits, each as sleekly monochromatic as the last. Dusty grays, opulent blacks, silky pale whites, rich navy blues, muted army greens. He told Kanye they'd mix up the singular color by playing with textures and tones. The goal was understated and casual, elevated and opulent.

Oh, this looks *right*, Kanye said. Let's do it! We got a fitting, right?

Jim knew how Kanye operated when it came to magazine photo shoots. The two men had known each other for nearly a decade; there was mutual trust there. They'd first met in 2005 when the men's magazine threw a big party for Jim's twenty-fifth company anniversary in Milan, back when magazine budgets were thick and sweet like honey. It was Jim's boss—*GQ*'s top brass, Jim Nelson—who asked Kanye to perform. After the rapper's set, as the party blurred into the after-party, Jim and Kanye met backstage, talking for nearly two hours about all things fashion. Kanye's first cover for *GQ* happened two years later when Jim put him in a slim Calvin Klein suit and Tom Ford sunglasses, pitch-perfect for the magazine's signature metropolitan look at the time.

But that was then, and this was now. With the rising adoption of athleisure and designer sportwear, the suit started looking stuffy and outmoded. The value system of daily fashion shifted; shoppers now considered comfort and functionality to be markers of style.

Jim, who had shaped how American men dressed for the past three decades, wanted to do something drastically different. "About three weeks earlier, I'd just come off a shoot with Drake, and I had put him in this kind of olive look, all head to toe, even down to the boots," recalled Jim. "For Kanye, I wanted just to do this monochromatic thing. It looked like the future. I showed him some mood boards, and he really loved it."

As Jim packed to leave the Mercer, Kanye mentioned he'd bring some clothes of his own.

Two weeks later, Kanye arrived at the West Village studio the evening before the photo shoot. He wore a dust-gray crewneck with a slightly scooped collar, skinny jeans, and Chelsea boots. With him were his longtime publicist, Gabe Tesoriero, and a newer face, a designer from Los Angeles named Jerry Lorenzo. Jerry was Kanye's creative consultant, a hybrid assistant and stylist of sorts. Waiting inside were nearly fifty racks of clothing. It was perhaps the most clothes ever pulled for a *GQ* photo shoot in the magazine's eighty-some years of existence.

Everything was organized by color. There was a $5,000 Calvin Klein camel coat, En Noir leather jogger pants that cost $1,400, and a nearly $4,000 Givenchy sports jacket by Kanye's friend Riccardo Tisci, the Italian fashion designer who brought streetwise silhouettes and graphic T-shirt motifs to French luxury label Givenchy. For footwear, there were sleek Bottega Veneta Chelsea boots, rugged Timberland boots, and classic Adidas Stan Smith sneakers, ranging in price from $75 to $770.

I don't know about this one-color thing, Jerry murmured from the back.

I love these looks on the board, but I want to try it all, Kanye told Jim.

All fifteen looks? asked Jim.

Nah, nah, Kanye replied, shaking his head. *Everything* in the room.

Over the next nine hours, they cycled through it all. By nightfall, Jim and Kanye had circled back to the one-color dressing looks that had been the original idea. The night-gray Balmain joggers with the Timbs. The chunky charcoal Bottega Veneta overcoat with a drab Calvin Klein sweater and washed-out black Levi's vintage tee. The cold-silver Fear of God bomber jacket—Jerry's new label—and the destroyed Rochambeau tee with leather Acne Studios pants. And finally, the threads that Kanye himself brought. A nubby, textured sweater and skinny jeans, both cream-colored and from the new A.P.C. KANYE collection the rapper had previewed in Paris earlier that year. Jim and Kanye paired that look with the white Stan Smiths.

There was something undeniably fresh about it. The monochromatic outfits looked incredibly modern and masculine. They felt tailored but informal, a new mode of dressing for the rap superstar.

The GQ cover hit newsstands in August 2014. The rapper looked stone-faced into the lens, wearing a camel coat and scoop-neck plain white tee with a delicate gold chain: "Kanye West Tells Us How to Dress Like a God." It was the latest milestone in Kanye's growing empire of influence. He was newly empowered as a creative force. He commanded rarefied space in pop culture: equal parts marquee rapper, bullish rabble-rouser, and poetic experimenter. Kanye had also recently married Kim Kardashian, one of the biggest celebrities in the world thanks to her family's bronzed reality TV empire and new-media savvy. The celebrity union boosted them both, propelling Kanye closer to the upper echelon he had been stretching for since rapping with his jaw wired shut. Anna Wintour had already featured the happy couple on the April 2013 cover of *Vogue*.

Two years earlier, Kanye had formed DONDA, an experimental design agency named after his late mother. He employed a collective of painfully hip creatives, led by Kanye's longtime creative director Virgil Abloh with support from Jerry Lorenzo, Matthew Williams, Heron Preston, Justin Saunders, Joe Perez, and others.

They traveled the globe with Kanye like salaried shadows in expensive jeans and enviable sneakers. Their Instagram feeds offered a peek into their jet-setting lifestyle. The group rarely worked out of a formal office; an ongoing joke among the group was that DONDA's headquarters was Virgil's laptop. A few of them—namely Virgil, Matthew, and Heron—started DJing at night under the collective name Been Trill.

Kanye kept the crew on their toes, always striving toward the next level. Nothing was ever enough. He didn't want to be the rapper with a vanity-project clothing label or to lend his celebrity to a liquor brand. He started the agency to ideate and create, not just to put a marketing spin on existing products. He wanted to be the next Steve Jobs, a claim he repeated ad nauseam.

But perhaps most of all, Kanye wanted to be a fashion designer.

Kanye's career as a fashion designer was full of fits and false starts. In 2004, it was rumored that he was launching Mascotte, with support from Jay-Z's Rocawear, then a commercial powerhouse; Mascotte never happened. A few years later, Kanye resurfaced with the brightly colored Pastelle, described as a mix between Polo Ralph Lauren and A Bathing Ape; the project made it farther than his last, but ultimately failed to reach the market. In 2011, Kanye finally got one off the ground: Dw by Kanye West, a women's collection full of skintight pants, low-cut dresses, and fur backpacks. The project lasted for only two collections before it was promptly shuttered. "It was the equivalent of Karl Lagerfeld launching a hip-hop career: i.e., absurd," wrote one fashion critic. When Anna Wintour was asked her thoughts, she replied, "Ask someone else."

Kanye fumbled to find success with clothing, but his arrival in the sneaker space was immediate and fierce. In 2007, he designed a limited-edition Bapesta sneaker for Nigo and spent two years working with Nike on developing the Air Yeezy 1, the brand's first collaboration with a non-athlete. Two years later, Kanye designed a three-shoe collection for Louis Vuitton that became sought-after collectibles, and the Air Yeezy finally dropped. Only nine thousand pairs were released, and they were gone in a flash. (An original prototype of the style later sold for $1.8 million, breaking the record for a sneaker sale at auction.) The Air Yeezy 2 came in 2012; the $245 sneaker sold out instantly, with secondary market prices reaching as high as $90,000. But his partnership with Nike soon soured to the point that Kanye wanted to spit it out. Kanye wanted royalties and more respect. Onstage during his Yeezus Tour, he frequently vented about the company and its CEO, Mark Parker; the Auto-Tuned rants generated their own news cycle. By the end of 2013, Kanye had signed a $10 million deal with rival Adidas to design not only sneakers, but a collection of men's and women's sportswear he would call Yeezy.

He had high hopes this could be what would lead to his big fashion break.

Kanye said Adidas gave him a budget of $500,000 to assemble his team of designers. "I don't know how I was supposed to put a design team together for that. But luckily, I was a multimillionaire rapper," he told the *New York Times*. Nothing was too grand or too expensive to achieve his dreams. Yeezy season 1 was his chance to prove to the fashion industry that his taste had evolved and he finally had what it took.

Kanye assembled a group that included Virgil Abloh, a fellow

Chicagoan, his loyal confidant and in-house creative director who ran his own graphic-heavy label Pyrex Vision; Jerry Lorenzo, whose Fear of God label was starting to make some quiet noise; Robert Geller, a German-born designer with his own cult-loved label and a résumé notch at Marc Jacobs; and Demna Gvasalia, a Georgian designer with stints at Maison Martin Margiela and Louis Vuitton. Demna had also just launched Vetements, a buzzy streetwise Parsian label, to much fashion industry fanfare; Kanye was fond of wearing a Vetements hoodie printed with a death metal–looking logo. The Yeezy season 1 team spent eighteen months working on the first collection; Kanye was deeply invested in every single stitch and color and fabric.

In February 2015, at New York Fashion Week, it was time to show the clothes to the world. The fashion show lasted twelve minutes, from the time Kanye's voice blared until all the models had walked and the designer took a bow. Even by fashion's avant-garde standards, the presentation felt closer to an art installation than a typical runway show. (It was choreographed by Italian performance artist Vanessa Beecroft.) Horns and lighting changed every ten seconds, and street-cast models walked to the front, line by line, staring into the distance. The collection included oversized tops and fitted bottoms, bomber-style jackets and washed-cotton jackets. There was a mélange of muted tones—fleshy shades, muted greens, beiges, bluish grays—often artfully distressed with raw seams. Toward the final minutes of the show, Kanye's newest track, "Wolves," played as the ceiling lights fully illuminated. Clad in a black hoodie and skinny sweatpants with his coin-gray suede Yeezy Boost 750 sneakers, he walked to the front row, nodded his head, a hint at the customary designer's bow, and then disappeared back into the darkness.

Kanye had done it. The collection—heavily influenced by vintage Helmut Lang and Martin Margiela—was wearable and thoughtfully designed. No one had compared him to a rapping Karl Lagerfeld. The clothes did not split the sky, but it looked like he might have threaded the needle between his perfectionist vision and wearable commerce. On the leading fashion website Style.com, Yeezy shot to the no. 1 most-viewed collection, dethroning iconic French luxury house Chanel, which had long occupied the spot. There were no especially high-profile rave reviews, but no ruthless critiques, either. After the show, the only thing left to do was wait to see how the collection sold once it hit shelves.

Lines formed outside of Barneys New York on Madison Avenue and the menswear shop Nomad in Toronto. There were some nerves from buyers about Kanye's price points, which ranged from $3,050 for a fur-hooded jacket to $180 for a stone-colored tank top. And yet customers happily paid the prices. The $235 camouflage T-shirt was a bestseller; one buyer theorized that it was because it was the item Kanye was most often photographed wearing. His new Adidas sneaker, the Yeezy Boost, cost $250, and Adidas sold 9,000 pairs in minutes, leaving people clamoring for more. The long-standing trade publication *Footwear News* gave the sneaker its Shoe of the Year award.

In the aftermath of the lines and quick sell-through times, the industry at large started to take Kanye the designer more seriously. It only took fast-fashion retailer Zara six months before it launched a Yeezy look-alike collection in its hundreds of stores. There was suddenly an influx of boxy, oversized T-shirts and slouchy cropped hoodies in drab colors walking around downtown New York. The rest of America soon followed.

The commercial success hinted at the truest asset that Kanye had. It was something that no other designer had, whether they were American or European or came from luxury fashion or streetwear. Kanye had his celebrity. "Everybody wants this collection for a piece of Kanye," said an executive buyer at Barneys New York. Being photographed on the cover of fashion magazines, having ultra-famous friends and songs on the radio, and being married to the world's biggest reality TV star drove shoppers into stores. Paparazzi photos became street-style lessons. Blogs wrote about his daily outfits with the precision of court stenographers. You bought a Yeezy shirt to buy into the world of Kanye the same way you bought a Polo shirt to buy into the world of Ralph Lauren.

The Yeezy look—understated, comfortable, and luxuriously casual—went beyond trends; it signaled a cultural shift. As a style icon and now fashion designer, Kanye had the power to change how hordes of men dressed. The second collection hit the runway later that year, another grouping of slouchy hoodies and cinched sweatpants in earthy tones of mud, clay, moss, and black. The monochrome head-to-toe look became a new signifier of dressing on the cutting edge. This was a whole new modern men's wardrobe to replace the old one.

The excitement surrounding Kanye and Yeezy floated outward, his star power proving bright enough to illuminate all the creative forces around him. By sheer proximity, some of his well-styled shadows—Virgil Abloh, Jerry Lorenzo, Matthew Williams, Heron Preston—were becoming next-wave fashion and social media stars in their own right. In the age of Instagram, no one was truly behind the scenes anymore. And a loyal digital following and celebrity association proved a formidable catalyst for a career as a fashion designer.

27.

The Plastisol Is Fading

Bobby Kim entered The Hundreds's headquarters and saw Tommy Hilfiger sitting in Ben Shenassafar's office. Just a few years earlier, Tommy had sold his behemoth of a namesake label for $3 billion to the same clothing conglomerate that owned Calvin Klein. Tommy's team had sent over some emails; the designer was interested in The Hundreds, and he wanted to tour their building. It was a seemingly odd pairing: Tommy, often described by press as "a bit of a square," and The Hundreds, a brand that referenced rappers and punk bands and the esoteric corners of culture like it was a sport. The whole headquarters tingled with excitement.

For the meeting, Ben and Bobby walked Tommy through the showroom and introduced him to some of the senior team. Tommy was focused and deliberate, soaking everything in. Ben and Bobby watched him as he moved around the showroom, thumbing through the latest samples that hung on the garment racks. Here was the American fashion establishment, showing interest in a brand that cut its teeth in graphic T-shirts and once sold their clothing out of a four-hundred-square-foot storefront located in an alley. Before he left, Tommy compared them to Supreme. It started to feel like this could *really* happen.

Negotiations progressed to preliminary due diligence. That was when Ben and Bobby took a magnifying glass to their slouching sales. The orders from Active and Zumiez had scaled back considerably; international sales had also shrunk and their own online shop had flatlined. They knew some areas of the business were sluggish but didn't really realize how much the brand had faltered until they were staring down the barrel of a spreadsheet. Six months later, Tommy's business partner Kenneth stared at Ben and Bobby with disappointment. The Hundreds had missed their sales projections by a mile. Tommy's team still sent an offer letter, but it wasn't what Ben or Bobby had hoped for.

"They put together one offer, and then that was the end of it for us," recalled Ben. "They wanted to pay half what we thought The Hundreds was worth." The two friends valued their brand based on what it had been a year or two ago, while Tommy Hilfiger valued them at their present state. The two parties politely went their separate ways.

But now, without Tommy or another outside deal to inject some much-needed capital into the brand, Ben and Bobby knew they had to take a long hard look at their business.

Just two years after The Hundreds hit an apex of nearly $22 million in annual sales, the number plummeted down to $10 million.

The aesthetic shift started when Kanye West gravitated toward gothic T-shirts and leather jogging pants in the early 2010s. Givenchy's $500 graphic T-shirts—with snarling Rottweilers and black-lettered fonts—became unmissable and sought-after. Suddenly, the colorful T-shirts from the likes of BAPE and Billionaire Boys Club or The Hundreds and Diamond looked passé. "All of a sudden, people didn't want loud colors. They wanted to go back to neutrals and dark colors," Bobby said. "They didn't want logos, because that didn't work well with traditional fashion. So all the logos went really small or disappeared completely." A new look had swept New York: zippered neoprene jackets and drop-crotch jersey pants paired with sleek, desaturated silk-screened T-shirts. The mode of dressing became coded as "street goth," unofficially fronted by the red-hot rap Harlem crew known as A$AP Mob, led by its charismatic front man A$AP Rocky. Alexander Wang, Rick Owners, and Yohji Yamamoto's Y-3 entered the hip-hop vernacular as Air Force 1s and Timberlands went from white and wheat to black. The aim was also to mix designer fashion pieces, such as velcro-strapped Maison Margiela sneakers or leather Hood By Air shorts, with the more downmarket T-shirts and baseball caps from Black Scale, Been Trill, and Vlone, a label founded by two A$AP Mob members.

Russ Karablin, a mainstay of the nineties New York scene who designed some of Supreme's earliest graphics, earned a hit of his own with his SSUR label: a flip of the Comme des Garçons logo that read COMME DES FUCK DOWN. (A$AP Rocky liked it so much he wore it in a music video.) Russ traced the lineage of the design back to the eighties: Dapper Dan's luxury knock-ups and Shawn Stüssy's riff on the Chanel logo. "It was a perfect example of street meeting high fashion," he said. "At one point we were talking to Comme des Garçons, to do an official sort of collabo. I presented her [Rei Kawakubo] with some ideas; she got a little nervous about it, because she was already not feeling the fact that people were appropriating her logo." Anti Social Social Club, a one-note label founded by Stüssy's social media manager, shot up in popularity when Kanye and Kim were photographed wearing the brand's caps and hoodies on numerous occasions. The buyers at boutiques and malls quickly picked up on the shift. "All of my salespeople and marketing people were like, *Where's our Hood By Air? Where's our Anti Social Social Club? When are we going to do something like that?*" recalled designer Jeff Ng of the New York brand Staple.

This sleekly grayscale look collided within another market trend. "There was this elevated idea coming along," recalled Bobby. "I really think it started with the denim thing." The streetwear boys had grown up; the graphic T-shirt and the fitted cap were replaced by selvage denim and heritage work boots (A.P.C. New Standards and Red Wing's Classic Moc, to be precise.) A new online subculture emerged: Hashtag Menswear (#menswear), led by street-style photos and essays on double–monk straps by bedroom bloggers. It bubbled up into the newly launched style website Four Pins, a sister website of *Complex* with internet-savvy prose that made caring about men's fashion seem less dandy. Street style made designer clothes look more wearable and, quite frankly, more masculine than they did on the runway. Suddenly, Rick Owens and Raf Simons entered the cultural vernacular the same way as Supreme and BAPE.

By 2015, these dual ideas of elevated and neutral colors had morphed into the *Yeezy look*. There was no need for logos or markers of any kind. Kanye's neutral-toned sweats, knits, boots, and outerwear became a new calling card for being in the fashionable know. "Kanye stopped wearing graphics," Bobby said. "Streetwear's core competency vanished overnight."

Ben and Bobby accepted The Hundreds's reality and sprang into action. It was pointless to fight it, although the growing pains of the last few years now stung with a sharper and more urgent jolt.

"We had employees, store managers steal from us. People that I never thought would take from us. Some of them got away with a lot of money," recalled Ben. They once discovered a scheme of theft in their warehouse: Employees were stealing merchandise to flip. Others nicked cash from the store register.

Ben and Bobby debated playing into the trends and demands of the market. The mall retailers and the brand's distribution partners asked for jogger pants, the slim, cinched-ankle sweatpants that had surged in popularity. "It was not authentic to us as a company and who we were and us as a brand in any way. And it was just something that we just didn't feel right doing," recalled Ben. "Looking back . . . *Was that the right decision?* I'm not sure. We could have made a lot of money selling jogger pants. But we just didn't feel in our gut that was the right decision for us." The same went for the brand's "Adam Bomb" character, a mascot that turned whatever garment it appeared on into a bestseller. Ben recalled a meeting with a European distributor who grew frustrated that they would not sell him more of the motif. *Yo, what are you doing? Just give me Adam Bomb everything. Why are we even playing games here?*

The Hundreds also dealt with what happens when your brand reaches a level of overexposure and your street credibility takes a hit. "I remember being in meetings as the store staff told Ben and Bobby, 'People hate the Adam Bomb. Nobody fucks with this thing anymore. Stop putting it on everything. This shit isn't cool anymore,'" recalled Jered "Red" Vargas, former manager of the Rosewood shop. "It becomes the trend for the fucking masses, and that's why the Zumiez of the world is like 'Give me more of that shit.' But by then, it's too late for everybody else. We're on to the next thing."

The Hundreds' boisterous presence—all of the online attention, their *The Hundreds Is Huge* tagline—ended up being sugar in the gas tank. "At that time when we were peaking, people thought we were at fifty to one hundred million dollars in sales because of the optics. We had just crazy optics. It hurt us," recalled Bobby. "That hurt us with customers because they were like, *Oh, you guys are mainstream.* It was so skewed and distorted. It fucked us in the end."

Instead, The Hundreds reined in its product design. Bobby no longer indulged every whim and fantasy. He strategized with Ben, their vice president Joey Gonzalez, and designer David Rivera to produce products that would be easier to sell to retailers and more palatable to a wider audience. Bobby introduced more sophisticated branding and pared-down graphics to meet the market where it stood. Then came the smaller stuff: no more flying first-class, reusable glass cups at the office instead of having to restock the red Solo cups weekly. Last came the toughest part, but the most inevitable: closing the stores and laying off employees.

These were stores that Ben and Bobby had spent months and months, hundreds of thousands of dollars, to build. Full of details and personal effects, physical gathering spaces for them and their friends, for the late-night parties and launch events, the smiles and cheap booze and loud music. The first two stores to close were New York and Santa Monica. They subleased the remaining five years they had left. After that, they shut down the San Francisco shop. Then came cuts to the office staff, reducing the team nearly by half.

"What happened during those years for us is we hit a ceiling with sales and then we had overhead. Our staffing, our rents, our lease. We were paying rent on four shops, two offices or three offices, depending on how you looked at it. Our warehouse. We owned a print shop. It was just insane," recalled Bobby. "We're hitting ceilings on sales and skate shops are dropping us. The aesthetic is changing. There was a confluence of reasons why we had to turn and the business changed."

Elsewhere in the industry, Greg Selkoe's once-unstoppable e-commerce giant Karmaloop was forced into a bankruptcy filing by a private investment firm. The company owed $116 million to creditors, a number caused by a maze of existing debt obligations, underperforming new business ventures, and declining sales revenue. Aaron Levant from the Agenda trade show guessed that from his conversations with brand owners, sales were down by more than 30 percent in 2015 from the year prior. Even Nick Tershay's Diamond Supply Co., which had seen growth year after year, felt the decline. "We were at $92 million and thought we were going to [break] a hundred next year," recalled Nick. "But we didn't . . . We leveled out and started going back down towards fifty." Competition in the space grew, too. The rise of a visual-centric social media platform like Instagram, coupled with e-commerce platforms like BigCartel and Shopify, made launching a brand easier than ever.

Ben and Bobby made an unusual but strong team built on a deep foundation of friendship. To the public, Bobby Hundreds was the creative one, the emotional artist, and Ben Hundreds was all business, cold and rational. That was partially true, but behind the scenes the two friends overlapped into each other's domains, helping lift each other up if the other was stuck. The biggest clash they ever had was over selling to the malls; Bobby left the meeting, got into his car, and drove off for the rest of the day.

"The thing that I'm maybe most proud of is the fact that Ben and I are still partners. We are in here every day," Bobby said. "Maybe the rarest thing of all is the fact that we still have this partnership. I can't think of any other streetwear brand that has that. I don't think that's existed. Shawn and Frank didn't stay together. I can't speak for some of the other brands, but can't think of a single brand where if there were partners, they stayed together."

The two cofounders sat ten feet from each other. Perhaps their differences were nowhere better personified than in their offices: Bobby's was overstuffed with art figurines, ceramics, toys, and skate decks, a fever dream of FAO Schwarz and Alleged Gallery. Ben's office looked more like a gentlemen's lounge, neatly decorated with a tufted leather couch, a bar cart, and mid-century chairs. One person said that Bobby's generosity and ability to hold a grudge came from the same well. He hired designers and illustrators he admired, often those whose phones had stopped ringing, to introduce their work to a new generation and to put some cash in their pockets. On the opposite end, if you ever wronged him, he would never forget it.

Both founders had started families and had young kids at home. Perhaps the two partners could have fought the change harder, but streetwear is a young man's game. The most significant difference between this moment in The Hundreds and the brand's previous challenges was that Ben and Bobby were no longer young men; they were both now husbands and fathers, with less time and energy than they had in their twenties.

There was some silver lining. Some clarity came. "Those are the years where I've made money, relatively, but I've also had the most difficult time reconciling my art with the business. It was the most fraught, in terms of people wanting things from me, not being able to discern who was my friend, who was an enemy," Bobby said. "Those were the worst years of my career. Just so, so complicated. Had nothing to do with art, had nothing to do with streetwear or the shit that we loved. It was just all about managing people and making money and negotiating."

In 2016, a luxury sportswear brand named Daniel Patrick took over The Hundreds's New York store space. The brand sold $500 jogger pants and plain hoodies for $250, tapping into the luxe-minimalist sportswear that shocked the industry. The walls were repainted white, like a slate wiped clean. It was as if The Hundreds New York never existed.

But the deep cuts that Ben and Bobby had made worked. With production downsized, stores shuttered, and employees let go, The Hundreds had stabilized. The business had readjusted to fit a diminished position in the contemporary market and was set up to continue and hopefully thrive again one day. As The Hundreds and its contemporaries scaled back, everyone wondered out loud, whispered at the trade shows and then drunkenly at dinners together: If their class of brands—the ones who made millions selling loud-print T-shirts in the malls—were the ones fading, then who was up next?

28.

A 700 Percent Markup

With his debut clothing project, Virgil Abloh managed to upset the status quo of streetwear and luxury fashion alike. After years of working in Kanye West's ultra-famous shadow, designing album covers and tour merchandise and everything in between, Virgil stepped out on his own with a new label, Pyrex Vision. The American designer, tall and friendly with a smooth head and trim beard, was thirty-two when he launched the brand. His clout already extended beyond that of a hotshot art director; he was a new-media figure and a cult celebrity with an influential Instagram account approaching seventy thousand followers. Virgil's feed was can't-miss content among a subsection of sartorially inclined men who idolized Kanye's personal style, Supreme Box Logos, and rare Nike sneakers.

Born in 1980 to Ghanian immigrant parents, Virgil grew up about a two-hour drive from Chicago in the Rockford suburbs. As a teenager, he became enamored with skateboarding and hip-hop, the specific cultural dichotomy of Ralph Lauren and Air Jordans. He sat with Martha Cooper's *Subway Art* book, emulating the "wild-style" lettering in his sketchbook alongside sketches of

Nike sneakers; at seventeen, he started DJing with his father's records. Virgil found the streetwear blogosphere and lurked on Samuel Spitzer's Splay forum, discovering the underground brands of downtown New York like Alife, SSUR, and aNYthing, who had cheekily branded their group as a collective called the "Retail Mafia." In college, he kept spinning records and skateboarding while pursuing a practical degree in structural engineering. He attended graduate school for architecture, started blogging for website The Brilliance!, and worked in a screen-printing shop that led to the gig with Kanye, then just a talented beat maker and upstart rapper with ambitions for hip-hop stardom to call his own.

By the time Virgil unveiled Pyrex Vision in December 2012, his list of design and fashion accolades had piled up. He had altered the contemporary aesthetic of hip-hop, orchestrating projects with George Condo and Riccardo Tisci; earned a Grammy nomination for his art direction; launched Chicago's trendsetting RSVP Gallery with fellow Kanye entourage member Don Crawley, aka Don C; and more recently had designed graphics for Shayne Oliver's New York fashion noisemaker Hood By Air.

The debut Pyrex Vision collection was concise and pointed. Virgil focused on streetwear staples like the T-shirt and the hoodie alongside hats and mesh shorts, and included a flannel as a sartorial outlier. The brand announced itself in tandem with a moody promotional video featuring A$AP Mob and friends. The guys took an aerosol can to a white wall while the song "Heart and Soul" by English post-punk band Joy Division played in the background. He titled the collection The Youth Will Always Win.

Virgil paired motifs and objects that didn't belong together, the way children sometimes play with toys, still full of untempered imagination. He printed Caravaggio paintings and blocky varsity fonts on the same garment. He had watched Supreme print George Condo's surrealist paintings on skate decks. Nothing was sacred. Acrylic, oil stick, and ground oil paint were no different to him than plastisol ink. The brand's name was a reference to Pyrex, the glassware product quickly adopted by crack dealers across the nation for its durability. The "23" printed on the back of the T-shirts, hoodies, and flannels referenced Michael Jordan's number for the Chicago Bulls. Each motif symbolized, as Virgil put it, "Pusha-T drug raps" and "Michael Jordan as God." The label's name directly referenced a lyric from the 2003 song "Dipset Anthem" from Harlem hip-hop group the Diplomats: *Back to the kitchen, that Pyrex vision.*

The Pyrex Vision T-shirts and hooded sweatshirts were printed on ready-made Champion blanks, Virgil's nod to American gym class, and sold for $100 and $275, respectively. (By comparison, Supreme charged $40 for a shirt and $168 for a hoodie.) The item that set social media and the fashion blogs on fire, though, was a flannel button-up, an average-looking plaid garment, with a bold screen-printed graphic on the back. It was priced at $550.

"This was sort of unheard of at the time," said Jian DeLeon, then a writer and editor at *Complex* who closely covered the launch. "That garments in this particular corner of the industry could demand such a high price . . . There was still this divide of what streetwear was and what streetwear should cost, what luxury is and what luxury should cost."

Virgil later said he took inspiration from a precise moment in New York culture. "At the time, my friends and I wanted to mix high fashion with street . . . a younger generation, the likes of A$AP Rocky and A$AP Yams, were mixing labels and brands and emotions to come up with a new aesthetic. I developed Pyrex

Vision out of that." No one else in hip-hop put it on quite like Rakim "Rocky" Mayers. The Harlem MC, who flowed in and out of the moment's monochromatic street goth look with ease, was quickly becoming rap's newest fashion prince. He evolved to be an intrepid and supremely fly dresser. Rocky paired $600 Hermès scarves with $28 Supreme Box Logo T-shirts, or wore $450 Hedi Slimane-era Saint Laurent skinny jeans with $12 HUF Plantlife socks. He anointed himself the "original Margiela madman." His "high-low" approach—more specifically, mixing streetwear with designer fashion—spread throughout most of contemporary menswear. VFILES, a fashion-focused social media site and SoHo storefront, turned lower Mercer Street into a micro-scene. The shop carried "the spirit of the old Patricia Field" and sold the latest wave of Been Trill, Hood By Air, and Pyrex Vision next to long-standing labels like Hysteric Glamour and Calvin Klein. Jian added, "The next generation of fashion heads were bubbling."

Digital sleuths connected some dots on Virgil's $550 flannels. The flannel was made by Ralph Lauren Rugby, and it appeared that Virgil had paid a clearance price of thirty-six dollars per garment. The product photography on the RSVP Gallery website revealed a clumsily executed Photoshop job; someone had attempted to remove the visible Ralph Lauren tag at the neck but left a trace. "It had been clone-stamped out, very sort of haphazardly," recalled Jian. Someone posted side-by-side screenshots of the flannel from Rugby.com next to the one from Pyrex Vision. Was it a Duchampian proclamation of art? Or was he just ripping off a bunch of hypebeasts?

In January 2013, Jian wrote the blog. One line in particular became intertwined with the designer's career for years to come: "It's highly possible Pyrex simply bought a bunch of Rugby flannels, slapped 'PYREX 23' on the back, and resold them for an astonishing markup of about 700%."

A year before Virgil launched Pyrex Vision, he printed and sold meretricious Been Trill T-shirts with Matthew Williams, Justin Saunders, and Heron Preston while all four were employed at Kanye's DONDA agency. Each had his own path into the Kanye West orbit. Matthew, a handsome man who grew up in Southern California, had designed a suit jacket for the rapper's performance at the Grammy Awards. Heron, born and raised in San Francisco, moved out east to attend Parsons, and eventually landed a marketing role in Nike's New York office. Preston first connected with Virgil online via Samuel Spitzer's Splay message board. Justin, a Canadian with a Jony Ive quality to him, ran a visual blog called JJJJound. Kanye sent Justin an email from Paris and swiftly hired him. The Been Trill brand was born from the group, which also included Florencia Galarza and the mysterious member YWP (rumored to be Kanye himself), performing DJ sets. "I think everybody on the internet thought we were taking Been Trill a lot more seriously than we actually were," Matthew later said. "Because of our social media presence, we can amplify a small, spontaneous idea so it seems much bigger than it actually is."

Been Trill had a connection with the mall retailer PacSun through Kanye and struck up a partnership deal in 2013. Soon, its T-shirts were widely available, and collaborations with brands like Diamond Supply Co. and The Hundreds followed. As PacSun tried to scale Been Trill, it became clear the guys had lost interest. "They were like, *Go ahead, do what you're going to do. Pay us royalties, but we're not going to wear it anymore. It's not us*," recalled one PacSun executive. The four stars of Been Trill moved on with individual projects: Heron founded a namesake brand out of New York; Matthew started a high-end label called Alyx with backing from Stüssy's longtime European distributor Luca Benini; Justin leveled up JJJJound from a blog to a freestanding creative studio; and Virgil was off chasing his own fashion dreams.

Pyrex Vision was short-lived. Virgil decommissioned the project when the parent company of the Pyrex trademark sent a cease and desist. This wasn't the nineties, when a small-time brand's use of a trademark flew under the radar; social media ramped everything up to warp speed. At a Givenchy fashion show, Virgil met Marcelo Burlon, a fixture of the late-nineties Milan nightlife scene and current influencer PR maven. On a Friday evening, Virgil told Marcelo he was looking for an investor and partner to produce his new fashion project. It moved fast; a meeting was set for that Monday with Virgil and his lawyers and Marcelo and his partner, Davide De Giglio.

When they met, Virgil was adamant about one thing. He told the room, This isn't a streetwear brand. This isn't a contemporary brand. This *is* designer.

He called it Off-White c/o Virgil Abloh. From the start, Virgil plugged his new label full of references and designed with a knowing sense of now. He built a sturdy visual language of identifiable motifs—bold Swiss typography, diagonal black-and-white stripes, and hovering quotation marks—that he paired with ironic expressions, creating a branded vernacular that recalled the conceptual word games of Lawrence Weiner or Jenny Holzer.

The name Off-White was meant to symbolize the gray space

between streetwear and luxury fashion. That meant graphic $210 T-shirts and hoodies for more than $500. Retailers in Paris and New York placed orders for the collection sight unseen due to the speed at which Pyrex Vision had sold out. In 2015, Virgil Abloh was the single American finalist for the LVMH Prize for Young Fashion Designers. He didn't win but described it as a pivotal moment for his career, because "it was streetwear that I was associated with at the time, and I think fashion hadn't decided whether streetwear was going to be a trend or something longer-lasting within it." Off-White was also where Virgil developed two other hallmarks: an urgent and unrelenting work ethic and a full-fisted embrace of social media.

He DJed upward of 250 dates a year, logging as many flights. His iPhone became his design studio, iMessage and WhatsApp his modes of communication. "The first thing that hit me working for Virgil is that ninety-to-ninety-five-hour weeks need to be normalized," recalled Samuel Ross, a British designer who worked at Off-White. "Virgil was just *designing, designing, designing*. We would go places, and Virgil would stay in the hotel and design," said Don C. Virgil once thanked Instagram for making it "possible for me to have a fashion brand without using the traditional system." It became a bit of a calling card, something the press would often fixate on, putting his digital social currency before his design acumen or work ethic. There was a change occurring; the way of running a fashion label was evolving. It needed to be quicker and more nimble. Virgil's grasp on social media was ahead of the curve; he'd post about Off-White fashion shows, inviting the "youth" to attend.

In 2017, Virgil became unmissable. W magazine dubbed him the "King of Social Media Superinfluencers" as he neared one million followers on Instagram. Off-White continued to skyrocket in visibility and influence as Virgil kept producing collections that were full of nice-looking womenswear and graphic-driven menswear that continued to sell through. The clothes showed up on everyone from supermodels and pop stars to the newest generation of street-fashion kids hanging out on stoops in deep SoHo, an area and scene that became jokingly known as the Clout Corridor. The label was stocked in 220 stores, including bona fides like Selfridges, Barneys New York, and Colette.

Virgil established himself as a master of the collaboration, working on clothes and accessories with Levi's, Chrome Hearts, Warby Parker, and Jimmy Choo. He released an entire collection with the furniture giant IKEA and elevated the Timberland boot, long an icon of hip-hop and New York City streetwear, to a luxury item that retailed for nearly $1,000. *WWD* reported that he was among candidates to fill Riccardo Tisci's post at Givenchy. His rise was not without discourse: Critics pointed to an oversaturation of simplistic commercial projects and that his Off-White collections trod well-worn ground; the revered Belgian designer Raf Simons dismissed his work as unoriginal. In response, Virgil titled an Off-White collection NOTHING NEW. But it was Virgil's first collaboration with Nike, released in September of that year, that sent his name into a new level of fame.

"We just knew we wanted to work with him, because he was emerging to be one of the strongest voices of his generation, really," recalled Marc "Fraser" Cooke, the Nike veteran who orchestrated the project and an original member of the International Stüssy Tribe. "We gave him some products and had given some other people some products, but it just really clicked with [Virgil]. We decided pretty soon that we would just give him all of them and let him do all of them, because it was just working so well."

Virgil made the prototypes by cutting up Nike sneakers with an

X-Acto knife and scribbling on them with Expo and Sharpie markers, mixing Martin Margiela's deconstructionism with the nonchalance of a graffiti writer. He added graphic print, a glossy plastic tag, and other high-design details. It came together at an Ablohian speed of ten shoes in ten months, a record pace for the sneaker giant. Nike applied Virgil's concept to ten iconic silhouettes, including the beloved Air Jordan 1 and Air Force 1, with prices ranging from $130 to $250. On Virgil's Instagram, fans watched him take a paint pen to "personal" pairs for his famous friends: Beyoncé, Drake, Naomi Campbell, A$AP Rocky, John Mayer. He even did a pair for His Airness, Michael Jordan himself.

The sneakers proved near impossible to get, with retail selling out in minutes and many boutiques implementing ticket lottery systems. Pairs sold for thousands of dollars on the secondary market. Shortly after the launch, the collection had its own dedicated Wikipedia page, where intrepid sneakerheads wrote academic paragraphs about Virgil's creative process and the project's significance. *Footwear News* awarded Virgil with the coveted Shoe of the Year Award for the Air Jordan 1, beating out Kanye's newest Yeezy sneaker and the unmissable Balenciaga Triple S, designed by Demna Gvasalia. Hypebeast later called it "objectively one of the most hyped sneaker collaborations ever."

The same year, Virgil gave two high-profile lectures at Harvard and Columbia—titled "Insert Complicated Title Here" and "Everything in Quotes," respectively—with both events posted to YouTube. His Harvard lecture was compiled into a booklet and published, billed as containing the "cheat codes" to his creativity. In the years after Jian DeLeon's essay—*No One Pyrex Should Have All Those Rugby Flannels*—Virgil did what Virgil did. He turned Jian's words into an object of design by commissioning street artist

Jim Joe to produce a minimalist rug that featured the full "700% markup" quote. Virgil offered up the one-off product without irony, or perhaps only with irony; he placed it in Off-White's Parisian showroom to greet buyers and other guests. The designer never hid his ace.

That year seemed unbeatable, but in March 2018, Virgil was announced as the new artistic director of menswear at Louis Vuitton, becoming the first African American artistic director at the influential European luxury house. Since Pyrex Vision five years prior, Virgil had built a personal brand and an aesthetic foundation so strong and sought-after that billionaire LVMH head Bernard Arnault wanted it for his portfolio's prize jewel. Two months after the announcement, Virgil attended the Met Gala, walking the famous steps next to supermodel and Instagram savant Kendall Jenner, who was dressed in custom Off-White. He debuted a cream tuxedo designed in the world-famous Louis Vuitton atelier and paired it with Air Jordan sneakers, FOR RED CARPET ONLY penned on the sole.

Virgil's debut collection was scheduled to go down the runway later that summer, and the entire fashion industry would be watching. So would the streetwear kids.

29.

Luxury Becomes Essential

In the early 2010s, the parking lot at PacSun's corporate office looked different. The drab three-story building was located in the northeast industrial section of Anaheim, California, among various wholesalers, plastic manufacturers, and construction companies. On any given day, a murdered-out Lamborghini Aventador sat in the parking lot, one of the most flamboyantly designed supercars that money could buy. There was at least one shiny G-Wagon, the six-figure luxury SUV preferred by rich rappers and well-heeled art dealers. The cars stood out among the rows of Toyotas and Hondas. These luxury vehicles belonged to PacSun's newest employees: Kanye West and his DONDA team, which often included some combination of Virgil Abloh, Matthew Williams, Heron Preston, Justin Saunders, and Jerry Lorenzo.

The project that brought the team into the building was adapting tour merchandise from Kanye's blistering sixth album, *Yeezus*, to sell at the hundreds of PacSun stores located in malls across the country. It was not going well. The only products the group mind agreed on were graphic T-shirts from the hand of contemporary artist Wes Lang, a heavily tattooed, motorcycle-riding painter who was largely an outsider within the art world. The menacing designs looked like something Metallica would have sold on its late-eighties tours: skeletal demons with scythes, skulls in war bonnets, and a grim reaper clutching roses. PacSun held out hopes for a larger collection from Kanye, but it felt unlikely. The rapper could be a whirlwind with his creative process, an uncompromising and indecisive bull in this corporate china shop. PacSun fronted money for sample after sample of jeans and plain T-shirts, but nothing ever seemed to please Kanye. He had a habit of only speaking to the designers in the room, rarely talking to or making eye contact with project managers or the sales and marketing executives.

To help lead the Kanye initiative, PacSun looped in Alfred Chang, Bobby Goodwin, Mike Viscusi, and Gary Wan, four longtime staffers within the company who had risen through the ranks to influential positions in design and merchandise management. They had noticed that young men were dressing like Kanye, Virgil, and Jerry: fewer graphics, more fashion-forward silhouettes. PacSun knew Kanye held that corner of the market in his hand like a marble. But this project was starting to feel like a money pit.

Out of everyone in the room, it was Jerry who stood out the most to the PacSun team. "He was Kanye's second eye. He was really quiet, very chill, and you could get answers from him," recalled the retailer's in-house designer Gary. Jerry was often outfitted in super-distressed skinny jeans and a slouchy oversized T-shirt from his own Fear of God label. He was handsome, with a muscular build, hyper-groomed beard, and closely cropped haircut. Grayscale tattoos covered his right arm like smoke.

Dude, this guy Jerry is cool, Bryan whispered to Alfred as they walked in the hallway after one of their Kanye meetings. Maybe we should do something with him.

They all knew about Jerry's label. The first Fear of God collection featured a dozen designs, including short-sleeve side-zip hoodies and T-shirts long enough to elicit a double take. Fear of God was sold at RSVP Gallery in Chicago, Union in Los Angeles, and Barneys New York. It showed up in Kanye's *GQ* cover shoot.

Jerry was friendly with a group of streetwear designers from the Fairfax scene: the guys from Diamond, Black Scale, and The Hundreds. At the time, he was working as a nightlife promoter. This was the boom years for the graphic T-shirt guys, the plastisol gold rush. at the mall. He clocked some of these guys spending five grand a night "when I'm busting my butt to leave with a grand."

"Everyone coming to the party spending money had their own brand. Narcissistically, I was like, *Man, if I can dress better than these cats, I should be able to figure this out, too,*" Jerry later said. "So I came downtown and figured out how to make a pattern, how to make a T-shirt, how to make a long tee. . . . I had this conviction that my point of view was missing from the marketplace."

PacSun watched the sales volume of graphic T-shirts shrink and had started to pay more attention to how the demographic was dressing on social media. They seemed to care less about big graphics and more about the trendy silhouette: baggy up top, skinny on the bottom. If they could take that look—simple, easy-wearing but fashion-adjacent—and hit the mall-friendly price points, they might have a winner. They approached Jerry with the broad idea of a partnership; he was open but firm about several points.

I don't want to water down Fear of God, he told them. But I also don't want to have an unconnected diffusion line. Let me do a version of this for the mall kid.

At the time, Gary Wan was the lead designer for Reign + Storm, one of PacSun's in-house labels that focused on elevated essentials: longline T-shirts with scooped necks, hooded sweatshirts with side-seam slits, crewnecks with zippered pockets. There was not a printed graphic in sight. "All of a sudden everyone was trending to be a minimalist," recalled Gary. "We knew Jerry was blowing up in Los Angeles. Luckily we got into business with him, and then we bagged Reign and Storm, because obviously Jerry's cachet was bigger."

Jerry built Fear of God by running around the Fashion District in downtown Los Angeles, going from factory to factory to cobble together his small-scale label. PacSun was just going to hand him the keys to a vast network of overseas manufacturers. Whatever he dreamed of, they could produce. "I would go to his house, and we would design in his garage," Gary said. "I was traveling to Tokyo and Korea at the time for sampling."

Jerry was also ready to break away from his famous boss. He felt burned out and slightly stifled; the hip-hop star's point of view had the ability to swallow the room and any other designer in it. Plus, Jerry felt outside of the true inner circle, once saying that he was brought into the DONDA team, "not necessarily as a friend, but more so an employee of Kanye." On top of access to PacSun's manufacturing, the deal came from a sweetened pot. Jerry would get a percentage of sales, and quite enticingly, it also came with a minimum guarantee—to the tune of seven figures. Even if the experiment didn't work and fizzled away, he'd at least have an extra million, likely more, in his bank account.

Instead of Fear of God, they agreed to call it F.O.G. The first collection contained an assortment of athletic fleece staples, flannels, and military-inspired pieces like jackets and vests. The lookbook's styling was aggressively layered: One look featured a pair of gray sweat shorts worn over beige thermal leggings; a gray longline T-shirt peeked out of a gray hooded sweatshirt, worn underneath a shiny black bomber jacket. All of the silhouettes were either boxy or elongated, or a bit of both.

When F.O.G. debuted in December 2015, PacSun put it in sixty of their top-tier stores and sold it on their website. They wanted to keep the first release small, to make it feel special. It was madness. Hundreds of people lined up outside of the stores, and small skirmishes ensued when the metal gates were lifted. Customers grabbed what they could get their hands on. "It was like tackle football," recalled one PacSun employee. The collection launched with inventory the retailer had projected would last six weeks on the shelves—it was all gone in six minutes. "It was for sure meant to sell out, but it wasn't meant to sell out in minutes," said Bobby Goodwin, then one of the retailer's leading merchandise managers.

PacSun was ready to kick things into high gear, sprint into a follow-up collection and print thousands and thousands more. But their new star designer did not see the need to rush. That was how he worked. So when Bobby and his team asked for more, they were surprised when Jerry told them he didn't want to chase that same product and needed time to think about what the next collection would be.

This idea of elevated essentials played into a larger reinvention of the male wardrobe that continued throughout the 2010s. It was not limited to the graphic-tee-and-sneaker-wearing set. Much of American menswear became less about classic tailoring and more about the ultra-modern sweatsuit. T-shirts became extra long with scooped hems; hoodies and crewneck sweatshirts were made from supersoft fleece and featured vented zippers; sweatpants were slim-fit and came with cinched ankles, designed to accent the sneakers, which held an increasingly important role in the modern man's closet. Guys on forums were talking about French terry cotton and Riri zippers. All these clothes often featured a limited palette of black, white, and shades of gray.

A New York label, Public School, run by Dao-Yi Chow and Maxwell Osborne, stormed the elite fashion scene and was an early crossover hit. The two city kids (and former Sean John designers) created a monochromatic uniform—an overcoat, sweatpants, and a T-shirt, often worn with a cap and Nikes—that became the era's defining silhouette. Ronnie Fieg, a former salesman and buyer at footwear chain David Z., launched Kith, both a store and brand that released monthly, line-generating sneaker collaborations. He started to design in-house athleisure to complement his sought-after kicks. The look was not limited to the East Coast; in California, a designer named John Elliott was selling millions of dollars of elite athleisure. It didn't take long before he was hailed as "the man who made sweatpants high fashion" as the likes of Kanye, Pusha T, and LeBron James became loyal customers. His namesake label eventually opened a store on Melrose Avenue in the former site of a Helmut Lang boutique, an apt metaphor in the form of retail real estate: Designer minimalism in the 1990s was $200 denim, and in the 2010s, it was $200 hoodies and $250 sweatpants.

Not long after that first F.O.G. collection, Jerry had more eyes on him than ever before. In 2016, his former boss Kanye wore $900 Fear of God jeans (with a couture Balmain trucker jacket) to the

Met Gala. Justin Bieber, a longtime wearer of Jerry's work, hired him to design an entire merchandise collection for the pop star's latest world tour. The grunge-inspired merch proved so popular that pop-up shops in New York City, Miami, and Toronto brought out lines of shoppers that spanned city blocks. The year delivered a palpable boost to Jerry's career and Fear of God's profile. Yet, Jerry put his head down and stayed the course.

Jerry and PacSun rebranded F.O.G. to F.O.G. Essentials in 2017; the following year, it became Fear of God ESSENTIALS. The less distance between this line and the Fear of God name, the better, Jerry felt. He embraced it the same as his more expensive mainline label. "I have more family members that shop at PacSun than at Barneys, to be frank," Jerry told *New York* magazine. Historically, diffusion lines were welcomed by the masses but largely looked down upon by elitists. Jerry never seemed to care much for what the luxury establishment thought about his work. Even for his high-end Fear of God mainline, he bucked the traditional structures and calendars of the larger fashion system, releasing collections when he saw fit.

ESSENTIALS stopped being exclusive to PacSun and expanded into other retailers like Nordstrom, Selfridges, and SSENSE. There was now enough stock to meet the demand; the brand released products in batches called "deliveries." Jerry's core vision focused on taking American staples like plain sportswear and denim and giving them a higher-fashion sensibility. His points of reference remained vintage finds at flea markets while he labored over materials, the fit, and the proportions of everything he produced. Little changes can make a garment stand out in the marketplace, and that uniqueness turned out to be a massive driver of success for the project.

"Because the T-shirt was heavier, the perceived value to the customer is, *Oh wow, this feels so different. You can't really find this anywhere else*," explained Gary, who worked as the ESSENTIALS head designer for three years before becoming design director for all of PacSun. It certainly didn't hurt that Kanye and Yeezy sold similar-looking silhouettes, further boosting the desirability of the oversized look. A Yeezy tee sold for under $200, and a Yeezy hoodie was around $350; PacSun sold Jerry's shirts for $40 and hoodies for $90. (A mainline Fear of God hoodie cost around $700.)

Season by season, Jerry's collections expanded and his ambition grew wider. Jerry landed a Nike collection—a new sneaker silhouette dubbed the Air Fear of God 1—and ESSENTIALS branched out to offer "Core" and "Fashion" sub-labels. The clothes remained true to the original vision: minimal and tonal branding, approachable silhouettes and price points. The mainline Fear of God collections continued to impress, even if they came came at an irregular cadence.

"I remember when Jerry announced that he was doing a collaboration with PacSun. It was pretty early on in developing his own collection and his own point of view. And I think there was a little part of him that felt like he had just sold to the devil . . . and then it just took off. To his credit, he really leaned into it and saw that this could be a way for him," said one esteemed fashion editor. "He's a very thoughtful designer."

Jerry built a cozy fashion empire on barely-there branding, sportwear staples, and zealous attention to detail. With Fear of God, Jerry created a new type of twenty-first-century American luxury, defined by $1,400 coaches jackets and $800 heavyweight hoodies. And with ESSENTIALS, he brought the same look to the mall, where it turned out that hordes of shoppers happily paid $40 for a shirt that looked like a $200 one.

30.

Supreme's Invisible Man

It was an early summer evening in 2018 at the Brooklyn Museum, an impressive beaux arts building that commanded an entire city block. Some of the most reputable names in fashion were inside, from Ralph Lauren and Tommy Hilfiger to Anna Wintour and Michael Kors. The Council of Fashion Designers of America's CFDA Awards, known as the Oscars of fashion, always brought a high-wattage crowd, and this night was no exception. This was not the CFDA Awards of ten years ago; the organization was trying its best to move with the times. Kim Kardashian West was summoned to receive the ceremony's inaugural Influencer Award. When it came time for the Menswear Designer of the Year award, comedian Trevor Noah took the stage to present. He mused on the decline of suiting: "We now live in a world where billionaires sport hoodies and Fortune 500 executives dress like rap stars." Then he opened the envelope and announced the winner: "Supreme."

The fashion-world audience clapped and orchestral music played as a fit man in his mid-fifties with a close crop of thinning gray hair, outfitted in a straightforward charcoal-gray suit and black dress shoes, walked to the podium. It was Supreme's founder,

James Jebbia. "Thank you," James said into the microphone. "I've never considered Supreme a fashion company or myself a designer. But I appreciate the recognition for what we do." Less than thirty seconds after walking onto the stage, he disappeared back into the dimly lit audience. It was a rare and quick glimpse of the man who avoided the industry spotlight. That night, James and Supreme beat out Raf Simons for Calvin Klein, Virgil Abloh for Off-White, Thom Browne, and Tom Ford to nab menswear's top prize at fashion's highest table. The *New York Times* chief fashion critic Vanessa Friedman called it "the biggest upset of the night." She continued, "The definition of a designer is changing, and Mr. Jebbia's win is the most potent expression of that shift."

It was a big moment for a man who felt long misunderstood and cast aside by the fashion establishment, a sentiment he had referenced multiple times in rare interviews over the decades. He often aspired for Supreme to be held in the category of Helmut Lang, A.P.C., or agnès b.—all driving forces of chic minimalism with what James labeled as "a consistent, cool look." But because of Supreme's origins and loudest demographics—a small skateboard shop and hypebeasts—they were almost never held in regard with those brands, even if Supreme had established a track record of delivering well-appointed basics season after season (alongside some more outré fashions and accessories). "A lot of people dismiss what we do. . . . They don't understand that just because skating is the culture we're working in, it doesn't mean that we can't make good things," James once told Glenn O'Brien in an interview.

Just five months before the CFDA Awards, Supreme had made its Paris Fashion Week debut, thanks to an official collaboration with Louis Vuitton. The project was orchestrated by British designer Kim Jones, the luxury brand's menswear artistic director. As a fashion student, Kim worked in the stockroom at Gimme 5, the distribution company founded by original International Stüssy Tribe member Michael Kopelman. The massive joint collection included skateboards, skateboard trunks, duffels, bandannas, denim, baseball jerseys, Box Logo T-shirts, hoodies, leather jackets, bottle openers, gloves, and phone cases. Louis Vuitton's iconic monogram print was reworked in Supreme's Kruger-inspired red-and-white. It was released at exclusive pop-up shops and Louis Vuitton stores around the globe; the fashion-industry trade publication *WWD* reported that the collaboration generated 100 million euro in a few months. Supreme x Louis Vuitton became an inescapable moment within the fashion and streetwear blogosphere; Highsnobiety founder David Fischer summarized the moment by saying, "It was like a bomb had hit."

"I think it opened us up to a different demographic, more of the Vuitton luxury customer," said Angelo Baque, Supreme's former brand director, who continued to work with James after he left to start his own creative agency, Baque Creative, and brand, Awake New York.

Then even bigger news broke: Supreme sold an approximately 50 percent stake in the brand to private equity giant the Carlyle Group for $500 million. The deal valued the brand at $1 billion. (The year prior, the brand generated around $200 million in annual sales.) In the years of Supreme's skyrocketing profile, James became increasingly elusive. Supreme—with the Louis Vuitton collaboration, the CFDA award, the $1 billion deal—became the capstone that signaled the official end of streetwear as an outsider to the fashion industry. The brand opened its second NYC store in Williamsburg, Brooklyn, bringing the company to a total of eleven stores worldwide. And the bigger Supreme got, the quieter did its owner.

James rarely granted interviews and pointed inward questions back toward the brand. He preferred it to speak for itself. A code of silence extended to those in his inner circle. His reputation for mystery weaved itself into the lore of the brand. It was not always like this. He showed up in a 1991 issue of *New York* dressed in a black Stüssy T-shirt and black jeans, with a buzzed head of dark hair, smiling next to then girlfriend and business partner Mary Ann Fusco in Union. Quotes from James appeared frequently in the *New York Times* from the early nineties through the mid-2000s, every year or so; the articles covered topics ranging from modern furniture to vintage skate T-shirts to the rebirth of the New York sneakerhead. Then he withdrew from the press. The timing, from the late aughts and onward, aligned with the rise of the internet and Supreme's growth.

Most of the photos of James on the internet are from Supreme's store openings or rogue cell-phone photos taken by fans: walking in SoHo beside Angelo Baque or sitting front row at Paris Fashion Week next to Virgil Abloh. He was known to politely decline selfies if asked. Fans traded stories of run-ins on forums. One spotted James shopping inside Dover Street Market; others mentioned seeing him on opening night for a David Sims exhibition, and once at a Depeche Mode concert. In the photos, James was usually dressed in what became his signature look: a plain white or black T-shirt, jeans, a denim jacket, and Clarks Wallabees. "He always had a fresh haircut and was well-dressed," recalled an early shop employee. "I remember he always had thousands of dollars in his pocket, and he'd break off cash from it." Even as his bank account grew, he still dressed with the inconspicuous precision of a man who knew not to signal too much. (Although it was later reported that he paid all cash for a $16.5 million "modernist hilltop castle" in Beverly Hills designed by renowned architect John Lautner.)

One of the first things James's friends and colleagues mentioned about him was his determination and ambition, as restless as a shark. Hung above his desk was a massive photograph of James Brown—the Hardest-Working Man in Show Business—leaning on a Rolls-Royce. "Part of his success is his work ethic," recalled Brendon Babenzien, James's first hire on the design team who spent fourteen years as Supreme's design director before leaving in 2015. "He works really hard. He doesn't front. He's constantly working." Another former designer added, "He definitely set high standards. There's no question about that. . . . There's no denying that James was always demanding."

The second thing some said was that he held excited passion for art, an avid collector himself. He took immense pride in Supreme's work with artists and the realization, as he once said, "that the art could reach regular people through apparel." There were stories of bravado and a short temper, what American writer Hilton Als might have described as boss-man theater. "There was always that kind of underlying pressure when you were working for him," Supreme's former production manager Augie Galan told *Complex*. He remembered a particularly sour interaction with James that took place on his second day. "He completely flipped on me, on a dime . . . and just started cursing me out. He laid into me for ten minutes, telling me that I should never tell him everything's good and that I should always be fucking working my ass off." James was also frequently described by former Supreme employees and people who have known him since the nineties as loyal, kind, and generous. A few mentioned his intensity has mellowed slightly with age, but not his sharply tongued humor. One wished he wouldn't work so hard.

The early Supreme employees mostly spoke with a deep reverence for the shop. "Supreme was family" was a repeated refrain. Almost all were shocked that the small skateboarding shop on Lafayette Street became a global fashion powerhouse and that they were still talking about it thirty years later. But the way they spoke about Supreme felt different than when they talked about James. With Supreme, the love was conceptual: the feeling of belonging to something bigger than yourself. When they spoke of James, it felt deeply personal. They seemed honored he had trusted these rowdy young skate kids with his shop. It was that respect that formed a two-way street, explaining why the front of the shop was always spotless, even if the back room was a madhouse. The twenties are a formative time in a person's life, and it is clear everyone was figuring themselves out with the backdrop of working and hanging out at this skate shop.

One former employee compared James to Andy Warhol and mega art dealer Larry Gagosian, adding, "James *is* pop art." Sam Spitzer, the creative technologist who helped James launch Supreme's e-commerce operation, said that after years of working closely with him, he started to understand how James perceived the consumer. "It's very special, it's not what people expect, and it's extremely unique to him. His point of view on commerce and culture and the way in which they can coexist. That is something that I think people don't understand about him, unfortunately, because they just don't. But that's something that he does better than anyone else that I've met in the world."

The mystery didn't always serve the brand. Especially in an era where blogs, forums, and social media gave streetwear devotees real-time access to figures like Virgil Abloh of Off-White, Bobby Kim of The Hundreds, and Nick Tershay of Diamond Supply Co. "There was a weird time I remember, even we were like, *Supreme is not that cool*. The young kids were just like, *Nah, fuck Supreme. Supreme is wack. Nobody even knows who owns it . . . and all the guys in there are rude*," recalled one brand owner. "And you'd even see a line of people that would be—not dissing anybody—but it would be the least cool people that you would see waiting in line."

Outside of Supreme's inner circle, James maintained a mysterious presence. "It's not like you're seeing James at the trade shows, or at the store, or in the street. It's like you had to know him to go visit him," recalled Greg Rivera, a cofounder of Mishka NYC. "I think there was that mystery, too, with Supreme. That even in the culture, you weren't really sure of the inner workings and how things got done." Over the years, James occasionally emailed Ben and Bobby from The Hundreds. Mostly just short notes, about what they were doing well, what they were doing wrong, "just bits of advice that really meant a lot to me as a kid who was trying to build a business," said Bobby.

In 2016, Tyrant Books published *Supremacist*, a very good novel by David Shapiro about a male protagonist named David who visits all the Supreme stores in the world. Over the years, Shapiro had also written about the resale aftermarket surrounding Supreme for the *New Yorker* and the brand's lawsuit against Leah McSweeney and Married to the Mob for *New York*. In promotional interviews, Shapiro played coy about what was autobiographical and what was fictionalized, but did cop to visiting "every Supreme store in the world at the time" and ruminated about being an "unwelcome customer." Still, he came across as a writer with a deep reverence for his subject. In an interview, Shapiro mentioned an email he once received from James: *Do you write negative bitchy one-sided articles about everything, or is it just Supreme?*

Brendon Babenzien, the long-serving Supreme design director, summed up his former boss: "At the end of the day, there are a million stories about James. He's got good and bad like everybody else does. But the one thing you cannot take away from James is he's the fucking heavyweight champ of retail."

News of Supreme's sale to the Carlyle Group ricocheted around the worlds of both fashion and business. There wasn't a true comparable moment in industry history. Quicksilver and Ecko had hit $1 billion in global revenue but both brands owned a maze of subbrands (Roxy, Hawk Clothing, Fidra and Zoo York, G-Unit, Avirex, respectively) and sold in thousands of retail stores. Supreme was just Supreme and its eleven stores. Neither Quicksilver or Ecko had the credibility or cachet of the New York "skate" label. Or, quite frankly, Supreme's acumen for fashion. James was in a starkly different situation, a new balancing act of culture and corporate.

There were layers of controversy when the deal was announced. First was the idea that Supreme had "sold out" and worries that the brand would be driven into the ground. The second, a little more nuanced, was about Supreme's investor, the Carlyle Group, a multinational private equity firm that held nearly $174 billion in assets. Since its formation in 1987, the company had profited from war, with numerous investments in the military-industrial complex and held stakes in companies that manufactured combat vehicles, artillery, missile launchers, and tear gas. It seemed at odds with a countercultural clothing label that one printed FUCK BUSH stickers in 2004.

These moves—the industry-shattering Louis Vuitton collaboration, the $1 billion evaluation—revealed a fashion world that was starving for something new. Supreme's creative output had not drastically changed. Just as the brand had done for the past twenty-five years, it still trafficked in the clothes of the New York skater: T-shirts, hoodies, jackets, and accessories with subversive undertones. This was the old world courting the new. It was Louis Vuitton, with its centuries-old monogram and VIP shopping suites, that needed the myth and mania of Supreme. It was one of the world's largest private equity firms that understood where there was smoke, there was fire. Where there was hype, there was money.

31.

Changing the Game

Inside a massive and darkened tent in the first arrondissement of Paris, a gritty corner of downtown New York started to materialize out of nothing but an idea. Raw materials turned into graffiti-covered stoops and gray concrete sidewalks and storefront façades. It was January 2019, in the lead-up to Fashion Week, and everything was happening under the watchful eye of the men's artistic director of Louis Vuitton, Virgil Abloh. The American designer, perhaps global fashion's hottest entity, walked around the tent as the chatter of hammers and hand drills filled the space. Virgil was dressed sleekly, a black hoodie worn under a black puffer jacket with black jeans and black Nike sneakers. He gave gentle commands to the staff, flashing his friendly gap-toothed smile and pointing at where to place the street signs, occasionally pulling out his trusty iPhone to show a reference. Every detail mattered, down to the city's iconic green trash can, a beloved impromptu obstacle of New York City skateboarders.

The previous year, Virgil's first Louis Vuitton collection had ushered in a new era for the French luxury house; the brand had newfound energy on social media and a fresh layer of red-hot celebrity, ranging from A-list reality stars and fashion-forward rappers to the next generation of Instagram savants. Virgil's designs stayed close to the world he built at Off-White, but he delivered grand menswear nonetheless: tailoring with playful proportions, vibrant hybrid garments like vests and harnesses, and sporty sneakers. He remixed the house's famed bags and accessories—the true moneymakers—to look both more utilitarian and more modern by adding ceramic chains and bold colors, like something out of the Whitney. At that first runway show, after taking the customary designer's bow, Virgil walked over to his friend and former boss Kanye West, and the two men embraced in an eruption of tears, accomplishment, and joy. Virgil's debut collection reportedly sold out faster than the Supreme collaboration, and LVMH's end-of-year report pointed to the brand's "exceptional performance." The former streetwear kid turned high-fashion designer came correct, and he was getting ready to do it all again.

With just over twenty-four hours until his latest show, Virgil floated through his Paris studio into his office, the walls lined with built-in shelves full of books, vinyl records, and family photos. He walked over to the set of turntables in the corner and began to play around, manipulating the beat to his liking. It looked like it calmed his nerves. This was only his second runway show for the esteemed luxury house, and it was a deeply personal one. There was pressure; the fashion establishment still looked at Virgil like he had something to prove.

The next day, as the crowd filtered into the dimly lit tent, they walked into a version of the Lower East Side—transported to a fictional version of Rivington Street, a nod to the neighborhood that birthed Alife Rivington Club, the pioneering sneaker boutique that opened in 2001. (The set's light-up sidewalk paid homage to

Michael Jackson's "Billie Jean" video.) Virgil had visited Alife's Orchard Street storefront when he was in his twenties, and it was this other Eden of everything he loved: graffiti and art and sneakers and T-shirts. "The day I stepped across on Rivington Street and Orchard Street the world shifted," Virgil wrote on his Instagram. He later called Alife a "real window into this culture."

The music started, and the models walked down the runway, zigzagging back and forth in the chaotic rhythm of a crowded city street. Elegant layers of monochromatic gray suiting, purple satin shirts, and artfully baggy pants. The cropped bomber jackets and vests so puffy the North Face Nuptse looks like a deflated Mylar balloon by comparison. The house's bags electrified into vibrant accessories in shades from ultramarine blue to highlighter yellow. About four minutes into the show, a man dressed in all black with white gloves, a red flannel cinched around his waist, sauntered to the stage. He stopped in front of a metal gate, shook the canister he held, and started spraying meandering lines on the gate. It was the graffiti artist Futura, now in his sixties and with the same youthful verve as when he was a teenage wagon writer.

Futura, who officially dropped the "2000" from his moniker at the turn of the millennium, had steadily risen since his art and design career was reignited by collaborations with BAPE and Supreme in the nineties and aughts. It brought a fresh new audience to his work. He went on to work with Levi's, Converse, Uniqlo, BMW, and the New York Mets and established himself as a regular presence on the pages of Hypebeast and Highsnobiety. A few of Futura's canvases from the eighties would become cherished, with one selling for $302,400, an explosion from the apex of $6,000 when he showed alongside Basquiat and Haring. Virgil championed Futura's work, enlisting him to do a capsule collection for

Off-White. Futura's first New York solo exhibition in over thirty years was scheduled to open later in the year, and in Futura's Rizzoli monograph, Virgil wrote that his work "distinctly shaped the visual world I grew up in."

"I'm enormously grateful for what Virgil did for me . . . he made it clear to me that I was someone that was enormously influential in his life," recalled Futura. "Seeing me as someone important in this whole bigger picture, I could never see myself that way, but I was so grateful."

Virgil's support of the New York downtown scene that inspired him was one of the foundations of his creativity. Just as Fab Five Freddy had cross-pollinated the worlds of uptown graffiti and downtown art in the eighties, Virgil did something similar for "streetwear" and high fashion. If you looked closer at Louis Vuitton's faux metal gate, you'd spot ROB 1970—a tag from Alife co-founder Rob Cristofaro. "Virgil has had the ability to take the same path that Alife did but inject it with celebrity. I love where he has taken us," Rob said. Virgil took to Instagram earlier in his career, shouting out Sam Spitzer's Splay.com forum, A-Ron's A New York Thing, KAWS, Supreme, Erik Brunetti's FUCT, Nom de Guerre, Russ Karablin's SSUR, Alife. Virgil collected both Birkin bags and vintage streetwear as if they held the same value to him; he told the *New Yorker* his collection boasted nearly five thousand T-shirts. He once called Supreme the "Margiela of its time." Angelo Baque recalled the sales spike after Virgil wore one of his brand's hats for a magazine photo shoot. "Virgil started wearing the Awake hat, and shit just cracked off for me. . . . It was just like, *Oh, this is dope. Here we go. It's 2003 all over again.*"

Unlike creative people who feared the blank page, Virgil seemed to embrace it. He could be precious about certain details and then move at the speed of light with others. Virgil worked at a hyperkinetic pace, as if this could all go away tomorrow. He was perhaps luxury fashion's first post-studio designer. "I have teams in Milan, Italy, London, and America, so as long as I have a fully charged iPhone, I feel like I can change the world," he once quipped. He continued to push his Off-White label to new heights. He dressed generational heartthrob Timothée Chalamet for the Golden Globes in a shimmering Louis Vuitton harness, the night's most talked-about look. Virgil designed more and more Nikes, from Dunk Lows to Air Maxes and Zoom Vapors. He remixed the midcentury armchairs by Jean Prouvé and designed a full collection for IKEA, including chairs, rugs, tables, clocks, and more. He collaborated on glass water bottles with Evian and luxury suitcases with Rimowa. He lived what he sold. Virgil promoted it all on his personal Instagram page, the grid a convergence of art and commerce neatly symbolizing the state of creativity under late capitalism. Yet, every project felt done in earnest, to his highest form of expression.

As one of Virgil's collaborators put it, "After years of working for Kanye and Kanye's slow perfectionist way of creating, once Virgil got a chance to do it on his own, it was like letting a greyhound out of the cage."

In 2019, Virgil Abloh, Heron Preston, and Matthew M. Williams were all on the official calendar of Paris Fashion Week. The arrival of the former Been Trill boys was a signal that fashion's home court had entered a new era. Matthew had kept busy with Alyx, now known as 1017 ALYX 9SM, developing a cult following for his slick layers of sleek black leather and nylon ballistic "chest rig" bags. (Williams would be named the artistic director of the French luxury house Givenchy the following year.) Heron's namesake label offered workwear staples like chore coats and ripstop pants with his signature orange tab. There was as much condescending chatter about their young and digitally savvy fans as the clothes; *Vogue* noted that "99 percent" of Heron's fanbase "lives and breathes" on social media, while the *New York Times* called Matthew "a hero to the hypebeasts who haunt forums and fashion resale sites." The revolution was not limited to the designers; an audience of fashion kids educated by platforms like Tumblr and Instagram, reading blogs like Hypebeast and Highsnobiety, had developed a keener eye for fashion. They were as interested in Martin Margiela as Supreme. It was now all at their fingertips. Social media accounts posted archival photos, and contemporary runway shows were immediately uploaded to YouTube. In a review of Virgil's latest Louis Vuitton show, long-running *New York Times* style reporter and cultural critic Guy Trebay said, "Fashion can't afford anymore to be precious or exclusionary. Instagram unlatched the gate to a once largely closed realm and the world rushed in."

The appointment of an American "streetwear designer" to such a prominent position at an old-world luxury house was met with contention and bickering from the start. Virgil's ascent and subsequent success within the fashion world, and now at Louis Vuitton, opened an industrywide discussion about a shift in fashion, an era defined by conceptualism and internet savvy over craft or classically trained skill. In part, the artist was judged by their audience: Virgil's archetypal follower was frequently knocked as a hypebeast, a streetwear-obsessed millennial male with money to spend—the slangy slight now commonplace in fashion-speak. In the eyes of the industry, the hypebeast was not a particularly sophisticated or desirable consumer, but they took his money just the same.

Virgil's younger audience and social media prowess led to plenty of hand-wringing over the death of the fashion designer and the rise of the multitasking, side-project hustling, Instagram-fluent, viral designing and branding virtuoso known as the creative director. In the eyes of the establishment, these two things were not equal. This was not a new critique; in 2000, Patrizio Bertelli, the Italian billionaire businessman and husband to Miuccia Prada, had proclaimed in the press, "Tom Ford is not a real designer. He's just good at marketing."

The old-guard establishment had been arguing about who qualifies as a *real* designer for decades, wary of those outside the European system of studying fashion at one of the prestigious fashion colleges in London, Paris, Rome, or Antwerp and then rising through the ranks from within one of the luxury houses. But CEO and chairman of LVMH Bernard Arnault took calculated risks, understanding that an avant-garde designer and his cachet could be bought; a young Marc Jacobs had held a reputation as a bad-boy designer—a "gay, sneaker-wearing, night-clubbing, temperamental New Yorker," as journalist Zoë Heller described him at the time—when the French fashion mogul hired him for Louis Vuitton back in 1997. The American designer had a successful sixteen-year run at the house.

Virgil brought an unconventional mode of working wherever he went, what he called the *3 percent rule*. He outlined this philosophy in his Harvard lecture and countless interviews: "introducing something new by changing a process, product, or perspective by only three percent." He often likened his creative approach to that of a beatmaker building a song from a sample. To him, his references were the same as Kanye remixing the chorus of a 1969 Hungarian rock song into the outro for "New Slaves." Not everyone saw it that way. On multiple occasions, Virgil was the subject of headlines and social media callouts with accusations of "stealing," from smaller labels to more well-known names. Sometimes it was specific graphics; other times, it skewed more conceptual and veered into instances of parallel thinking, like the similar use of a color, fabric, or motif.

For an Off-White collection, Virgil remixed a 1966 graphic by Italian architect A. G. Fronzoni, which landed him a scolding from Diet Prada, a widely followed fashion watchdog Instagram account; this reading pointed to a fundamental misunderstanding of genre. Virgil's deep-cut reference and graphic flip harkened back to the early days of streetwear—a tradition carried from generation to generation, as seen in T-shirts from FUCT, SSUR, Not From Concentrate, Supreme, Alife, The Hundreds, and countless others. In his IKEA collaboration, Virgil included a near-exact design of a famous midcentury Paul McCobb chair, only adding a door stopper at the leg; the precise math is hard to decipher, but perhaps he counted the glossy addition as his requisite 3 percent. As Doreen St. Félix wrote in her magazine profile of Virgil, "His work is often referential, and some critics have accused him of 'stealing' designs. But [he] sees it as rooted in the ethos of streetwear."

The Belgian fashion designer Walter Van Beirendonck, a member of the acclaimed Antwerp Six, accused Virgil of producing Louis Vuitton designs with a motif copied from one of his collections: stuffed figurines sewn onto the garments. Walter went one step further in a pointed interview: "It's very clear that Virgil Abloh is not a designer. He has no language of his own, no vision." Virgil pushed back, citing an older Louis Vuitton menswear show as the source, which he outlined in the show notes, and released a statement labeling Walter's claims as "a hate-filled attempt to discredit my work," stopping short of calling a spade a spade. Three years prior, a gentler critique came from the venerable Raf Simons, who called Virgil unoriginal in an interview with *GQ Style*. (Virgil had openly shown his reverence for Raf's work, even speaking to *Vogue* about his eighty-piece collection of the designer's clothes.) Virgil later reflected on Raf's put-down in an interview with *SNEEZE Magazine*: "With the flick of his wrist, he contextualized me as not being a designer. But he called my European counterparts, Gosha [Rubchinskiy] and Demna, designers by name. It struck me how he expressed that bias so nonchalantly."

Some of the prejudice Virgil experienced—the insinuation that his work and journey were less valuable than his peers'—called back to the othering of the "urban" label ascribed to Black designers and brand operators of the nineties and early aughts. "I don't come from where I'm supposed to come from," Virgil told *W*. "So I have to prove that this is design, that this is art, that this is valid." Streetwear lacked the prerequisites of fashion—as with any true and worthwhile subculture, sincerity and participation were the only credentials required for entry.

One of Virgil's favorite talking points in interviews was to link streetwear with the prominent French painter and conceptualist Marcel Duchamp, who died in 1968. "It's this idea of the readymade. I'm talking Lower East Side, New York. It's like hip-hop. It's sampling." Duchamp became known for his "readymades," which he explained as "everyday objects raised to the dignity of a work of art by the artist's act of choice." (In 1917, the Frenchman famously signed a porcelain urinal and presented it as a sculpture.) Calvin

Tomkins, the legendary arts writer and author of the definitive Duchamp biography, wrote, "The readymades defied any attempt to define art, and this turned out to be what contemporary artists needed most—complete freedom to *make it new*. Art became much easier for mediocre artists and a lot harder for good ones."

In June 2019, when Virgil was thirty-eight years old, the Museum of Contemporary Art in Chicago opened a mid-career retrospective of his work, complete with a pop-up store. Eight racks displayed clothes Virgil had designed for Louis Vuitton and Off-White. There was a five-foot plexiglass re-creation of Kanye West's *Yeezus* album cover. Dozens of Nike sneakers sat on raised stages. A full-scale replica of the half-pipe from Pharrell's "Frontin'" music video. Elsewhere were DJ turntables, a cease-and-desist letter, and a playful pile of his furniture. Within the exhibition was a piece by the artist and filmmaker Arthur Jafa: a screenshot of Virgil FaceTiming his friend the rapper Theophilus London. In a darkened room, the 2012 Pyrex Vision video played on a loop as a rug printed with the "700% markup" quote from the blog post heard around the streetwear world lay in the middle of the floor. It wasn't all warm welcomes from the art world; the esteemed contemporary art magazine *Frieze* ran the headline "Don't Buy What Virgil Abloh Is Selling."

The criticism from any angle did little to diminish Virgil's star power and demand as he closed out 2019. His fans tracked all of his work with the same intensity: fashion, sneakers, mixtapes, furniture, and collaborations. (His Instagram account now neared four million followers.) The sprawling exhibition proved to be one of the highest-grossing shows in the museum's history; it later traveled to other museums in Atlanta, Boston, and Brooklyn. The French e-tailer Farfetch acquired the New Guards Group—licensee of

Off-White, Heron Preston's eponymous label, and several other contemporary brands—for $675 million. LVMH reported record results, hitting over $59 billion in annual revenue, and credited "exceptional growth at Louis Vuitton" and Virgil personally for bringing "new life" to the brand in an end-of-year report.

"For so long I didn't see artists or designers that looked like me in spheres of high art or high fashion, so I believed I couldn't do that," Virgil said that year. "But now, in this moment, in a way, I've become part of the establishment."

32.

The Hype Machine

The line at Supreme's New York store became almost as famous as the brand itself. It often ran down Lafayette Street, around the corner and down another block, and sometimes around yet another corner. Hundreds of young men would be lined up the night before the Thursday morning drop; the diehards would arrive sometimes as early as Monday. There were security guards and often a self-regulated system that included a list of names and what position in line you were. It still became a spectacle. *Complex* sent a host and video team to the weekly drops, interviewing the people waiting in line. In broad daylight, resellers pulled up in cars, handing out cash to people in line to purchase on their behalf.

The prize possession was the Supreme logo. They called it the *bogo*—Supreme-speak for the Box Logo, the iconic red box printed or embroidered at the center chest on T-shirts and sweatshirts alike. The late writer Gary Warnett, of the blog *GWARIZM*, an authoritative and dedicated voice of the nascent streetwear industry since the nineties, once wrote, "That logo future-proofed the brand and acted as a visual manifesto of sorts with regards to Supreme's appropriately downtown merger of skate and art." The bogo was timeless, and it drew the biggest crowds, the longest lines, and commanded the highest resale value. Without the Box Logo, Supreme was a gun without bullets.

Reselling had long been a nuisance and an accepted part of the limited-edition sneakers and T-shirts. Ever since Japanese shoppers took to Supreme in the late nineties, filling their duffel bags with T-shirts to resell back in Tokyo, the practice burrowed itself within the ecosystem like a tick and never left. The earlier rise of eBay and PayPal bolstered the practice. You no longer had to meet in person and exchange cash in hand—everything was done over the internet. Social media accelerated the practice to new heights.

"It created a whole secondary economy where young kids can make money. . . . That's what really, at first, ballooned," recalled Supreme's former design director Brendon Babenzien. "The volume we saw had more to do with kids reselling than anything else."

A tipping point in fervor for Supreme came from a collaboration with Nike in 2014, an opulent riff on the Foamposite One, a jolie laide basketball sneaker that debuted in the late nineties, priced at $250. The word was the sneakers could fetch upward of $1,000 if you resold them online. Hundreds of people flooded Lafayette Street, blocking traffic, rushing the store and being generally rowdy. "I'm not doing this for the sneakers, this is for the money. I could care less about the sneakers," a twenty-four-year-old named Carmelo told a local news outlet. The NYPD shut down the release, with reports of mace and batons being used to disperse the crowd. Supreme announced that Thursday's in-store launch had been canceled, and the Foamposite sneakers would only be sold via the website. On the morning of the online release, the shoes sold out in under a minute.

Fashion's embrace of Supreme's "drop model," where an entire seasonal collection is pieced out over weeks and sold in more limited quantities, played in harmony with the resale model. Luxury houses introduced quick-strike product drops and limited-edition capsules with increasing frequency. In 2019, Hypebeast teamed up with PricewaterhouseCoopers's in-house consulting firm to publish the joint Streetwear Impact Report, which highlighted how the fashion subculture had been overtaken by big business. "Exclusivity and desirability are conferred by scarcity and insider knowledge rather than high prices. In short, streetwear has redefined how 'cool' is made profitable," stated the report. Supreme, Nike, and Off-White were dubbed the top three streetwear brands of the moment. That same year, The RealReal, the world's largest marketplace for authenticated luxury resale, reported searches for "streetwear" at an all-time high, with a 281 percent increase from the year prior. Resellers found an immovable spot in the new global fashion system.

There was a primal and humanistic layer to this level of materialism. The scarcity principle, a proven psychological concept, simply states that scarcity confers value on objects. If what we desire appears to be in limited supply, the perception of its value increases significantly. This thinking caught on within consumerism in the late eighties due in part to the bestselling book *Influence: The Psychology of Persuasion*, by behavioral scientist and marketing professor Robert Cialdini. Resellers simply tapped into the scarcity created by streetwear's mode of operating and exploited simple psychology to turn a profit.

Nike wanted in on the hype. In 2015, the company launched the SNKRS app, which reworked the mechanics of the sneaker drop. The interface played off the look of Instagram and other social apps, a feed-based design that featured product. Instead of leveraging existing product photography, the team shot what they described as "sneaker porn" to populate the app, looking to "to level up how we romanticize sneakers." Dennis Todisco, who previously worked for Diamond Supply Co. and Karmaloop, was brought in by Nike for his insider expertise on fashion, streetwear, and sneakers. "They were looking for somebody who kind of sat in that intersection of digital marketing and living within that space," he recalled. When a user successfully purchased a pair, they received a "You Got 'Em!" screen. The act of buying sneakers had been fully gamified. There were clear winners and losers.

By 2019, SNKRS was on pace to generate more than $750 million in annual sales. That was just a fraction of the sneaker behemoth's $39.1 billion in revenue, but deliberately so. As the company's chief financial officer said on an investor call that year, "We still supply a very small percent of the demand that we're seeing."

Buying Supreme or rare Nikes online became harder by the season. An onslaught of "shopping bots"—automation software—were used to speed through checkout. Often coded and then sold by computer savvy teenagers, the bots connected directly to Supreme's servers, bypassing the front end of the website entirely. These rogue developers spent hours studying and disassembling Supreme's source code like it was a Swiss clock. Payment and shipping information was prefilled, outpacing those navigating the online shop who have to go through the checkout process manually. The milliseconds it saved were the difference between scoring a Supreme item that Thursday or not. On a Thursday drop in

December that year, the Supreme Box Logo sweatshirt sold on the website received 9.8 million page views and 1.9 billion purchase requests. Sam Spitzer, the man who launched Supreme's e-commerce business, worked with his team to keep the bot makers on their toes, playing a programmer's game of cat-and-mouse. They constantly changed variables within the checkout sequence, adding a captcha or obfuscating products with numeric sequences.

Aftermarket streetwear became a big business. Venture capitalists poured a collective $800 million into leading online marketplaces and media platforms, expanding the category twenty-one times faster than regular retail since 2016. These investments went to peer-to-peer marketplaces that sold hard-to-find menswear, and to platforms that acted as middlemen between buyers and sellers while vigorously verifying the authenticity and condition of each product. Each company had its niche and differing business model, but they all aimed to dethrone eBay, the original secondhand online superstore, by appealing to a younger and more culture-oriented audience.

The breakout star was StockX, which started as a sneaker resale marketplace and then expanded to include streetwear staples and art-adjacent collectibles. Matt Powell, a well-known sneaker industry aficionado and analyst, said at the time, "The internet and eBay made reselling into a cottage industry. Platforms like StockX made it into a business." In 2019, the company achieved rarefied unicorn status, Silicon Valley parlance for a startup valued at more than a billion dollars, and Google became one of its most prominent investors. The next year, StockX reported that it saw over $1 billion in transactions on its website. As with contemporary art, all of a sudden the focus was more on the potential value of the sneakers and clothes than on the actual sneakers and clothes themselves.

It echoed something the famed art dealer Mary Boone once said: "There are more people collecting for the wrong reasons, basically as the latest get-rich-quick scheme. They buy art like lottery tickets."

Between the bots, the apps, and the resale platforms, buying and reselling streetwear and sneakers now emerged as a potential full-time job. Sneakerheads signed up for lotteries at boutiques or set alarms for exact release times. There was a real-time price tracker on StockX monitoring a growing resale network that extended beyond eBay to include platforms like Grailed and GOAT, which acquired the sneaker retailer Flight Club. Resellers populated social networks with photos—Instagram grids full of Yeezy sneakers, Supreme T-shirts, Balenciaga hoodies, Chrome Hearts denim—and short clips promoting their personalities. Consignment and reseller stores started to pop up in malls and shopping centers across the country. It became nearly impossible to buy high-ticket styles from Supreme without the aid of a shopping bot.

Despite all of this, the brand's most loyal fans remained undeterred. An often-overlooked feature of the Supreme line was the camaraderie. You'd spot friends and strangers alike waiting together and joking around, vibrating with excitement like they were waiting in line for a concert. While a large swath of the label's audience bought to flip and turn a profit, many still bought and revered Supreme like it was art. A handful of Instagram accounts and websites meticulously cataloged Supreme seasons, like art-punk archivists cataloging Raymond Pettibon's flyers for Black Flag in the eighties. The two most prominent were SLN, or Supreme Leaks News (with 2.1 million followers), and Supreme Community (800,000 followers), both of which archived the brand's seasons and even tracked sell-out times. They also would leak what products would be released on upcoming Thursdays—called drop lists in Supreme-speak. The account administrators made connections with store employees who leaked the photos the night before. Sometimes money was exchanged for the intel.

There were also more niche concerns: Supreme Copies was an Instagram dedicated to unearthing the brand's far-flung design references, created by an eighteen-year-old high-schooler from Oregon. He traced the source inspirations for a pair of sunglasses from 2019 to a nineties Arnette design worn by Ad-Rock from the Beastie Boys; a "666" patch donned by the late Notorious B.I.G.; a pair of panther-printed jeans inspired by Santa Monica Airlines; or gradient track pants that referenced an old FUBU design.

Then there were the super-collectors. Two Supreme collectors, Ryan Fuller and Yukio Takahashi, teamed up with an art gallery in Los Angeles to display their collections. "We met through Supreme," said Ryan. "The community of Supreme collectors is kind of a tight-knit community." He amassed a trove of 248 Supreme skateboard decks that spanned over twenty years. Yukio's assemblage of over 1,300 objects focused on Supreme accessories. Sotheby's sold Ryan's collection for $800,000 (the initial estimate was $1.2 million) to a Chinese collector who also owned works by Picasso and Monet. The following year, Vancouver fashion student James Bogart—who had spent eight years assembling a "complete archive" of 252 Supreme Box Logo T-shirts—offered the set to Christie's for sale; it was expected to fetch $2 million. To collectors of all stripes, Supreme remained sacred and special, even as the aftermarket price on a $30 bogo T-shirt rose to over $1,000.

The momentum around Supreme surged, even if it was indeed bolstered by the new industry of reselling that had popped up beside it. In November 2020, it was reported that VF Corporation—

the American apparel and footwear conglomerate that owned Vans, Timberland, The North Face, and others—purchased Supreme for approximately $2.1 billion. To borrow from an internet meme: the Carlyle Group became the world's most successful Supreme reseller, landing approximately a 2x return on their $500 million investment less than three years earlier.

33.
Armed with a Mind

Brendon Babenzien had opened his own store in Nolita, a small downtown neighborhood that bordered SoHo, less than seven blocks from the Supreme office where he spent much of his twenties and thirties. This marked the second coming of Noah, the menswear label he first launched and then shuttered in the early aughts. The eight-hundred-square-foot space was a cozy shop decorated with vintage rugs and an oxblood red Chesterfield sofa. The clothes—preppy and classic with delightfully offbeat details—hung on brass-and-leather racks suspended from the ceiling. Graphic T-shirts were folded neatly on built-in wooden shelves. There was no massive line outside, no wall of skateboard decks, and the shop employees did not shoot daggers if you dared to touch one of the T-shirts.

When Brendon first left Supreme to launch Noah in 2002, the brand never rose above a small-scale operation, with sales never exceeding $50,000 a year. (He returned to Supreme four years later.) This time around, Brendon brought in his wife, Estelle Bailey-Babenzien, a British Ghanaian interior designer who had graduated from Central Saint Martins. The two raised funding to build the store, hire staff, and purchase inventory, and opened Noah's doors on Mulberry Street in late 2015. A year or so prior, Brendon walked into James Jebbia's office and told him he was leaving Supreme. The company was getting too big; he didn't like working somewhere that promoted what he considered irresponsible consumerism. "Brendon was disillusioned by the hype culture of Supreme," Estelle said.

"The allure of being a rich man for me was not strong enough," Brendon recalled. "You can have tremendous financial success that way, but my belief is when you get that big, it's much harder to maintain a true sense of your brand. It just turns into a totally different thing. I'm not sure I would ever . . . I don't know what I would do, because there's a point where it gets beyond your control."

The core idea of Noah was to build a business to prove that you could be successful and still act responsibly. Brendon had become fed up with the larger system at play. "I wanted to make clothes with better materials that I thought would be longer-lasting." He used to be able to get so much made in New York City for Supreme in the nineties, trekking around the Garment District and Brooklyn in one of the company SUVs. Now almost everything had moved overseas. More than 60 percent of fabric fibers are now synthetic, which Noah largely avoided even though it was more expensive to do so. "It makes all the difference in a garment. It basically determines how long a garment will last. A ripped seam can be resewn, but if a cheap fabric tears or wears through, it is a bit more difficult to repair properly," Brendon said. Noah manufactured in countries with stronger environmental and human rights regulations, like the United States, Italy, Portugal, Canada, and Japan. The brand used high-quality materials: Shetland wool imported from Scotland, Japanese selvedge denim, organic cotton from Spain. This meant higher prices: a T-shirt sold for $52, chinos for $258, a sport coat for $998.

Noah's relaunch came at what felt like a flash point in the fashion industry. Fast fashion, globalization, and technology had combined to create a greater level of consumption than ever before. Burberry revealed it burned $37 million of unsold product to protect "brand value," which spurred global backlash; the fast-fashion industry—a growing segment led by Zara and H&M—produced an estimated ninety-two million tons of textile waste. As journalist Dana Thomas encapsulated in her 2019 book *Fashionopolis: The Price of Fast Fashion and the Future of Clothes*, "fashion has been a dirty, unscrupulous business that has exploited humans and Earth alike to harvest bountiful profits." Since the eighties, propelled by the rise of fast fashion, the industry grew from a $500 billion trade to "a $2.4 trillion-a-year global behemoth." *Sustainability* became a hollow buzzword. While many brands participated in "greenwashing," or making misleading statements about their environmental impact, Noah ran in the opposite direction. On the brand's website, an eye-catching graphic stated, WE ARE NOT A SUSTAINABLE BRAND. All of fashion was talking about how to run a more conscientious fashion brand, a mindset Brendon wrestled with for years. In interviews with fashion magazines and national newspapers, Brendon was direct about the fact that he wanted his customers to buy less and to buy better. His focus was less on the singularity of sustainability and more on running a clothing company with "responsible business practices."

Noah swiftly found a loyal audience. The clothes united fashion editors, grown-up skaters, reformed hypebeasts, and menswear aficionados under one roof. Brendon admitted that the attention on the label's relaunch was more intense than he had imagined. The résumé notch at Supreme meant feverish press coverage and a preconceived narrative impressed on his new brand. The brand held a tight network of retailers, including fashion-oriented ones—Dover Street Market, Saks Fifth Avenue, SSENSE, Mr Porter—but also sold to skate shops like Black Sheep in North Carolina and Premier in Michigan. Noah opened two stores in Japan, which remained a crucial market to win over. (It was not with Ken Omura, the man who brought Supreme to Japan in the nineties; "James would never have allowed that," Brendon said.) Noah rose from a cult menswear label to a beacon of how American men now looked to dress. It grew to a staff of nearly fifty employees while the Mulberry Street flagship generated up to $300,000 in monthly sales.

The aesthetic tastes of a generation were shifting once again, from a graphics-heavy and sometimes juvenile style toward something more sophisticated. Some labeled the shift as "post-streetwear" or "the prep revival." Of brands like Noah and another rising label called Aimé Leon Dore, *GQ*'s Sam Schube wrote, "They provide thoughtful, legible clothing to men who've outgrown either hyped-up streetwear or limited basics." It looked a lot like the City Boy style coined by *Popeye* magazine: a mix of certain streetwear, classic American workwear, and preppy staples. Even Tyler, the Creator, who rose to fame in a Supreme cap, T-shirt, and cut-off shorts, now dressed like he'd stepped off a page of *Take Ivy*, the seminal photography book that documented the fashions of Ivy League students from the 1960s.

Then one day in 2020, Brendon got a call from his attorney, who had an unexpected question. Would he be interested in leading the menswear division at J.Crew?

One block away from Noah on Mulberry Street was another store that sat in reflection of the times: the nostalgia-heavy and sharply streetwise Aimé Leon Dore. Founded in 2014 by Theodore "Teddy" Santis, the New York label was a fever dream of Ralph Lauren and Supreme, a blend of classic American menswear and the grittier New York nineties. The brand's printed T-shirts sold for $85, caps for $65. There were also sport coats for $800 and trousers for $350. The clothes were not necessarily groundbreaking, but Teddy and his team had some of the best styling and marketing photography in the game. Overcoats with hoodies, cable-knit sweaters with sweatpants, and scarves paired with baseball hats, all part of the high-low balance that made the brand feel fresh: a step up from streetwear, but not as fussy as classic menswear.

The early years of the brand were a learning curve. "I didn't know how to make clothes; I wasn't classically trained," Teddy said. "It was a lot of just trial-and-error, just falling on my face a bunch until I figured it out." But by 2016, the label had found its stride. Teddy ran successful pop-up shops in downtown Manhattan and landed glowing write-ups in *GQ*, and later, in *Vogue*. Within another couple of years, Aimé Leon Dore managed to emerge as a generational force, appealing to a broad swath of streetwear devotees, menswear loyalists, and sneakerheads alike. The brand was also a social media powerhouse, swiftly building a devout contingent of over one million followers on Instagram and earning a loyal audience on TikTok.

Aimé Leon Dore—known simply as ALD among the label's acolytes—followed the Supreme model to a near T: collaborations with the right brands, splashy campaign imagery, releasing a slow trickle of product week by week throughout the course of a season. After a stint with retailer partners, the brand eschewed the wholesale model. By 2019, it had opened a permanent flagship on Mulberry Street featuring an installation of deflated basketballs by artist Tyrrell Winston. An early pop-up shop doubled as a gallery show, with over a dozen photographs hung in white frames, artifacts of Teddy's life growing up in Queens: Timberland boots, Air Force 1 sneakers, Krylon spray paint cans, a trio of Phillies Blunt boxes, a stack of cassette tapes from Nas and Mobb Deep. He launched the label within a highly specific universe.

"With us, you have this component where maybe a kid will come in and buy a white tee with a Phillies Blunt image, but then you have a guy who is a bit older who is buying a $1,000 coat," Teddy later said. "Nom de Guerre was one of the biggest inspirations behind my brand. They made it okay to go and buy a pair of Dunks, to wear them with a pair of trousers, a knit, and a wool zip-up.... There was also Supreme, who birthed our whole streetwear culture. They've done a ton for New York."

It only took one meeting and two phone calls for Brendon to land the top menswear post at J.Crew. When his lawyer first called him about the opportunity, Brendon didn't think much of it. He told himself he had no shot and assumed he'd never hear about it again. The company was probably talking to a dozen other industry insiders who probably had deeper experience at legacy institutions like Ralph Lauren or Gap. But when his name came across the desk of Libby Wadle, the chief executive officer at J.Crew Group, she recognized it.

That's the Supreme guy, right? she thought.

Brendon did not play it coy in his interview; he had been wearing the brand since 1984.

Look, I don't want to be rude or come off as this obnoxious guy, he told her. But I'm the right person for this job.

Libby was impressed by his conviction.

"When you do what I do, and you grew up in America, you look at brands that were once the pinnacle of American style that are no longer, and you literally cannot stop yourself from making the plan in your head for what you would do if you got the call," Brendon said. "I was fully ready."

It was a peculiar time to join the long-standing American retail chain. In May 2020, the company filed for Chapter 11 bankruptcy after years of slumping sales. By August, it had officially exited bankruptcy, thanks to an infusion of capital from investment firms. "We need to disrupt the business," Libby told the *Wall Street Journal* at the time. Brendon's appointment was announced in May 2021. J.Crew's hiring of Brendon made national newspapers and fashion magazines alike. It was more press than J.Crew had received in years, not since the days of high-profile designers like Jenna Lyons and Frank Muytjens, back when the brand's Ludlow Suit reigned supreme in the world of hashtag menswear. Everyone was asking the same questions: "Can Hypebeast Magic Revive J.Crew?" (*New York Times*); "Can J.Crew's CEO Get Men Excited About Khakis?" (*Wall Street Journal*); "Can Brendon Babenzien Make J.Crew Cool Again?" (*GQ*).

The answer appeared to be a resounding yes.

Brendon's first collections earned quick sell-throughs and praise from both the press and customers. J.Crew held an industry cachet it hadn't seen in years. Two standout products—the wide-fit "giant" chinos and a slouchy $700 suit—became beloved by the menswear set. Brendon was pleased, and there was a sense of a purpose he got from working with J.Crew that was different from Supreme or even Noah. It was not lost on him that he'd been given a chance to lead the menswear program at a company he wore as a teenager on Long Island.

"Everything I do refers back to my youth in a way," he said.

Brendon wanted Noah and J.Crew to change behavior at a consumer level. Buying smarter and buying better. He knew there were limitations to what was possible at J.Crew, but the size of the platform was worth the concessions. For Noah, he was in no rush to scale the company. He estimated the brand's annual sales to be around $10 million, a size he was more than happy with. "It's more about spreading ideas and culture," he explained, nodding to the delicate balance of art and commerce. "I've been dealing with that my whole life, and I am walking this really fine line between, how do we build a business that is a viable business, supports my family, supports the people that work in the organization, but also doesn't bastardize the things we love?"

Even if the ethos and aesthetic of Noah were different than Supreme's, it was clear that Brendon's time there had stuck with him and informed how he worked. "I think what James believed, and I think I probably got some of this from him, was like, you just can't really stop. It takes work to continue to be good," he said. At Noah, Brendon orchestrated collaborations with bands like the Cure and New Order and artist estates like Tom Wesselmann and Barney Bubbles. The label used a project with Timex to raise awareness about pollution in waterways and ghost nets, and released more traditional collaborations with brands like Barbour, Puma, and Adidas. He introduced "Not Dead Yet," a program where shoppers could trade in unwanted Noah gear for cash; the brand either repaired and resold, donated, or upcycled the materials into new clothes.

"I never quite fit in, no matter where I go or how old I am. When you spend most of your life being the underdog and the outcast, it is hard to shake that feeling. Even at my age, I feel like the outcast, right?" Brendon, now in his fifties, said. He had aged well and had held fast to his dedication to independence and youth. "I still don't fit in, even with our business. People are still like, *What the fuck is Noah? I don't understand*. Quite frankly, it used to bother me. But now, I think of it as weirdly my skill. That's how it's supposed to be."

That misalignment, the thing Brendon wrestled with for his whole life, had, in some strange way, worked in his favor. He had a brand to call his own, one he was deeply passionate about, and a brass-ring job at an institution of classic American style. Perhaps being out of step had paid off in the long run.

34.

Virgil Was Here

The workshop that made Louis Vuitton's footwear was a horizontal building of concrete and steel with a sprawling central courtyard. It looked like a giant shoebox of brutalist design. Over 250 artisans crafted the luxurious shoes—glossy pumps with chic block heels and classic penny loafers made from calf leather—primarily by hand. It was located in Fiesso d'Artico, a sleepy Italian village outside of Venice that had been making shoes since the thirteenth century, when the region's artisans established a school devoted to the craft. In the summer of 2021, they were doing something that had never been done before. The Italian shoemakers were making the Air Force 1, one of Nike's most beloved sneakers and an eternal icon of New York street style.

It marked the first time in the sneaker's forty-year history that the model was produced outside of a Nike factory, another meaningful project Virgil Abloh brought to Louis Vuitton. To him, the Air Force 1 was infinite. "It's completely not a shoe. It's an art object. . . . It distills everything I'm saying into an object," Virgil said. "The Air Force 1 is a basketball shoe, but through hip-hop culture, it has energized a representative sculpture. It means a lot to very specific people."

Debuting in 1982, the Air Force 1 (or AF-1) was the first Nike basketball shoe to feature the company's groundbreaking "Air" technology. Two years later, the sneaker was set to be decommissioned until a few Baltimore sneaker stores stepped in. It was a bestseller within the city limits, with the beloved nickname "Airs." One local buyer flew to Nike's Portland headquarters, persuading the company to keep selling the style to the city's stores. Nike agreed. It was enough to keep the Air Force 1 from an early grave, and by the mid-nineties, Nike had given the AF-1 a national rerelease, and the sneaker never left the shelves.

The sneaker held omnipresent status within hip-hop hubs nationwide, especially in New York, where idolized rappers like Jay-Z and Fabolous championed the style. In the city, the sneaker earned the name "Uptowns," because they were ubiquitous in Harlem, and New Yorkers took the subway line to upper Manhattan to get 'em. "People want to analyze it to death, but it's really just that it looks great on your foot," said sneaker aficionado Bobbito Garcia, author of *Where'd You Get Those? New York City's Sneaker Culture: 1960–1987*. By the mid-aughts, the AF-1 was Nike's bestselling sneaker, mainly because of its popularity off the court, earning status as a style icon instead of a basketball shoe. A footwear industry expert estimated to the *Baltimore Sun* that the style generated Nike roughly $1 billion annually.

Within the street fashion circles, designers took the AF-1 and upgraded the Swoosh with Louis Vuitton's signature monogram print, sometimes from real luggage but mostly from bootlegs bought on Canal Street. Supreme's Alex Corporan remembered wearing a pair in the nineties. It could all be traced back to the innovative handiwork of Daniel Day, better known as Dapper Dan, and his Harlem atelier. The "knock-up" designer had been creating pairs since the eighties and immortalized the remixed sneaker on the cover of a Rob Base & DJ E-Z Rock album. But this was the first time the Louis Vuitton Air Force 1 was official. And Virgil insisted that the sneakers be made by the luxury house itself.

"He was adamant that they had to be made in the Atelier LV, and I wasn't so sure that that was necessary," recalled Nike power player Marc "Fraser" Cooke. The two had worked closely together on Virgil's mega-successful "The Ten" project a few years prior. At first, Fraser was frustrated; he told Virgil that nobody makes a Nike sneaker better than a Nike factory.

No, no, no, Virgil typed back. It had to be Italy; it had to be Fiesso d'Artico. It had to be made at Louis Vuitton's shoemaking atelier. "We got into a back-and-forth," he recalled. "Not an argument, but a debate." Fraser tried to convince Virgil to go with a specialized Nike factory in Taiwan, but the designer held firm. "He wouldn't budge. He was adamant."

Ultimately, Nike sent product and manufacturing experts to Italy to teach Louis Vuitton workers how to make the AF-1. "Of course, they can make anything," recalled Fraser. "The reason why he was right is what made him who he is, which was not just about the product. He was already imagining all of the storytelling that was going to drive a much richer backstory. I had to say to Virgil afterward, *You were bloody right.*"

Later that year, forty-seven bespoke pairs were made for his Louis Vuitton Spring/Summer 2022 collection, which went down the runway in the summer of 2021. Virgil named the collection Amen Break, a reference to a widely sampled drum break from a 1969 B-side track by the American soul group the Winstons. It was used extensively in early hip-hop and became one of the most sampled drum breaks ever, appearing in N.W.A.'s 1989 hit "Straight

Outta Compton," and, decades later, on Tyler, the Creator's 2013 song "Pigs."

Virgil told *Vogue*'s chief critic Sarah Mower, "People don't know that the drum pattern in their favorite song was from a very specific soul song—and it's a sampler that makes it possible."

Fashion tends to award legacies by major paradigm shifts and aesthetic revolutions. Coco Chanel transformed the little black dress from working-class origins into a chic and covetable status symbol. Yves Saint Laurent dressed women in pants with elegance and grace. Rei Kawakubo of Comme des Garçons turned jet-black misfit clothing into a thing of romance and beauty. Giorgio Armani and Thom Browne successfully altered the acceptable proportions of the suit, and Hedi Slimane elevated the androgynous look of indie rockers like no one before him. A designer who came from the school of streetwear was unlikely to implement a seismic shift or woo the industry. In fashion's hierarchy of genres, it sits at the lower rungs. Streetwear is a completely different game with a completely different set of rules. It is about remixing, not reinvention.

"In a way, streetwear really doesn't have a single piece that it brought to the market itself," explained Nick Bower, the longtime Stüssy designer who came from the world of traditional fashion. "The North Face, they brought the puffer to the business . . . Carhartt brought the work jacket, and Levi's brought the jeans. What streetwear does, it takes all of that, mixes it up in a palette, and offers it in a new way. I don't think there's a single piece that you could say, *Hey, that piece was never seen before streetwear existed.*" If a "streetwear designer" was to earn a fashion legacy, it would be a different kind of fashion legacy.

In November 2021, Virgil died in Chicago, where he was born, after a two-year battle with a rare cancer known as cardiac angiosarcoma. He was forty-one. It shocked the world. Just two months prior, he had attended the Met Gala, wearing a white tuxedo jacket with MODERNISM airbrushed across the chest. His wife, Shannon Abloh, later confirmed to the *New York Times* that they knew of his prognosis in July 2019 and chose to keep his illness a secret from all but his closest friends. Many of Virgil's collaborators were not aware that he was ill. "Even though we knew the challenge of what he was fighting, it went a lot faster than we thought it was going to," she said. It was an early end to a prolific career; his original Louis Vuitton contract had already been extended before it had expired, and LVMH had reached a deal with him to acquire a majority stake in Off-White. As with many artists, the press was kinder and more generous to Virgil in death than in life.

A Louis Vuitton fashion show just days after his passing functioned as a celebration of his life. The Arnault family flew in, as did celebrity friends like Kanye West and Kim Kardashian West, Rihanna and A$AP Rocky, and countless others. To close out the show, a drone-choreographed light display created the form of a paper airplane and then spelled out *Virgil was here*. The next month, Virgil's friends and family gathered in the atrium of the Museum of Contemporary Art in Chicago for a memorial service. The crowd included artists, professors, designers, rap stars, supermodels, and old friends alike. "They recalled the sacrifices V made for his art, the endless flights and far-flung DJ sets, the constant WhatsApp messaging, the Instagram account he used as an open studio," remembered his friend Antwaun Sargent. (Many friends called Virgil V.)

Virgil treated the friends and collaborators he had made in the past decade with grace and generosity. He was known to answer a high number of direct messages on Instagram from fans and aspiring creatives alike. Even in success, Virgil remained something of an outsider, with one foot in the establishment and another in the underground. The elite fashion industry could be sniffy toward him, and his popularity meant he had long since lost the cachet of the underground.

"It just was the coolest thing ever to see your friend live out his dream and to do it to such a degree that he did," said Benjamin Edgar, who met Virgil in 2006 when the two wrote for The Brilliance! together.

"I wasn't aware of his condition, the severity of it. I was caught off guard as were many, and I was just heartbroken," recalled Futura. "In the almost twelve years I knew Virg, I was enriched by his presence. . . . He took the time out to talk in places where you never really knew what time zone he was in or where in the world he might be."

"I learned so much from him," said Tremaine Emory, a close friend and designer who also worked with Virgil at Off-White. "The greatest thing I learned from V is it don't matter what anyone say. That motherfucker had supreme confidence. In the most trying times, people hating. He just knew what he wanted to do and that it was valid."

"When I talk about generations who got to make the most of that information they were given, Virgil's at the *nth degree* on the edge of that curve," said Eric Haze, the graffiti artist and pioneering designer. "Nobody's come along even close to Virgil with the acumen, ability, and contemporary sophisticated ability to curate instead of micromanage, which is very important as a designer. Virgil shifted the paradigm by clearly honoring every component of history and culture that's sort of added up to his own personal grasp and intelligence."

Even after his death, Virgil's work kept coming. Collaborations with Mattel, Alessi, Cassina, Mercedes-Benz, Burton Snowboards, the NBA, and a Louis Vuitton book. Shannon Abloh took on the role of chief executive and managing director of Virgil Abloh Securities, a corporation that unites his creative ventures.

"To me, design always has the inherent idea of being a bridge from the past, with an eye toward the future," Virgil once said. He honored a highly specific past in a way that no other designer ever did. A lion of synthesis who mixed Black street culture with highbrow design and luxury fashion. The Nike Air Force 1, a sneaker made famous by Black youth in Baltimore and Harlem and then rappers, was made in the Louis Vuitton factory in Fiesso d'Artico. He brought out Futura—the man who bumped elbows with Warhol and Basquiat and worked on the Supreme logo—to throw up a tag on a Parisian runway. He published coffee table books, printed zines, and built robust educational websites to give away what he called the "cheat codes" of streetwear, breaking down systemic walls and inspiring an entire generation of creative teenagers, especially those of color, along the way.

Virgil was a rare breed of fashion designer, an eternal optimist who seemed hardwired toward the bigger picture. His visual language was unique to his worldview: Pioneer CDJ and DJM, Apple MacBook and iPhone, Supreme T-shirts and Air Jordans, American sports and Swiss typography, Photoshop and JPEGs, X-Actos and Sharpies, Air Force 1s and Louis Vuitton monograms. He was a cipher for a generation that spoke mostly in Instagram captions and products and logos. He placed these motifs within ateliers and runways unlike any single name that came before him. Virgil was fashion's greatest sampler and he did his remixing with the most Duchampian wink the industry had ever seen.

35.
A Stüssy Succession

Frank Sinatra proved to be vigorous rootstock for the Stüssy brand. The former accountant acted as wise shepherd and held true to much of what it symbolized in its heyday. In the decades since Shawn Stüssy left his namesake label, Frank and his team had weathered many storms—changing marketplace trends, the pivot from in-store retail to e-commerce, the ambush of digitally savvy brands like Diamond Supply Co. and The Hundreds, the convergence of streetwear and luxury fashion. Most of all, Frank navigated sustaining a label without its namesake founding designer. Stüssy became a journeyman brand throughout these years—never the most covetable within America, but it held a regular presence within the marketplace and remained a strong performer overseas. Its staying power was also a testament to the foundation the brand laid in the nineties.

"Shawn gave them everything they needed to keep that thing going for a very long time because that graphic language is so strong," said Noah designer Brendon Babenzien, who discovered Stüssy in the eighties at the small surf-skate shop he worked at as a teenager.

Frank's son, David, was born in 1986 and spent much of his childhood running around the Stüssy business. When he was six, Frank brought him to the company ski trips at Mammoth Mountain, where David snowboarded with the international buyers. As a teenager, he tagged along with the skate team—Danny Montoya, Keith Hufnagel, Scott Johnston—filming footage on a handheld camcorder as they traversed the globe. David seemed destined for a career in the family business. He was homeschooled along with his two sisters and graduated when he was sixteen. He went to junior college while working at Stüssy in the sales department. It gave him a view into a new side of the business: interacting with buyers, seeing how design and production teams worked. One day, he approached Frank and told him he wanted to quit Stüssy to focus on his college education. He graduated from the University of Southern California and then worked within the Los Angeles entertainment industry. The experience proved to be an eye opener for David; working in Hollywood wasn't for him.

David came back to Stüssy in the early 2010s, right as Frank and the team were in the midst of a digital fiasco. The web developers erroneously built the brand's new website with Adobe Flash, and it had tanked the Google rankings. David approached his father and told him that he'd take the lead on fixing the website. It proved to be trickier than the younger Sinatra might have thought; it took nearly two years to launch the new Stüssy website. Still, Frank was impressed by his son's determination. Not long after, David looped himself into the actual clothing design.

David eventually took a larger role within the company, elevating some of the younger design team members and bringing in fresh talent. Paul Mittleman, who was hired by Frank after Shawn's departure and rose to the brand's global vice president of design and creative direction, exited the company in 2011 after nearly eighteen years. Nick Bower, the brand's head designer who was hired right after Shawn quit, left in 2014, clocking seventeen years. "It's hard to plug new ideas into an old team. It was very hard for Nick and Paul to accept the relationship with younger people that didn't have their senses," Frank recalled. "It represented conflict, it represented criticism. It represented pressure."

"I was kind of pushed out, but it wasn't in a horrible way," said Paul, who quickly landed a new job at Adidas. "I was pissed off at first, but who wouldn't be?"

David brought on a new global brand director in Fraser Avey, who previously worked at the exclusive Toronto boutique turned label Ransom. Fraser met American designer Tremaine Emory on a night out in London and the two kept in touch; Tremaine started to freelance for the brand as a creative consultant. He relocated to Los Angeles and started working for Kanye West and Yeezy before proudly being fired by the whirlwind rapper. This opened the door for Tremaine to take on a larger role at Stüssy, rising to become the brand's art director at large. Other hires included Jayne Goheen, a style blogger turned artful designer; Israel Gonzalez, an apparel industry veteran; and Ryan Willms, a former magazine editor with a stint at the venerable New York boutique Totokaelo. Collectively, the design team nudged the brand slightly toward a more fashion-oriented focus.

By the time David took on more significant responsibility at Stüssy, Frank, who was well into his sixties, knew a change was necessary. He was burned out. "The market's changed, it's very hard. We weren't able to bring in a new customer," Frank recalled. "I'm not going to sell out, so I'm either going to wind down to zero, or I'm going to sell the name to somebody that would reasonably be a caretaker." Around 2014, David became Stüssy's new chief executive officer, taking the reins from his father.

The brand had grown to annual revenues of $50 million, the biggest it had ever been.

David flew to Europe and met with longtime international distributors Michael Kopelman and Luca Benini, and later with stakeholders in Japan. The brand downsized its retail network and focused on its flagship stores, cutting tens of millions of dollars of wholesale accounts, including pulling out of the mall retail chain Zumiez. They were prepared to take the revenue drop in order to solidify its foundation. Some distributors scrambled.

"There was a moment when Stüssy cut off all their distribution globally just to go direct. The word was, especially in Europe, distributors had built their whole business on Stüssy, and they were like, *We need the next Stüssy*," recalled one brand owner. "But no brand from our generation was at the caliber of what Stüssy was in terms of global recognition."

The brand still sold to some select retail partners but put a renewed focus on its online shop and boutiques, or "chapters" in Stüssy's parlance. The year 2020 marked forty years of Stüssy. To commemorate the anniversary, the brand produced a limited-edition varsity jacket and T-shirt, designed by new-wave International Stüssy Tribe members Tremaine Emory and artist Cali DeWitt, with an editorial shot by original IST member Mark Lebon. The celebratory collection also included T-shirts and garments in partnership with the biggest and buzziest names in fashion: Comme des Garçons, Marc Jacobs, Rick Owens, Virgil Abloh, and Martine Rose.

The same year the Stüssy brand celebrated its fortieth anniversary, Shawn Stüssy found himself in the fashion spotlight for the first time in years. Kim Jones, the British designer who orchestrated the Louis Vuitton and Supreme collaboration, called Shawn out of "retirement" to work on a collection for the French luxury house Dior. Shawn's recognizable scribble appeared on everything from knitted sweaters and bucket hats to shorts and pants. It was a high-profile project that included a runway show in Miami. Shawn attended the show outfitted in an immaculate black suit and sunglasses, with long surfer hair. "He started it all," Kim told supermodel Kate Moss in an interview for *i-D*. "You know, James at Supreme or Nigo at A Bathing Ape, [Shawn] was doing it even before them. They all look up to him and respect him."

In the years since Shawn left his namesake label, he lived a charmed life, raising his sons and dipping his toes in and out of the industry as he pleased. In 2008, he founded S/DOUBLE, a brand that was born out of his connections in Japan and lasted for six years. The founding designer held a prickly relationship to his former company in the decades since. He occasionally aired grievances on his Instagram, calling out Stüssy for *still* using his handwriting and design. "They can rerun my old work to death but something about holding an original piece that is the real thing just cannot be overstated . . . no matter how much things are sliced and diced, photoshopped into submission, tweaked for financial gain, the real is always going to be the real," Shawn wrote alongside a photo of a 1991 T-shirt he designed. He often posted old photographs on his Instagram and reminisced about the good old days. He still shaped surfboards. In a 2019 interview with *Vogue Italia*, Shawn offered a rare comment on his relationship with Frank: "We had no falling out. I sold. And I walked away with a big bag of money. I just walked out the door and never looked back. So I haven't seen him for twenty years."

After news of the sale of Supreme to VF Corporation, the industry was hot with speculation about which streetwear brands were next to be bought. "All the bankers came running once they did that Supreme deal," David told the Business of Fashion. Frank had only considered selling Stüssy once before, back in the early aughts. He was approached by Italian billionaire Renzo Rosso, the founder of Diesel and president of OTB Group, which owned Maison Margiela, Marni, and Jil Sander. They flew Frank out from California; he found them likable and capable, but they didn't understand the brand or the market. Frank received an official offer letter, which he politely declined.

The Stüssy brand was at an age where teenagers who grew up wearing it now ran their own labels. Our Legacy, a Swedish menswear label with an unrivaled following, was founded by one of those teenagers, Jockum Hallin. "A nice Stüssy T-shirt was just the coolest thing you could have," he said. "I loved the connection the brand had to surf, street, and music culture." Our Legacy represented the new guard. It is decidedly a fashion label, with $2,000 leather jackets and $400 trousers, and backing from LVMH Luxury Ventures. In 2020, Stüssy and Our Legacy released a summertime collaboration full of striped button-ups, earthy plaid outerwear, and artful suiting. The collection was raved about by Hypebeast and Highsnobiety, but also bubbled up into *Vogue* and *GQ*. In a short time, Stüssy showed up on contemporary celebrities like supermodel Bella Hadid, pop star Justin Bieber, and rapper and fashion tastemaker A$AP Rocky.

David was running an entirely different business than his father did. "Back in the day, we made everything in California and sold it in California," recalled Frank. "Global supply chain didn't exist. Global customers didn't exist." Stüssy was bigger than ever before, and David and his team were navigating how to grow the label to new heights while keeping it full of soul. But how big? "Let's just say that we're moving towards $100 million," Frank said. "We really don't want to be that big, and we're doing everything to maintain the discipline. We're cutting orders. We're not opening up channels. We're limiting how much product we make. On the other hand, my son is very passionate about serving customers. He'll say, 'I've got all these people waiting in line at my stores, and they get inside and there's nothing to sell them because we're out.' So he's trying to balance having things for people to buy when they want to buy it. . . . It's a philosophical, ethical, practical balancing game."

In 2022, Stüssy's eight-ball motif, a design first introduced by Shawn in the early nineties, surged in popularity among Generation Z, boosted by Instagram and TikTok's algorithm. The feverish demand was specific to the sherpa fleece and windbreaker jackets. They sold out within minutes on the brand's online shop and were soon listed on resale websites for double the retail price. (Highsnobiety called it "a proper viral hit.") Videos on TikTok became bragging rights, with users showing off the jacket with a covetableness that Stüssy was once known for but perhaps hadn't seen in decades.

"Just the fact that you've been around long enough makes you automatically cool. Stüssy is emblematic of that to me," said Bobby Kim, a cofounder of The Hundreds. "There isn't anything that's necessarily remarkably different than what they've done in the past. They just have stayed. And the longer that they stay, they just get stronger."

"I'm delighted with what David's done. I'm proud, I'm happy for him.... There's no second-guessing. There's no, *I wish*. There's none of that," said Frank.

Over forty years after Shawn made the first Stüssy surfboard in that tiny Laguna Beach shaping studio, the label has endured. It now has thirty storefronts across the globe, with more than half located in the loyal Asian market. Perhaps most crucially, it has won over a younger generation and a fresh new audience. The majority of the graphic T-shirts still feature Shawn's handwriting, and signature collage-esque style. Plaid shirts, relaxed-fit jeans, chino work pants, baseball caps of all styles. A contemporary Stüssy collection does not differ greatly from one the brand would have released in the nineties, although the color palette skews richer and more monochromatic. It's a balancing act: to create styles that wear like American vintage and still carry the air of exclusivity that has become synonymous with streetwear. It was a strategy that worked back in the brand's original heyday. Decades later, it worked again. Even with a different Sinatra at the helm and Shawn Stüssy himself nowhere to be found.

36.

World Famous

One billion dollars a year.

That was the goal VF Corp.'s chief financial officer told investors after the company acquired Supreme. The New York label had annual sales of around $500 million at the time. To double the current revenue felt like an ambitious proclamation. Supreme had come far from a small skate shop where selling a few hundred bucks of T-shirts and hard goods was considered a *good* day. The brand and its new corporate owner agreed that Supreme's core leadership team would stay the same. Founder James Jebbia was to remain heavily involved, just as he had for the past twentysomething years.

But one cannot double a business with scarcity. A new era of Supreme had begun.

In early 2019, before the VF Corp. acquisition finalized, Supreme closed the original Lafayette Street store for renovations and pointed customers toward a temporary location at nearby 190 Bowery. The move turned out to be permanent, and by September of that year, the first Supreme store that James had opened in 1994 closed its doors for good. The Bowery shop opened inside a legendary downtown building, one that Keith Haring used to cover with his radiant baby motif. In the gray light of a late-winter day, a man who looked to be in his mid-sixties—dressed in a white painter's jacket, tiger-stripe camo pants, a black beanie, and black latex gloves—walked up to the exterior's limestone façade. A cameraman followed his every move. He pulled out a paint pen and scribbled something in a deep red: FUTURA. The graffiti artist and longtime Supreme collaborator was ushered inside, where a machine lift and dozens of spray cans awaited him. Over the next week, on a grand marble wall, Futura painted a sprawling mural over six feet tall and forty-five feet wide, nearly touching the ceiling.

"They always go and mess it up," said Neil Logan, Supreme's longtime architect, who also worked on the Jebbia family loft in Greenwich Village. "After we do a nice job of the architecture and care about every little finish, they come and have a guy with spray paint just do something there." Neil explained how Supreme differed from the industry standards; James did not follow the traditional rules of detail design. "They kind of made it up themselves. . . . Every store that they have goes through a rigorous back-and-forth. The reason it's important is that they put an emphasis on the visitor to the store, what they see first, what they see second, what they see as they leave and so on."

In early 2023, the brand moved its Los Angeles store from Fairfax Avenue to the Sunset Strip, setting up shop in the historic former Tower Records building. Over the next few years, the company opened new stores in San Francisco, Milan, Berlin, Chicago, Seoul, and Shanghai, among other cities, bringing the total to eighteen Supreme stores: six in the United States, six in Japan, and six scattered across Europe and Asia. All the new stores stayed true to the vision of the Lafayette Street original: an ideal white space of culture and commerce.

"A gallery is constructed along laws as rigorous as those for building a medieval church," wrote Brian O'Doherty in "Inside the White Cube," a landmark *Artforum* essay published in 1976. "The work is isolated from everything that would detract from its own evaluation of itself. . . . Things become art in a space where powerful ideas about art focus on them." As in the tightly controlled environment of the modernist gallery, James invented strict laws for the Supreme stores. Inside, the space was often stripped to its bones, exposing raw materials and traces of the past that were then polished. There was a unique vocabulary of floating racks and shelving, carefully placed sculptures and installations. The T-shirts were folded so tightly it was like art. Music blared so loudly that the windows sometimes shook. While Martin Margiela required his staff to wear long lab coats, Supreme employees were required to wear a New York attitude. James invented a new type of fluorescent-lit retail minimalism. The shopping experience made it so that Supreme was not sold—Supreme was acquired.

At around eight thousand square feet, the Supreme Bowery store was a supercharged version of what the original 600-square-foot Lafayette Street shop was. In many ways, the Bowery and Sunset stores were the same as the Lafayette and Fairfax ones, just bigger. Similarly, Supreme was still the same, just bigger. It still sponsored a team of world-class skateboarders, and it still employed a close inner circle of friends in the shops and main office. It designed and sold clothes that looked nearly the same as they did thirty years ago. The stores sold skateboards, hard goods, and a small selection of other brands, usually friends or friends of friends, and they still served double duty as unconventional art galleries. Between all the Supreme locations, there were works from Mark Gonzales, KAWS, Rita Ackermann, Weirdo Dave, and Nate Lowman, among others. James remained heavily involved in the day-to-day of Supreme. For each Thursday drop, he worked with longtime Supreme e-commerce technologist and partner Sam Spitzer to select the designs to be featured on the brand's signature preview page. Even the website remained largely the same as it did when it first launched.

"Still to this day, I go in before every collection is released and [James] asks me what I think of every single product. We edit it together, and I make every thumbnail personally," recalled Sam. "There's no single individual that would represent the brand the way that I do, because I *was* the kid. I'm not a kid anymore, and the brand is not a little skate shop anymore. . . . That's the truth. Keeping it real is really important to James. . . . We have every resource to make our website look like everyone else's. We intentionally don't want that."

"I don't want to speak for James, but he won't speak. So maybe this is the time to say this," said Brendon Babenzien, Supreme's former design director. "To the best of my knowledge, and I can say that he has said this to me in the past . . . he did not expect this to happen. There's no world where James ever thought a two-billion-dollar valuation would be possible. He may have kept hopes and dreams alive in the back of his head, but he never once would vocalize something that crazy. He always told me he didn't believe anything like this would be possible." As predicted, Supreme's invisible man did not respond to interview requests for this book.

There was one massive change that happened to the brand in this new era, and that was a designer named Tremaine Emory. He was selected by James to be Supreme's first-ever creative director. Tremaine—eloquent and opinionated, an idiosyncratic and immaculate dresser with broad shoulders, a big beard, and dreadlocks—had quickly established himself as a force within the streetwear and fashion worlds. He launched Denim Tears in 2019, a punchy and stylish fashion-art project that quickly gained momentum and collaborated with Dior and Levi's. Tremaine was born in Georgia in 1981 and moved to Queens, New York, before his first birthday. He became enamored with style while in high school and often hung out in front of Union. At one point, Tremaine was supposed to meet with James for a job at Stüssy, but the interview kept getting pushed and never happened. Instead, Tremaine took a job in the stockroom at Marc Jacobs in 2006 and worked for the fashion label for nine years, moving to the front of the shop and eventually relocating to London to open a new store for the brand. It was there that he cofounded No Vacancy Inn, a loose creative agency, with Ade "Acyde" Odunlami and started to work with Frank Ocean. Tremaine returned to America and worked freelance gigs that led to a job as the brand director at Yeezy and the art director at large for Stüssy.

As a designer, Tremaine was a bomb thrower, using fashion to weave brutal truths within his work and push forward the energy of social and racial justice movements. "I wanna start uncomfortable conversations," the designer has said. One of the first high-profile collaborations under his Denim Tears label was a 2020 collection with Levi's in which he printed cotton wreaths on classic 501 blue jeans. The wreath motif was inspired by a Kara Walker painting. "That's just one of the ways I use iconography to bring social awareness to systematic racism, paying homage to what Black people have been through," he said at the time. The cotton wreath motif has become perhaps the brand's most recognizable design. Tremaine produced a Denim Tears sweater with artist David Hammons's *African American Flag* knitted on the front, a reimagined version of the United States flag with the red, green, and black of the Pan-African Universal Negro Improvement Association. Tremaine's fashion riffed on the iconic Ralph Lauren Polo American flag sweater that was first released in 1989. That year, the brand also released sleek, monochromatic hoodies and sweatpants to a graphic flip on John Pasche's famous Hot Lips logo for the Rolling Stones. Like his friend Virgil Abloh, Tremaine also held an appreciation for an older generation of T-shirt brands, once telling a story of buying a SSUR hoodie from Union when he was younger.

"If I lived in the fifties or sixties, I probably would have been a writer. . . . And if I lived a bit later, I would've maybe been a painter. But I didn't grow up in those times," Tremaine said in an interview with the writer and cultural critic Touré. "I grew up in a time when one of the most important expressions to young people and humans is fashion because of consumerism. Capitalism pushed fashion as a vehicle to make money. You can try to Trojan horse inside of that to get messages out."

Tremaine's first day at Supreme was in February 2022. The year prior, he had suffered a lower aortic aneurysm. Eight out of ten people don't survive such an event, and it was a real scare, he said. He was in a wheelchair until he regained more strength in his legs, and then eventually started to walk with the aid of a cane. Tremaine seemed to appreciate and acknowledge the situation he was in at a brand the size of Supreme. "I was probably the first Black kid in Jamaica, Queens, wearing Supreme in 1999," he once recalled. "To become the creative director twenty-five years later is just a story for the ages."

Supreme still had a long way to go toward $1 billion, but VF Corp. had predicted the label would soon hit a more modest $600 million in annual sales. In June 2023, financial reports showed a dip in revenue; sales trended down instead of up. Supreme reported

$523.1 million in annual sales, a $38.4 million decline from the same period a year prior.

Tremaine's run at Supreme was shorter than both parties expected. After two collections, in August 2023, Tremaine resigned, citing "systematic racism" within the company; the rift stemmed from a dispute over a forthcoming collaboration with visual artist Arthur Jafa and a work of photomontage that depicted the 1920 lynchings in Duluth, Minnesota. Tremaine told the *Washington Post* that James removed the imagery without telling him, after a Black employee sent an email to the team questioning the usage of such violence for a commercial apparel project. Supreme issued a statement "strongly" disagreeing "with Tremaine's characterization of our company and the handling of the Arthur Jafa project."

In an interview with *Complex* after he left, Tremaine summarized a larger misalignment: "James couldn't let go. . . . He would never admit that he was the creative director of Supreme, but he had been for thirty years and he's done a damn fine job of it. . . . But when it came time to give the reins, he did not do that. I don't think he understood psychologically what it was to truly let go of it and let someone else run it." After his exit, Tremaine released a capsule collection with Arthur Jafa under his Denim Tears label. He also took a venerable Supreme design and flipped it, changing the original text to read: SYSTEMIC RACISM CONTROLS AMERICA.

By 2024, with $1 billion in annual revenue still far away, rumors swirled that VF Corp. was looking to sell Supreme.

Before the sale rumors, *GQ* and Highsnobiety pointed to a Supreme collaboration with The North Face from its spring and summer collection as a sign of the new corporate change and perhaps the brand's stagnation. ("Supreme Is Dead, Long Live Supreme," proclaimed the Highsnobiety headline.) In previous years, Supreme and North Face products would have sold out in seconds. This time around, stock sat available on the Supreme website for days. Online critics suggested the brand was increasing production by too much in an attempt to meet investor growth expectations. StockX reported Supreme doubled the number of Box Logos they had dropped over the past two years; the *Wall Street Journal* analyzed a drop and found that by the following week, fifty-three of the fifty-five products from that drop were still in stock. The headline asked: "Is Supreme Still Cool?"

"I think that what you've seen with Supreme is as they've gotten bought and sold and then bought and then sold again, people are trying to take that coolness and scale it. Make it more profitable," said Brahm Wachter, Sotheby's head of modern collectibles. "We're not selling nearly as much Supreme as we were, and the market has really gone down."

Jerry Lorenzo's Fear of God Essentials, the diffusion line of basics the designer launched with PacSun, now brought in between $200 million and $300 million a year and had scaled up its seasonal collections to include over one hundred garments. In 2023, StockX reported that Fear of God had dethroned Supreme as the most searched brand. Aimé Leon Dore, the Queens label that now had stores in New York and London and the backing of LVMH Luxury Ventures, continued its dominance. Jon Caramanica, the *New York Times* pop music critic and longtime men's Critical Shopper columnist, wrote, "Aimé Leon Dore has stepped into a void that perhaps could have been filled by Supreme but wasn't ever quite."

In July 2024, a surprise deal was announced: French-Italian eyewear giant EssilorLuxottica purchased Supreme from VF

Corp. for $1.5 billion in cash, a steep $600 million decline from the $2.1 billion VF valued the brand at four years prior. Supreme's sales trended upward again, increasing by nearly $15 million from the year before, to an annual total of $538 million. If anything, the sale suggested that Supreme, which still operated on a foundation of controlled scarcity, did not fit into VF's core business model of extensive distribution. Yet the sale became an industry-wide, alarm-ringing symbol of the "cooling streetwear market."

Supreme is Supreme.

It was a phrase that came up time and time again in the streetwear industry. From the skaters and free-roaming city kids who worked at the original shop back in the nineties to the generation of brand owners that came in Supreme's wake and made millions of dollars along the way. There was a reverence for the New York label that no other brand or designer in the space had.

"Supreme is coveted. . . . If you're seventeen years old, getting into a Supreme store, buying that first T-shirt, something you never want to lose for the rest of your life, it doesn't matter if it's thirty dollars," the late designer Virgil Abloh once said. "That seventeen-year-old kid is going to remember Supreme for the rest of his life."

Almost as often as "Supreme is Supreme" came up, so did the notion that two things could be true at once. A T-shirt can just be cotton and plastisol ink. It can also be a powerful symbol for belonging. Clothing is coded in meaning, and dressing up was not something superficial; it was about knowing yourself and about expressing yourself. There was a reason why streetwear's core audience was always young men. Teenage angst was eternal. The fraught moments of being a teenager—the time when one is grasping at an identity and longing to feel a part of something bigger than oneself. Two things *could* be possible at once. Supreme was still a sacred thing, worthy of protection and preservation. It was also a willing participant in America's image-driven, capitalist culture. Yet, at a certain volume, a project crosses the threshold into the mainstream and it risks becoming, as the late American critic Dave Hickey said, "pop masquerading as art, as opposed to art masquerading as pop."

"I really believe that the sneaker drops and the skateboards and the limited T-shirts were the excuse. People were shopping for friends. They were shopping for like-minded individuals, people who looked like them, felt like them, listened to the same type of music," said Bobby Kim after The Hundreds closed their Fairfax Avenue store in 2025 after nearly twenty years. "It was just a space where you could feel a little bit more in your element of *I want to be a part of this.*"

As a brand like Supreme built a fortress around itself and its owner, Bobby and Virgil shared everything out in the open, dissolving the barrier between designer and customer. There was something about Bobby's blogging and Virgil's frequent Instagram-ing that felt communal. For aspiring designers and brand owners, that level of access was both an education and a call to action. It was a means to pass a baton and keep a creative lineage alive.

Streetwear was so many things, more an amorphous idea that kept redefining itself. To this day, the term itself is still bucked by those within it. There is an argument to be made that streetwear was defined less by aesthetics, and more by the origins and ethos it carried. It was born from graffiti, breakdancing, hip-hop, punk rock, skateboarding, and surfing. It came from kids who didn't have a regular income and had to create their own fashion identity. It was kids remixing wares from army-navy stores. It was Willi Smith collaborating with Barbara Kruger and Keith Haring on T-shirts. It was graffiti writers wearing painter caps and homemade Rust-Oleum T-shirts. It was Youth Crew bands wearing varsity jackets and high-top Nikes. It was Black and brown teenagers wearing Polo Ralph Lauren. It was skaters dressing like rappers dressing like drug dealers. It was Dapper Dan and Supreme. It was Alstyle 1301 T-shirts heavy with plastisol, New Era fitted caps, and Nike SB Dunks. It was Virgil Abloh and $500 screen-printed flannels. It became a deeply American phenomenon, the repackaging of rebellion into commerce. It went from the clothes associated with subcultures to a culture of its own design. It was a looking glass and a medium to sell a culture back to itself. Or as one of Supreme's earliest employees put it, "It went from a subculture to a culture to a commodified fucking corporate animal."

Streetwear successfully reshaped both culture and commerce. An entire generation now looks at a red box with white Futura text and thinks of Supreme, not Barbara Kruger. The "drop" model is now embedded within American consumerism, and brand collaborations have become so ubiquitous that they've lost potency. Fashion went from the four-season calendar to releasing things fifty-two weeks a year. Vanessa Friedman, the chief fashion critic for the *New York Times*, wrote, "It's that those hoodies and sneakers and T-shirts have become so fully absorbed by the high-fashion establishment that the line between streetwear and fashion has effectively disappeared.... Streetwear has become fashion—or fashion has become streetwear, depending on how you want to look at it." In 2019, PricewaterhouseCoopers estimated the size of the global streetwear market at $185 billion by sales, making it by some estimates about 10 percent of the entire global apparel and footwear market. But it felt like streetwear's attitude and aesthetics now commanded nearly every corner of the marketplace. Its designers and disciples ascended to the upper echelon of corporations.

A Bathing Ape founder Nigo was appointed as the artistic director of French luxury fashion house Kenzo; Louis Vuitton announced Pharrell Williams as its new men's creative director, the polymath stepping into the role Virgil Abloh once held. The Hundreds co-founder and designer Bobby Kim was hired by Disney as VP of creative for consumer products, overseeing the design of everything from toys to apparel. Samuel Spitzer's e-commerce platform—the one he developed for Supreme—was now used by Dior, generating hundreds of millions in sales for the brand. Even Erik Brunetti and his label FUCT became national news when the designer fought the USPTO's ban on "immoral" and "scandalous" trademarks, leading to a high-profile case that rose to the Supreme Court, which ruled in Erik's favor. Elsewhere, designers who came up within the streetwear world were plugged into fashion gigs high and low, everywhere from fast fashion retailer H&M to Italian house Givenchy.

Toward the end of 2024, Supreme launched a major campaign featuring Tyler, the Creator. The rapper was no longer a loudmouthed teenager but an auteur and a polymath, a cultural tastemaker, and a generational voice in hip-hop. It was as full-circle of a moment as it got for the kid from Hawthorne who used to post on the Hypebeast forums and run wild on Fairfax Avenue. "Supreme was our Louis Vuitton. It was like our top-of-the-line shit," Tyler once said. "Especially knowing not everyone had it. It only made it more special." Tyler's own trajectory is a classic story of a rise to the American mainstream: from the margins of youth culture toward the center of popular culture. He did it all while wearing Supreme. The musician had landed two Grammy Awards and three no. 1 albums. His own clothing labels, Golf Wang and GOLF le FLEUR*, have transcended side projects and become fashion entities of their own. Many signs point to Tyler being destined to end up as an artistic director for Louis Vuitton one day, following in the footsteps of Virgil and Pharrell. (In 2024, Tyler designed a capsule collection for Pharrell's Louis Vuitton.)

Now in his sixties, the Supreme founder was still playing a young man's game. The man who changed fashion forever was more of curator than a designer, more of a perfectionist than a prophet. James was always au courant with New York City, and Supreme could have only come from nineties New York. A city where painters and gallerists and skaters and truant teenagers all hopped on the same subway. His dedication to nineties New York style was absolute even as consumer tastes evolved. "I guess a lot of what we do comes from the nineties era, because that's when we opened and started," James once said. "But I also feel that was a golden era for clothes, for music, for art, for a lot of things." He couldn't have known it at the time, but as technology smoothed and hyper-optimized our world, the spit-polished ethos and aesthetics of a downtown yesteryear grew more alluring by the decade. Something found a foothold at 274 Lafayette Street in 1994. An era of "train-hopping, taxicab-jumping, runaway kids" who wanted nothing more than to scream at the moon. James and Supreme managed to put it in a bottle and sell it for the last thirty years. In the end, the brand's power was supercharged by its refusal to explain itself. And this is to say nothing of the quality and style of the clothes the brand designed and produced year after year. A contemporary Supreme collection does not look all that different from "golden era Preme," as devotees lovingly, and sometimes longingly, call it.

Every counterculture is eventually exploited for commercial purposes, first by the artists and participants themselves, and then by new jacks and opportunists. Streetwear was a deeply complex, fast-evolving form ripe with aesthetic possibility. It was an inversion of power that turned graffiti writers into blue-chip artists and raw-nerved misfits into sought-after designers, and made small-time T-shirt brands into bona fide fashion labels. That turned the Air Force 1 and the Supreme Box Logo into generational objects of design and desire. The T-shirt will have a place in youth culture forever, and owning the right one also made you feel like you belonged to something that was bigger than yourself.

Streetwear took our existing and often unoriginal world, mixed it up on a palette, and offered it in a new way. It had a propensity to stay the same, but it became bigger than any brand or designer. There was a markedly masculine attitude, complete with territorialism and traditionalism. There were brotherhoods and community and jealousy and beefs. These designers—most without formal training—copied without shame and brought a scorched-earth approach to appropriation that would have made Warhol flinch. Many also represented their world, a world that the fashion institution largely ignored, with the fidelity of an artist. At some point, this group turned an assemblage of existing cultural motifs into a constellation of codes and references. It was simultaneously a movement and a mode of culture deeply intertwined with commerce. One that started as a rebellion against a form but, perhaps inadvertently, became a new and marketable genre of clothing on its own.

But above all, it was a whole new fashion world—built by rogues and outsiders from the undergrounds of American culture—ready to replace the old one.

Notes and Sources

This book blends dialogue and scenes drawn from interviews, documents, and memories, presented without quotation marks. I attempted to speak with every key figure within the text, though some declined or did not respond. In these instances, I read and listened extensively—reviewing past interviews, profiles, monographs, lectures, panels, podcasts—and spoke to those who knew the subjects firsthand.

Among the invaluable sources: Christian Beamish's piece on Shawn Stüssy in the *Surfer's Journal*; Jeff Spurrier on Erik Brunetti in *Details*; Noah Johnson's Q&A with James Jebbia and Thom Bettridge's oral history of Virgil Abloh's career for *GQ*; Elena Romero's book *Free Stylin'*; W. David Marx's *Ametora*; Karizza Sanchez and Lei Takanashi's reporting for *Complex*; the *Touré Show* interview with Tremaine Emory; and the late Gary Warnett's blog GWARIZM. Others, too.

Much is owed to the quiet, steady work of the editors, writers, and archivists at publications—including, but not limited to Hypebeast, Highsnobiety, *Complex*, The Brilliance!, Four Pins, *Jenkem Magazine*, Sabukaru, DampMagazines. The archives of the *New York Times, Los Angeles Times*, the *New Yorker, New York, WWD,* and *California Apparel News* also provided a decades-long trove of business and cultural reporting.

As this book covers fifty years, the full citations run long. I've included an abridged version here; the full, extended notes are archived online at tylerwatamanuk.com/bigger-than-fashion-extended-notes.

Act One

Lara Chan-Baker. "Interview: Shawn Stussy." *Acclaim Magazine*, 2013.
Christian Beamish. "When the Bassline Thumps: Woodshop to Hip Hop with Shawn Stüssy." *Surfer's Journal*, 2016.
James Oliver. "Interview: Shawn Stussy." *New Order*, April 2020.
"A Chat With Shawn Stussy." *Empire Ave*, July 2013.
Luke Leitch. "Shawn Stüssy: L'uomo Che Ha Inventato Lo Streetwear." *Vogue Italia*, December 2019.
Jason Crombie. "The Shawn Stussy Interview." *Monster Children*, 2011.

Notes and Sources

Ari L. Goldman. "City to Use Pits of Barbed Wire in Graffiti War." *New York Times*, December 1981.
Cathleen McGuigan. "New Art, New Money." *New York Times Magazine*, February 1985.
Glenn O'Brien. "1981: 'New York/New Wave.' " *Artforum*, March 2003.
R. J. Rushmore. "The Mudd Club and 'Beyond Words.' " *Viral Art*, February 2014.
Calvin Tomkins. "Up From the I.R.T." *New Yorker*, March 1984.
Suzanne Slesin. "An Artist Turns Retailer." *New York Times*, April 1986.
Peter C. T. Elsworth. "The Art Boom: Is It Over, or Is This Just a Correction?" *New York Times*, December 1990.
George "Rack-Lo" Billips. "Life and Times of Rack-Lo: The Silk Crizzy Rush." RACK-LO YouTube, October 2017.
Jackson Blount and George "Rack-Lo" Billips. *Lo-Life: An American Classic*. powerHouse Books, 2016.
Victor "Thirstin Howl the 3rd" DeJesus. "Bury Me With the Lo On." *Victory Journal* Vimeo, 2017.
Rose Apodaca. "The Stussy Style: Irvine Clothier Heightens Hype by Playing Hard to Get." *Los Angeles Times*, July 1992.
Neil Feineman. " 'Dude Clothes' Ride Big Wave in LA and Abroad." *Los Angeles Times*, June 1989.
Jason Jules. "The Lexicon of Street Culture." Styled/Vocal Media, September 2018.
Cara Greenberg. "Where the Clothes Match the Music." *New York Times*, June 1993.
Jeremy Abbott. "Supreme Genius James Jebbia on Creating the Coolest Streetwear Brand." *GQ Style*, October 2017.
Robert Sullivan. "Charting the Rise of Supreme, From Cult Skate Shop to Fashion Superpower." *Vogue*, August 2017.
"Eddie Cruz of Undefeated: You Have to Stand for Something." Rebel Radio, YouTube, July 2020.
Enid Nemy. "Style Makers: Camella Ehlke, Clothing Designer." *New York Times*, June 1991.
Jian DeLeon. "The Oral History of Stüssy" (Parts I and II). *Complex*, December 2012.
Rebecca Mead. "Stupid Hip Stüssy." *New York*, December 1991.
Fraser Cooke. "Hiroshi Fujiwara." *Interview*, March 2010.
Joe Goodwin. "Last Orgy: Tracing the Legacy of Japan's Most Important Fashion Column." *Sabukaru*, March 2024.
Takashi Suzuki. "Nigo." *PIGMAG*, May 2005.
Carrie Donovan. "Fashion View: Much Ado About the Japanese." *New York Times Magazine*, July 1983.
Gary Warnett. "Erik Brunetti: The Outsider Artist." *Inventory Magazine*, 2016.
Erik Brunetti. *FUCT*. Rizzoli, 2013.
Erik Brunetti. *Oval Parody Book*. Kaleidoscope, 2022.
Martin Pearson. "FUCT in the U.S.A." *i-D*, July 1994.
Ian Michna. "Discussing the History of FUCT & the Current Streetwear Market." *Jenkem Magazine*, May 2019.
Anna Scott. "The Comeback of Freshjive." *Los Angeles Downtown News*, October 2009.
Russell Simmons with Nelson George. *Life and Def: Sex, Drugs, Money, and God*. Crown, 2001.
Lewis McAdams. "Loose Threads." *Los Angeles Times*, June 1994.
Ian Fisher. "Phat City." *New York Times*, April 1993.

Josh Franklin. *Subblueminal.* Invasion Studios, 2022.
Bruce Vielmetti. "Not the Kind of Smoke They Had in Mind." *Tampa Bay Times,* February 1993.
Louis Menand. "Before Roy Lichtenstein Went Pop." *New Yorker,* July 2021.
Michel Marriott. "Hip-Hop's Hostile Takeover." *New York Times,* September 1992.
Marguerite T. Smith. "Sustaining WilliWear's Spirit." *New York Times,* May 1987.
Robert Wynne. "At 26, Designer Karl Kani Sits Atop His Own Fashion Empire." *Los Angeles Times,* December 1994.
Lauren Goldstein. "Urban Wear Goes Suburban." *CNN Money,* December 1998.
Nancy Hass. "The Ups and Downs of Mossimo." *Los Angeles Magazine,* June 1997.
Bobby Hundreds (Bobby Kim). "The Man. The Myth. Mossimo." The Hundreds, October 2016.
William Kissel. "Catching on Fast: Stussy and Mossimo Start Up New Lines to Spread Their Success." *Los Angeles Times,* December 1992.
James Jebbia. *Supreme.* Rizzoli, 2010.
Roberta Smith. "Barbara Kruger's Large-Scale Self-Expression." *New York Times,* January 1991.
Mary Tannen. "The Rules of Attraction." *Vogue,* March 1995.
Glenn O'Brien. "James Jebbia Is Supreme." *Interview,* February 2009.
"Young Designers are Dressing SoBe." *Miami Herald,* June 1993.
Phillip J. Lavelle and Sandi Dolbee. "Across America, a Nomadic Band Quietly Recruits Brothers and Sisters for the 'True' Church." *San Diego Union-Tribune,* November 1997.
Dana Thomas. *Deluxe: How Luxury Lost Its Luster.* Penguin Press, 2007.

Act Two

Richard A. Martin. "The Rebirth of the New York Sneakerhead." *New York Times,* July 2004.
"The Suckhour Episode 19: New York Stories." SUCKLORD CITY, YouTube, June 2016.
Shaila K. Dewan. "With Lights Out, Looters Set Sights on Sneaker Shops." *New York Times,* August 2003.
Ariel Levy. "Chasing Dash Snow." *New York,* January 2007.
Noah Johnson. "The Untold Story of IRAK, Downtown New York's Most Legendary Graffiti Crew." *GQ,* August 2021.
Eric Swisher. "Chrome Ball Interview #94: Ryan Hickey." Chrome Ball Incident, July 2016.
Aaron Bondaroff and Virgil Abloh. "My Lives in T-Shirts, Act 2." *SNEEZE Magazine,* Fall 2021.
Rob Walker. "The Brand Underground." *New York Times Magazine,* July 2006.
Thom Bettridge. "Hypebeast vs. Highsnobiety: A Journey Toward the Heart of Content." 032c, May 2017.
Susan Carpenter. "Sole Searching." *Los Angeles Times,* July 2006.
Andrew Pulig. "The Wild Wild Web: The Chronicles of the HYPEBEAST Forums." Hypebeast, August 2014.
"The Fall of 'TRL' and the Rise of Internet Video." WNYC Soundcheck/NPR Music, November 2008.
Chuck Anderson and Benjamin Gott. "Interview!: Wayne of Superfuture®!!" The Brilliance!, 2005.

"Pigeon Dunk Interview." *Sneaker Freaker*, August 2008.
"Pharrell and Jacob the Jeweler Interview." JOOPITER TV, YouTube, October 2022.
Ariel Levy. "Enchanted." *New Yorker*, August 2008.
Suzy Menkes. "Louis Vuitton: Blinded with Commerce." *New York Times*, October 2004.
Mike Albo. "Charge That Tee on My Platinum." *New York Times*, December 2007.
Kelly Wetherille. "Nigo Opens Up About Bape." *WWD*, February 2011.
Kari Hamanaka. "Nick Tershay, Diamond in the Rough." *WWD*, August 2018.
"Nicky Diamonds." *Premium Pete Show* (podcast), 2019.
Andrew Asch. "Streetwear Demand Growing." *California Apparel News*, June 2014.
Karizza Sanchez. "How Fairfax Became the Mecca of Streetwear: An Oral History." *Complex*, February 2019.
Sarah Wolfson. "Supreme Sues Married to the Mob." *California Apparel News*, May 2013.
Foster Kamer. "Barbara Kruger Responds to Supreme's Lawsuit." *Complex*, May 2013.
Blair Alley. "Zumiez 100K 2012." *TransWorld SKATEboarding*, January 2012.
"Building Diamond Brands with Nicky Diamonds." *Berner's Round Table* (podcast), June 2019.
Kristie Bertucci. "Diamond Life." *DUB Magazine*, May 2014.
"Crooks n Castles." Ismail Maiyegun, Vimeo, November 2015.

Act Three

Clover Hope. "Kanye Has a Dream: Inside His Creative Agency DONDA." *Vibe*, August 2013.
Karizza Sanchez and David Cabrera. "The Untold Story of Pastelle, Kanye West's First Clothing Line." *Complex*, July 2018.
Ian Hundiak. "A History of Kanye West's Sneaker Collabs." *Sneaker News*, February 2014.
Virgil Abloh. *Figures of Speech*. DelMonico Books/Prestel; Museum of Contemporary Art Chicago, 2019).
Emilia Petrarca. "Meet You on the Corner of Hype and Mercer." *New York*, January 2018.
Jian DeLeon. "No One Pyrex Should Have All Those Rugby Flannels." *Complex*, January 2013.
Thom Bettridge. "Group Chat: The Oral History of Virgil Abloh." *GQ Style*, March 2019.
Diane Solway. "Virgil Abloh and His Army of Disruptors: How He Became the King of Social Media Superinfluencers." *W*, April 2017.
"Kerwin Frost Talks to Jerry Lorenzo." Kerwin Frost, YouTube, April 2021.
William Van Meter. "The Point Men for Public School." *New York Times*, January 2014.
Jake Woolf. "How Kith's Ronnie Fieg Became the King of Sneakers in 2016." *GQ*, December 2016.
Vanessa Friedman. "Fashion Gives Its Top Award to a Man Who Says He Isn't a Designer." *New York Times*, June 2018.
Evan Clark, Aria Hughes. "A Supreme Deal: $1B Valuation from Carlyle." *WWD*, October 2017.
Gary Warnett. "The James Jebbia Interview." Hypebeast, December 2013.
Lei Takanashi. "Supreme Team: The Story Behind the Brand's Original Design Crew." *Complex*, April 2020.
David Shapiro. "Flipping Supreme." *New Yorker*, November 2013.
Doreen St. Félix. "Virgil Abloh, Menswear's Biggest Star." *New Yorker*, March 2019.
Matthew Schneier. "They Been Trill. Now the Rest of the World Is, Too." *New York Times*, January 2019.

Guy Trebay. "At Louis Vuitton, Michael Jackson Forever." *New York Times*, January 2019.
Zoë Heller. "Jacob's Ladder." *New Yorker*, September 1997.
Ezra Marcus. "Belgian Designer Accuses Virgil Abloh of Copying. Again." *New York Times*, August 2020.
Mario Abad. "LVMH Revenues Surge Again Thanks to 'Exceptional' Performances at Louis Vuitton and Dior." *Forbes*, April 2019.
Dan Hyman. "Virgil Abloh Has Designs on High Culture." *New York Times*, May 2019.
Gary Warnett. "Knowledge Reigns Supreme." GWARIZM, May 2013.
Liz Warren. "Streetwear Resale Show Unstoppable Growth, New Report Finds." *Sourcing Journal*, August 2019.
Shoshy Ciment. "Inside SNKRS: How a Group of Nike Employees Went 'Unconventional' to Build a Chart-Topping App That Would Transform Sneaker Culture." *Business Insider*, November 2020.
Lauren Schwartzberg. "The Botmakers Who Rule the Obsessive World of Streetwear." *Wired*, May 2017.
"Carlyle to Flip Streetwear Icon Supreme in $2.1B Deal." PitchBook, November 2020.
Thom Bettridge. "The New York We Fuck With: The Life and Times of Aimé Leon Dore Designer Teddy Santis." *SSENSE*, January 2017.
Peter Saltsman. "At Louis Vuitton's Footwear Atelier in Italy, an Extreme Commitment to Craftsmanship." *Sharp Magazine*, March 2020.
Fred Bierman. "The Nike Air Force 1 Sneaker Turns 25 Years Old." *New York Times*, December 2007.
Zoë Vanderweide. "The History Behind the Louis Vuitton Nike Air Force 1 by Virgil Abloh." Sotheby's, September 2022.
Sarah Mower. "Louis Vuitton Spring 2022 Menswear Collection." *Vogue*, November 2021.
Vanessa Friedman. "Shannon Abloh Is Ready to Talk." *New York Times*, November 2022.
Antwaun Sargent. "In Search of Virgil Abloh." *GQ*, February 2022.
Luke Leitch. "Into the Sky Above: Virgil Abloh Stages His Last Show for Louis Vuitton." *Vogue*, November 2021.
"Tremaine Emory on Denim Tears, Why He Quit Supreme, and Illustrious Career in Fashion." *Touré Show*, DCP Entertainment, YouTube, September 2023.
Rachel Tashjian. "How Stüssy Became the Chanel of Streetwear." *GQ*, May 2021.
Samuel Hine. "Meet Know Wave and No Vacancy Inn, the Crews Behind Art Basel's Wildest Party." *GQ*, December 2016.
Jonathan Michael Square. "Fashioning an African American Lexicon." Metropolitan Museum of Art, February 2022.
Charlene Prempeh. "The 'Cultural Lightning Rod' Taking Over at Supreme." *Financial Times*, June 2022.
Vikram Alexei Kansara. "Tremaine Emory Exits Supreme, Alleging 'Systematic Racism.'" Business of Fashion, August 2023.
"Tremaine Emory on Denim Tears, Virgil, Kanye, and Leaving Supreme." *Complex*, YouTube, July 2023.
Jacob Gallagher. "Is Supreme Still Cool?" *Wall Street Journal*, May 2023.
Mik Awake. "The Near Death and Rebirth of Tremaine Emory." *GQ*, November 2023.
Jon Caramanica. "How Aimé Leon Dore Took New York." *New York Times*, July 2023.
Noah Johnson. "Supreme Leader: The Extended James Jebbia Interview." *GQ*, July 2019.
Vanessa Friedman. "Streetwear Is Dead." *New York Times*, February 2022.

Acknowledgments

With thanks to William LoTurco of LoTurco Literary for his steadfast belief in my writing and this project; Yahdon Israel, senior editor at Simon & Schuster, for the sharp thinking and support throughout this process; Stuart Roberts for the book's original green light; Khalid McCalla, Yvette Grant, and the rest of the team at Simon & Schuster for your hard work in carrying this forward; Shaker Samman and Nikki Shaner-Bradford for the team effort of fact-checking; No Ideas for the cover design. To the editors I've worked with over the years—thank you for the assignments, the notes, and the space to grow as a writer. Every piece mattered. To my parents, brothers, family, and friends: Thank you for supporting me and my work.

My endless gratitude to the artists, the designers, the brand owners, the stylists and retailers and editors, and everyone else who let me into their world for this project: Your time and your candor made this book possible. Even if not every conversation found its way onto the page, you helped give form and texture to an unforgettable story.